EDIBLE WILD PLANTS
OF
PENNSYLVANIA
AND
NEIGHBORING STATES

EDIBLE WILD PLANTS
OF
PENNSYLVANIA
AND
NEIGHBORING STATES

RICHARD J. MEDVE and MARY LEE MEDVE

Illustrations by Kimball S. Erdman

The Pennsylvania State University Press
University Park and London

Some recipes are from other printed sources and permission to use these recipes is greatly appreciated. Recipes of walnut-honey balls, hickory Christmas balls, elderberry wine, crab-apple-mint jelly, and gooseberry preserves are from *Edible Wild Fruits and Nuts of Canada* (1979) by Nancy J. Turner and Adam F. Szczawinski, published courtesy of the National Museum of Natural Sciences, Ottawa, Canada. Nancy Hall gave permission to use the arrowhead spread recipe from *The Wild Palate: A Serious Wild Foods Cookbook* published by the Rodale Press. The white pine bark candy and pawpaw ice cream recipes are from *Wild Food Plants of Indiana and Adjacent States* by A. McPherson and S. McPherson, published by the Indiana University Press. Freda Gibbons gave permission to use the blueberry cobbler, cranberry whip dessert, and sassafras jelly recipes that appear in *Stalking the Wild Asparagus* by Euell Gibbons and published by the David McKay Company, Inc. The beach plum and peach pie, barberry-apple jelly, dock clam soup, gooseberry pie, and no-cook hazelnut candy recipes were reprinted from *Feasting Free on Wild Edibles* by Bradford Angier with permission from Stackpole Books. The recipes for cherries jubilee and Indian cucumber-root pickles are from Alyson Hart Knap, *Wild Harvest: An Outdoorsman's Guide to Edible Wild Plants in North America* (New York, NY, Arco Publishing Company, Inc., 1975). The birch beer recipe is reprinted with permission from *Field Guide to Edible Wild Plants* by Thomas S. Elias and Peter A. Dykeman, Grolier Book Clubs, Inc., Sherman Turnpike, Danbury, Connecticut 06816.

Library of Congress Cataloging-in-Publication Data

Medve, Richard J.
    Edible wild plants of Pennsylvania and neighboring states / by
    Richard J. Medve and Mary Lee Medve ; illustrations by Kimball S.
    Erdman.
        p.   cm.
    Includes bibliographical references.
    ISBN 0-271-00690-0
    1. Wild plants, Edible—Pennsylvania—Identification.   2. Wild
plants, Edible—Middle Atlantic States—Identification.   3. Cookery
(Wild foods) I. Medve, Mary Lee. II. Title.
QK98.5.U6M43   1990
581.6'32'0974—dc19   89–22830

It is the policy of The Pennsylvania State University Press to use acid-free paper for the first printing of all clothbound books. Publications on uncoated stock satisfy the minimum requirements of American National Standard for Information Sciences—Permanence of Paper for Printed Library Materials, ANSI Z39.48–1984.

This book is dedicated to our children, Pam, Steve, Ken, Kathy and Dave, who made beaver walks, picking blackberries, and eating "weeds" even more fun.

WARNING

There are risks involved in consuming edible wild plants. To minimize them, it is necessary to obtain positive identification of each plant, to collect the proper plant structure at the correct stage of development during the proper season, and to prepare it in a specific manner for consumption. Even though these steps may be followed exactly, the possibility exists that the consumer may be allergic to the plant, or that the plant may in some way be anomalous. The authors have been conscientious in their efforts to alert the reader to potential hazards of consuming edible wild plants, but the reader must accept full responsibility for deciding whether to consume any particular edible wild plant.

The descriptions of medicinal uses of edible wild plants given in this book are for educational purposes only. The authors are not recommending the use of these plants in self-medication. Always consult a physician about such use.

CONTENTS

PREFACE

In 1968 at the annual meeting of the American Institute of Biological Sciences at Ohio State University, Dr. John Wolfe announced that President Lyndon Johnson was going to use the word "ecology" in a presidential address. Today the term is a household word and its use by a president does not generate the type of enthusiasm demonstrated by the biologists in attendance at that meeting. At that time, however, the use of "ecology" was an important event, for it reflected the growing political pressure of the environmental movement that was sweeping the country.

From this movement the first Earth Day developed in 1970. Earth Day expanded to Earth Week as the movement grew, but later shrank to Earth Day again. In 1989 few Earth Day programs were conducted, and it received only passing mention by the media. The 1990s, however, show promise for an environmental resurgence.

During its peak period, the movement focused on broad environmental problems: air and water pollution, endangered species and habitat, soil conservation, safe disposal of municipal and toxic wastes, nuclear power, and the use of pesticides. In response to this outpouring of environmental concern, all levels of government bent to the demands of the citizenry and passed numerous environmental laws. New governmental regulatory agencies, such as the Environmental Protection Agency, were formed, and other agencies, such as the National Park Service and the United States Army Corps of Engineers, had their missions expanded and guidelines redefined to include environmental concerns. While the broad environmental movement has lost some of its energy, an enthusiasm for a return to nature and a simpler lifestyle has been steadily growing. This personal involvement in nature is demonstrated by the number of people attending nature programs, park visitations, and the 62.5 million people who have backyard bird feeders. It also includes a range of activities as diverse as having a house plant and making a wilderness trek across the Colorado Rockies.

Eating edible wild plants is a part of this individual response to return to nature. It is a part of a desire to get "back to basics." People want to learn to identify plants, prepare natural dyes, make clothes from natural products, prepare wild edibles for consumption, and in general learn how to be self-sufficient in this highly technological society.

New York City is about as far removed from nature as one could imagine, but it serves as a good example of the interest in getting back to the basics. Since 1982,

"Wildman" Steve Brill has led edible-wild-plant field walks for the public. His "hands-on" approach often means picking some plant specimens from Central Park. However, it is against the law to pick plants in New York City parks, and on March 29, 1986, the "Wildman" was arrested. As incongruous as it may seem, the end result of this encounter with the authorities was the employment of the "Wildman" by the City of New York Parks and Recreation Department. In 1987 he scheduled over 100 field walks for the Parks Department, where he described how to forage and prepare edibles in such wilderness areas as Manhattan, Long Island, Brooklyn, the Bronx, and adjacent metropolitan New Jersey. If New Yorkers are excited about foraging for wild edibles, the country as a whole must be ecstatic.

We hope this book will serve as a valuable resource tool for those individuals living in the mid-Atlantic region of the United States who want to get back to nature by being able to forage and prepare meals from edible wild plants.

ACKNOWLEDGMENTS

We would like to recognize two groups of people who have made contributions to this book. They can be categorized as "the obvious" and "the not-so-obvious."

In the latter category are those individuals who have affected our lives in some way and indirectly played a role in the development of this book. They helped to nurture our interest and appreciation of the outdoors. Without this focus, we would have had no inclination to attempt this project. Parents, children, other relatives, friends, teachers, scout leaders, casual acquaintances, and colleagues are among this group. To all of these "not-so-obvious" contributors, we extend our thanks for the impact on our lives that helped make us what we are.

"The obvious" individuals are those who made some direct input to this book. Some have made knowing contributions while others are completely unaware of their efforts.

The senior author has led field trips for thousands of individuals over a span of thirty-eight years. These field trips included everything from Boy Scout hikes to university graduate classes. Since 1976 he has conducted numerous outdoor-oriented workshops at Slippery Rock University. In 1979 a workshop on edible wild plants was added to the annual summer offerings. In each of these activities, participants always managed to teach the teacher. Their contributions were a welcome addition to the learning process. The transferral of the students' information to the teacher was followed by a subsequent transmittance of that material to new students. In time the origin of much of the material faded, and unfortunately there is no name to associate with the material and no individual to acknowledge. Much of the information in the remarks and recipes sections came from this group of unknowing contributors.

The junior author has been a cook for more than thirty years. She has adapted many of the edible wild plant recipes from those that she uses for cultivated plants. Many of these cultivated plant recipes originated from friends and relatives. In some cases it is difficult to associate a particular recipe or idea with a certain individual. Marian Medve, however, was a major source of cooking information, and modifications of her recipes are evident throughout the book. Betty Purvis, Gail Blakely, Judy Tucker, and Edelene Wood also contributed recipes.

Other individuals who made various contributions to this book are Keith Witherup, Jamie Yost, Mary Paoli, Todd Weber, Dr. Frank Pugliese, Ken Medve, and Dr. N. L.

Gamberoni. Most of the typing was done by Claudia Hart, but Pat Snyder and Janice Daughtery helped considerably. To all of these people we extend our sincere thanks.

The edible wild plant illustrations are the work of the very talented Dr. Kimball Erdman. Some of his suggestions were also incorporated into the book as welcome additions. His illustrations are a valuable asset to the book. We value his artwork and his friendship.

The nomenclature used in this book is taken from *A Synonymized Checklist of the Flora of the United States, Canada, and Greenland* by Kartesz and Kartesz and the USDA *National List of Scientific Plant Names*. For the actual identification of plants, however, we used *The New Britton and Brown Illustrated Flora of Northeastern United States and Adjacent Canada* by Gleason. Appreciation is extended to Drs. Gleason and Britton, along with Judge Brown, for producing such a botanical work of art.

The senior author is grateful to Slippery Rock (PA) University for the sabbatical leave that was granted to him to continue work on this project.

A special thanks to Edelene Wood, President of the National Wild Foods Association, who on September 16, 1988, at the annual meeting of the NWFA had the insight to declare foraging for edible wild plants to be a national sport.

Products and commercial enterprises mentioned in this book are not endorsements, but are included for information purposes only.

INTRODUCTION

Frustration is often a problem for a novice. There is not only a lot to learn, but also difficulty in finding the information in order to learn it. The novice may also need to master certain information but be unaware of other important, pertinent aspects. To paraphrase Albert Hague of the TV show "Fame," knowing that we do not know something is bad enough, but not knowing that we do not know something is even worse.

The novice plant forager experiences these types of problems. Most know that plants must be accurately identified, edible parts collected and prepared, and recipes obtained. Many people are completely unaware that edible parts should be collected at a certain stage of development, or that female flowers of some plants should be collected and not male flowers, or that some delicious potherbs contain high concentrations of oxalic acid, which can cause health problems, or that a rootstock is really an underground stem and not a root. Where to obtain all of this information is often a problem. The usual solution is to use a reference book or to consult with another forager. However, a single reference book is usually inadequate, and erroneous information is often passed from one person to another. We have tried to reduce the frustration of the novice forager by including botanically accurate, up-to-date information that is essential for the person starting on the edible wild plant adventure.

Two reasons why dictionaries and encyclopedias are so valuable as references are that they are well organized and that they contain predictable information. These two features served as the basic framework for this book. For each described species, the reader can easily locate the species entry and be certain of the type and location of that information within the entry.

Each plant is alphabetically cross-referenced by common and scientific names in the index. Every species entry conveniently contains the same categories of information on two facing pages: common names, scientific name, family, illustration, characteristics, habitat, distribution, edible parts, food uses, precautions, preparation, recipes, and remarks.

This book presents a complete package of information for more than 100 edible wild plants found in the mid-Atlantic region. The frustration that a novice experiences while trying to prepare that first dish of wild edibles should be minimized with the use of this book. As the forager gains experience and wishes to include other plants and try new recipes, additional resources will have to be consulted. To aid the reader in this regard, a list of recommended books has been included.

1

FORAGING FOR EDIBLE WILD PLANTS

Why Forage?

Reasons for foraging for edible wild plants vary from the practical to the etheric. For some it is an economic necessity because cultivated crops are simply unavailable. Others consume edible wild plants because many are more nutritious than their store-bought relatives. Edible wild plants are organically grown and relatively free of pesticides and other pollutants. For the outdoorsperson who faces the possibility of being lost or away from provisions, knowledge of edible plants may also be the difference between survival and death.

Some enjoy the fun of foraging. Spending the day outdoors foraging and preparing a new recipe can be an enjoyable experience. It is also very gratifying. There is a self-fulfillment in the knowledge that we can roam the fields and forests and confidently eat from nature's kitchen.

Self-sufficiency is a common philosophy today. Woodburners, clothes from natural fibers, wind-powered generators, gardens, and collecting edible wild plants are all evidence of this interest in being self-sufficient. Part of this philosophy has emerged because of a desire to be less dependent, but a deeper motivation appears to be the fear of a major disaster.

Another reason to forage is the taste of the food. While some edibles are little more than survival foods, others are delightful to the palate. Their unique flavor cannot be obtained from plants sold in the market.

For many people, foraging and consuming wild plants gives a feeling of oneness with nature. There are no people, machines, or preservatives between the individual and the plants. It is a return to the very basics of nature, where herbivores live off the land.

Emerson defined a weed as a "plant whose virtues have not yet been discovered." There seems to be something contemptuous in calling a plant a weed. To a wild-plant enthusiast who has discovered the virtues of many plants, there are relatively few if any weeds. By recognizing the edible virtues of plants, foragers are raising them from the lowly status of "weed" to the respectful stature of edible wild plant. After using this book and trying the recipes, you will never again call lamb's-quarters

3

a weed. Instead you will nurture it with respect and even encourage its growth in your garden.

Edible wild plants provide alternatives to a rather limited choice of domesticated plants. Of the approximately 20,000 plant species that have been identified as being edible, about 150 are used extensively and three (wheat, rice and corn) provide humans with more than half of their bodily energy requirements. The availability of edible wild plants in the grocery store, however, is growing. Purslane, Jerusalem artichokes, ostrich fern, dandelion, watercress, and many berries and nuts are already available. Amaranth is growing in popularity as a flour source and is predicted to be a commonly cultivated plant of the future. If this trend continues, the forager of the twenty-first century may look at this book with some amusement and disbelief as he wonders about the wisdom of his ancestors, for today's edible wild plants may well be tomorrow's cultivated plants.

Rules of Foraging

Encounters with bears, poisonous snakes, chiggers, ticks, and the usual array of accidents are among the possible types of hazards faced by the wild plant forager. In addition, the plants themselves are a formidable obstacle.

Some plants are poisonous while others produce allergies. Allergic reactions include diarrhea, hives, vomiting, cramps, asthma, and headaches, and may even be violent enough to cause death. One out of six Americans is allergic to something. Allergies that usually come to mind are ragweed pollen and bee venom, but food allergies also exist. Among the common foods that most often cause hypersensitive reactions are gluten, nuts, fish, peanuts, soybeans, shellfish, eggs, and milk. Gluten is a protein found in wheat, rye, oats, and barley. A person having gluten intolerance must avoid all foods containing any of these grains. Food allergies are difficult to identify because commercially prepared foods contain such a large number of components and symptoms may not appear for as long as 24 hours after consumption.

Some people feel quite safe when consuming edible wild plants because the plants are "wild" and "free" from the manipulations of humans. The gluten allergen is a good refutation of this belief. This wheat protein is a naturally occurring compound that no doubt occurred in "wild" wheat plants that were the ancestors of our modern genetically and agriculturally manipulated cultivated wheat. Imagine that wheat had not been domesticated and today was categorized as an edible wild plant. It would still contain gluten and still be a problem for foragers. If humans can be allergic to cultivated crops, why should we expect anything different from "wild" plants?

In addition to those plants that produce allergens, there are those that contain toxins. Poisonous plants are troublesome in two ways. Some poisonous plants, such as poison hemlock and water hemlock, are a problem to the forager because they resemble edible plants. Even edible wild plants may be vexing because they may be poisonous at some stage of development or have particular organs that are toxic.

No doubt about it, "it's a jungle out there." Eating edible wild plants is not a spur-of-the-moment activity. Foraging requires much mental preparation. Avoiding plants with allergens or toxins could be a life-or-death matter. Therefore, the rules of foraging must be strictly followed.

1. Be positive of the identification of the plant. Many plants that are eaten at an early stage of development are difficult to identify at that growth period. Check the plant against an illustration, photograph, or herbarium specimen. When researching the plant, use the scientific name. Common names are too confusing. There are many common names for the same species and the same common name may be used for several species. Plants have one scientific name and that name is unique.
2. Collect during the proper season.
3. Use freshly collected plants. Some plants produce toxins when wilted.
4. Collect the correct plant organ and make sure that it is at the proper stage of development.
5. Avoid collecting from areas that may be contaminated with pesticides, heavy metals, polluted water, excess fertilizer, or human or animal excrement.
6. Adhere to the warnings described in the precautions section of each plant entry.
7. Follow the directions described under the preparations section. Some plants require boiling in several changes of water.
8. If you are allergic to some cultivated plants, avoid eating closely related edible wild plants. Anything in the same family may cause an allergic reaction.
9. A species that is described as being edible refers to an average plant and an average human. Remember that each of us contains a unique set of genetic information and so does each plant. Your unique set of genetic information may vary enough from the average human that you may be allergic to certain plant species. On the other hand, an unusual genetic combination in the edible wild plant may have made it different enough from the average that it may be toxic to the average human.
10. The first time that you consume a new edible wild plant or a new part of a plant, do so in moderation. A teaspoonful is a good starting amount. Although the plants may be 100 percent natural, you can still get sick.
11. Until you have progressed beyond the scope of this book, avoid experimentation on untested, potentially edible wild plants or undescribed parts of edible plants.
12. A wild animal feeding on a plant is no guarantee that humans can eat it safely. More than fifty bird species eat the fruits of poison ivy. There is no general test for poisonous plants or edibles.
13. Only collect from plants that are available in abundant quantities. Replant corms, bulbs, tubers, rhizomes, and seeds. Try to collect edible parts without destroying the plant.
14. Obtain permission from the landowner and check on state and federal regulations before foraging.

15. Much of the information obtained about edible wild plants has been gained mainly from the experiences of Indians, pioneers, outdoor enthusiasts, and European immigrants. Few scientific investigations have been conducted on wild edibles. Therefore, don't expect everything that you read to have scientific backing. Also, don't be surprised when the Food and Drug Administration reports that a commonly consumed edible plant, such as sassafras, has been found to contain a carcinogen. Keep up to date by reading the latest information on edible wild plants.

If you can't remember all of these foraging rules, keep this mnemonic in mind:

EDIBLE PLANT PARTS TAKE *TIME* TO *PREPARE*

Make sure that you have correctly identified the *EDIBLE PLANT,* have the correct edible plant *PART,* have picked it at the right *TIME* (season and stage of development), and have followed the recommended *PREPARATION* procedure.

Optimal Foraging

Could we return to a simpler life and forgo the convenience of foraging at the local grocery store? A few individuals have voluntarily made this commitment and are almost totally self-sufficient. Others, especially in the Third World Countries, have had this commitment forced on them.

There is a joke about a pig and a chicken who wanted to do something for Farmer Jones to show their appreciation for all of his kindness to them. The two animals considered many possibilities. The chicken finally suggested that they make a breakfast of ham and eggs for Farmer Jones. The flabbergasted pig said, "That sounds fine, but for you that's only an involvement while for me it's a total commitment."

Most of us are occasional wild plant foragers. We are involved, but not totally committed. To make the galinsoga cheese soup recipe, most people would forage for galinsoga in the wild, but probably forage for the flour, milk, cheese, and salt and pepper at the local grocery store. Making an edible wild plant dish from all wild edibles requires an extremely large amount of time and energy in addition to a lot of planning. Did you remember to burn coltsfoot leaves in June for salt and collect pennycress seeds in July for pepper? Try sometime to prepare an edible wild plant meal without using a single store-bought food item.

Even the occasional edible-wild-plant enthusiast should try to maximize the benefits from time spent foraging in the field. To do so requires the application of an ecological concept called the "optimal foraging theory."

The "optimal foraging theory" states that animals consume forage items that give them the best return for time and energy spent. To function optimally, the foraging animal must

1. Decide where to look for food
2. Go to the site and search for food
3. Evaluate observed food for potential food value

4. Pursue the food
5. Capture the food and prepare for consumption
6. Consume and digest the food

The "optimal foraging theory" appears to describe a predatory relationship. Usually we think of a predator as an animal that kills and consumes another animal. If the definition is broadened to one organism killing and consuming another organism, herbivory and omnivory can be included as well as carnivory. Therefore the plant forager, whether deer, bumblebee, grasshopper, or human, must forage optimally. The forager that spends a great deal of time searching for food, eating small food items, unsuccessfully trying to capture large prey, or eating nutritionally poor food will soon show some effects from this net loss of energy. This type of foraging is not cost effective and will be reflected by loss of body weight, ill health, and fewer surviving offspring. In a worst-case scenario, the ultimate result is death for the individual and extinction for the species.

As humans have progressed from hunting and gathering to agriculture to industrialism, the "optimal foraging theory" has become highly refined. Most twentieth-century humans are far removed from direct foraging. Instead, we rely on a very specialized group of foragers, called farmers, to do the foraging for us.

On an energy basis, however, the present-day farmer is not in compliance with the "optimal foraging theory." Producing one pound of lettuce that contains 56 calories requires 400 calories of fossil fuel. Another 1,800 calories of fossil fuel is used in shipping the lettuce from California to New York. Other crops are subsidized with an even greater amount of energy. The result is an average expenditure of twenty units of fossil fuel for every one unit of food energy produced. Contrary to the "optimal foraging theory," cost effectiveness for the modern farmer is not measured in energy and time, but in dollars. Cost effectiveness for farmers is thus measured in economic rather than ecological terms. In either case, not getting your investment back is bad business.

As with many other examples of man's failure to comply with ecological principles, current agricultural practices do and will continue to have a negative impact on the ecosphere. Whether totally committed or just an involved edible wild plant forager, as a practical ecologist, you should resolve to comply with the "optimal foraging theory." Here is how to do it.

Decide Where to Look for Food

Each plant entry in this book lists distribution and habitat. The distribution description will indicate where you can expect to find the plant in the geographical area covered by this book. Habitat will identify certain biological communities and geographical or geological features.

Every species has tolerance limits for each environmental factor that affects its existence. The amount of light, water, nutrients, acidity, etc., that a plant can tolerate is set by its genetic makeup. The area where the environment contains these factors within the plants' limits are reflected generally by its distribution and specifically by its habitat.

Important information is also contained in the listing of the plant's characteristics.

7

It includes life span and flowering time. Knowing that a plant is a perennial means that the plant will be there the entire year in some form. If you are after flowers or fruits, the flowering time is important.

For example, suppose that you want to collect purslane. A check of the index shows that it is described on page 26. Consulting this page reveals that it is distributed throughout the mid-Atlantic region and that its habitat includes gardens, vacant lots, waste sites, and recently disturbed areas. Its characteristics show it to be an annual that flowers all summer. Where and when to look now becomes much easier. Putting all of this information together means that if you live in Pennsylvania and it is July, you can start your foraging for purslane in your garden.

Remember that foraging for edible wild plants does not require a trip to a virgin forest. Many of the "wild" edibles are considered by some to be "weeds." These "weeds" occur as far away as your vegetable garden, lawn, flower garden, or vacant lot.

Knowing how to read a topographic map is a great asset when deciding where to look. General vegetation types, slope, exposure, stream size, and sizes of lakes are only a few of the helpful bits of information that can be obtained from topographic maps. Community names are also helpful in inferring types of biological communities. A town named "Heath" would show the possibility of a nearby bog and the presence of blueberries and cranberries. For example, a botanist at Slippery Rock University mentioned in casual conversation to a new colleague that a bog exists within one mile of the campus. That afternoon the botanist found a cranberry in his mailbox. The new colleague just consulted a topographic map for the area, identified the most likely drainages in which a bog could occur, and went to the spot.

Searching for Food

The time to search for food is not the day when you want it for a meal. Noticing a patch of red raspberry plants in the fall while rabbit hunting, observing an elderberry bush while on a spring bird walk, or seeing the white lacy flowers of Juneberry while on a drive in March is when the search for food starts. Keep a log or map with a notation of these observations. Trying to find the asparaguslike shoots of Japanese knotweed in May is fairly difficult, but the eight-foot-tall plant in July is obvious. A map with the July observation noted will make next May's search easy.

When exploring likely habitats for a particular species, remember that some plants have fairly restricted habitats which result in isolated populations. Where moist areas occur along a hillside is a good place to find wild ginger. Hazelnuts are often found at the edges of forests and not in the forest interior unless there is a canopy gap. Spatterdock, cattail, white water lily, and pickerelweed may all occur in the same lake, but at different water depths. Knowing that watercress grows in water is not good enough. You must search in the most likely habitat, which is the clear, shallow water of springs and brooks.

Conduct the search in a systematic manner. If looking for hickory, walnut, sugar maple, beech, or white oak in a mature forest, walk the area in a grid pattern or follow a series of imaginary parallel lines laid out at a right angle to the contour and a certain distance apart.

Evaluate the Plants

Now that you have located the plants, you must decide which to pick. The edible parts, precautions, and preparation sections of the plant entry provide information to evaluate an edible wild plant. Among the factors that need to be considered are size of the population, possible contamination by toxic substances, health of the plant, insect damage, age of the plant, stage of development, and part to be consumed.

For example, suppose that you want to prepare the recipe for stuffed grape leaves. The entry for grape shows that only the young leaves are to be used and that the best time to collect the leaves is late spring and early summer. This means that June is probably the best time to get to the correct habitat and look for leaves that are not quite fully expanded.

Many plants that are used as cooked greens can be collected through most of the year. Older leaves, however, tend to be bitter, stringy, and tough. Careful evaluation of the leaves of dandelion, dock, ox-eye daisy, and similar plants can mean the difference between a delightful meal and just filling your hungry stomach. Be as selective with wild edibles as you are in the grocery store.

With some wild edibles, proper evaluation of the plant is a life-or-death decision. Selecting young dandelion leaves versus older ones may affect the palatability of the dish, but it is not life threatening. With plants such as mayapple, however, you can't afford to make a mistake in evaluating the plant. Only the ripe, yellow, soft fruit is edible. The unripened fruit, as well as all other parts of the plant, is poisonous.

Pursue the Food Item

Pursuing a plant sounds a lot easier than pursuing an animal. After all it is just sitting there. Digging enough spring beauty corms to make a meal, tapping sugar-maple trees in knee-deep snow, or slopping in the muck to collect cattail rhizomes may change your mind. Pursuing takes time. Mosquitoes can make the pursuit of high-bush blueberries a real test of dedication.

There are a lot of shortcuts to pursuing edibles: use scissors for watercress, shake berries onto a sheet, use a rake for cattail, sweet flag, pickerelweed, and spatterdock rhizomes, wear leather gloves when collecting nettles and thistles, use a shovel for spring beauty corms or Indian cucumber-root rhizomes.

Capture Food and Prepare for Consumption

The capture of most plants does not have the inherent problems that capturing an animal does. Follow the directions under precautions, preparations, and remarks for those plants that pose some unusual problems.

Collect edible plants that are available in abundance. Most plant foragers conduct their activities as a hobby and not as a means of survival. It does not make either ecological or ethical sense to destroy a plant population for a hobby. Where possible, replant corms, bulbs, tubers, rhizomes, and seeds. Try to collect the edible parts without destroying the plant.

For each of the edible-wild-plant entries, there is a description of how to prepare the plant, a list of its food uses, and two recipes. Some plants can be eaten raw with no preparation while others require a great deal of preparation. Plants such as nuts, dandelion, wild onion, and partridgeberry, can be eaten raw. Others, such as amaranth, lamb's-quarters, and purslane, can be eaten as a cooked green after boiling or steaming for just a few minutes. Wild lettuce, spatterdock, and poke must be boiled several times to remove bitterness, toughness, or poisonous properties. Even after all of that treatment, they are at best considered a survival food. Especially for plants that are in the latter category, always follow the directions described under preparation and be sure to heed the precautions section. Even when you follow directions explicitly, only eat a teaspoonful of a plant that is being consumed for the first time. Preparation recommendations are for the average person. In regard to this plant, you may not be average.

Don't become dependent on special recipes for wild edibles. Instead, focus on a substitute list. In other words, what can be substituted for green beans, spinach, potatoes, or broccoli? Knowing that stinging nettle can be used as a spinach substitute makes all of those spinach recipes into nettle recipes. Try wedding soup with nettle, ravioli with nettle, or cooked nettle greens with butter and salt and pepper.

Consumption and Digestion

There is a story of two depression-era hoboes who were never without their large soup pot as they rode the trains from one town to the next. About dinnertime they would get off the train at the closest town and soon, in a central location, they would have a pot of water boiling over a nice bed of coals. Inquisitive townspeople would inevitably stop and ask what they were making in the large pot. "Stone soup," would always be the reply. "How do you make it?" To that question one of the hoboes would remove a shiny white stone about the size of a golf ball from his pocket. "I just put this stone in the boiling water and about an hour later the soup's ready to eat. Why don't you stay and have some?" Of course the inquisitive townspeople always stayed because they had never tasted stone soup. One of the hoboes would suggest that the stone soup would taste a little better if there were some carrots in it, and the obliging townspeople would run home to get the carrots. The next townsperson might be convinced that a stalk of celery would flavor the soup, or an onion or a soup bone or a few potatoes. When enough items had been added and thoroughly cooked, the shiny white stone was removed from the soup, carefully dried, and returned to a pocket for safekeeping. The hoboes and townspeople all marveled at the wonderful-tasting stone soup.

Many edible-wild-plant dishes are similar to "stone soup." Either so many other items are added to the dish or such a small amount of wild edible is used or the edible is so bland that the wild edible plant adds nothing more to the dish than the shiny white stone.

A common question concerning wild edibles is, What does it taste like? Some plants compare quite easily with a cultivated plant. Lamb's-quarters does taste like its cousin, spinach. Others, however, have their own taste. Persimmons taste like persimmons.

Some of us have trouble digesting cucumbers, milk, or peanuts. We can expect much the same thing for wild edibles.

Problems may be avoided by not consuming wild edibles that are closely related to cultivated plants to which you are allergic or cannot digest. If wheat flour bothers you, avoid reed grass. If you are allergic to mangoes, don't try staghorn sumac. If tomatoes give you a rash, why eat ground cherry? Also, if you are allergic to some medications, avoid plants with similar components. If aspirin gives you problems, don't use wintergreen or birch.

THE NEED FOR PRECISION

A local newspaper recently carried an article on edible wild plants. In the article the reporter stated that poke roots were edible. Discerning readers, we may hope, noted the error or at least checked other sources before trying to eat the poisonous poke roots. But what about the edible wild plant neophyte who believes everything in print? When queried about the error, the journalist stated that the word processor had "eaten" her story, and to meet her deadline she had rewritten the story from memory. Unfortunately she could not recall whether it was the poke root or the shoot that some people ate. When informed of the error, the reporter wrote a followup article correcting the inaccuracy and detailing the paradox of poke. She received several letters from people who were hospitalized after having tried poke roots. Fortunately, these mishaps did not occur as a result of reading the original edible-wild-plant article.

Another article in a large metropolitan newspaper carried a story about feasting on forest edibles. The article contained at least fifteen errors or half-truths. In this case a letter to the author and a later letter to the editor asking for a correction brought no response.

Whom can the wild food forager trust? Where can we obtain reliable information? A problem is that few scientific studies have been conducted on edible wild plants, and those studies usually remain buried in scientific publications.

When dealing with edible wild plants, a little knowledge can certainly be a dangerous thing—especially when some of that knowledge is suspect. Armed with a paperback, a newspaper article, or a few words of advice, the novice forager is anxious to take that suspect knowledge into the field to forage in Mother Nature's garden.

All of us have conveyed some type of information to another person. We assume an awesome responsibility when sharing information about wild food plants. Our friends are willing to put parts of those plants into their bodies on the basis of our advice. Vagueness and inaccuracies cannot be tolerated when dealing with the life of the person with whom we have shared some of ourselves.

The poke-root article is an example of an inaccuracy that was due to carelessness. Reasons for other inaccuracies are varied. A recent book on the market interchanged the titles of two plant illustrations. In another book a recipe for hot clover and rice shows an accompanying drawing of white clover, but the title identifies the plant as "white clover: *Melilotus alba.*" Is white clover (*Trifolium repens*) to be used, or is it white sweet clover (*Melilotus alba*)?

Another problem with references is that they often lack preciseness. One example is the lack of precision in identifying a plant. Common names are often used instead of scientific names. Which plant do you know as pigweed, black snakeroot, ironwood, or poke? Each of these names is commonly used for several species. Some names such as sorrel, dock, lily, violet, and turnip include plants from several families. A recipe for sorrel cobbler may fail to designate which sorrel to use. Some references also use common names in a generic sense. For example, a reference to goldenrod as a source of tea is too general. There are more than sixty-five species of goldenrod in the northeastern United States and Canada, and not all are good for tea. A popular edible wild plant book lists sumac for making tea. Is poison sumac included? Poison ivy is also a sumac.

Another problem area is the misuse of standard botanical terms. Perpetuating the misuse of botanical terms destroys our ability to communicate. Several popular publications describe the use of cattail "roots" when the authors probably mean the horizontal, underground stem (rhizome). Others mention spring beauty "potato root" when they mean corm (another underground stem) or burdock "stem" when petiole (leaf stalk) is implied. (White potatoes, by the way, are tubers [stems] and not "roots.") The inner bark of the young twigs of some trees is edible, yet cambium, inner bark, and sapwood are often used synonymously, which should not be done. The incorrect use of these terms exemplifies the need for precision. Their misuse is confusing to the knowledgeable reader but more importantly could result in the neophyte forager chewing on the wrong part of the plant.

More than 1.2 million poison exposures were reported to U.S. Poison Control Centers in 1987. One in thirteen of these exposures involved plants. Poke and poison ivy are among the most commonly cited. As with many medicinal plants, some edible wild plants are also considered poisonous. Edible wild plants listed in *Poisonous Plants of Pennsylvania* include mayapple, black cherry, poke, pawpaw, asparagus, elderberry, crab apple, stinging nettle, oak, milkweed, burdock, and amaranth. A similar list of poisonous cultivated plants could also be developed that would include tomato, potato, rhubarb, cabbage, cashew, and apples.

Just as with cultivated plants, wild edible plants may have some toxic properties. The farmer and grocer have already selected the edible part of the cultivated plant for us. The selection of the edible portion of the wild food plant is our responsibility. Be absolutely certain of the edibility of any plant before putting it into your mouth. Double-check what you have read or heard. Use the correct terminology and scientific name in order to be precise and avoid confusion.

HOW TO USE THIS BOOK

If you are certain of the plant's identity, go directly to the index and find the page number of the entry. Compare your plant with the illustration and the characteristics to verify your identification. Remember that this book contains a limited number of plants and that you may have one of the many that are not included in this book.

Once you are positive of the identification, carefully read through the other parts of the entry. Use the illustrated glossary when unfamiliar terms are encountered. Be sure to read the "Rules of Foraging," which begins on page 4, and "Optimal Foraging" on page 6 before you begin to do any collecting.

For additional information, consult the remarks section. Usually this section will include some explanation of the origin of the scientific and common names, historical importance, medicinal uses, nutritional value, and economic importance. Further detailed nutrition information of selected plants can be found in the nutrition composition table on pages 218–19. The remarks section will be very useful to field-trip leaders.

The medicinal uses cited for plants are reported as educational information. Historical and contemporary uses by physicians as well as herbalists are a part of this information. The authors are *not* recommending the use of these plants in self-medication. Always consult a physician.

If uncertain of the plant's identity, you have two options. The first is to consult with some authority. This may be a knowledgeable person or a plant identification book. A technical book will probably require the use of dichotomous keys. A second, less desirable option, is to page through this book and compare the unknown plant to the illustrations and then verify it as previously described. To help those people who like to page through books, the plants have been arranged according to size from the smallest to the largest. The average sizes are indicated along the page margin.

The Index of Food Uses, which begins on page 235, will aid the person who wants to prepare a certain type of food but does not know the plants that can be used for that type of dish. Boldface indicates that recipes are included with the plant description.

The precautions section for each plant entry may mention some poisonous plants that resemble the edible plant. Toxic Look-alikes, on pages 221–23, contains a more detailed description of these poisonous plants.

EDIBLE WILD PLANTS

WHITE WATER LILY
(White pond lily)

Nymphaea odorata Ait.
Nymphaea tuberosa Paine
Nymphaeaceae

N. odorata

Characteristics: These are aquatic, herbaceous perennials with leathery green leaves on very long petioles that arise from stout rhizomes. The round leaves have a single break from margin to leaf center. The leaves and flowers float on the surface of the water. Numerous white petals that may tend toward pink, four green sepals, numerous yellow stamens, and a single ovary compose the flower, which blooms from June to September. *N. odorata* has fragrant flowers, leaves that are commonly purple or red beneath, and a petiole that is not striped. *N. tuberosa* usually has a striped petiole, leaves that are commonly green beneath, and a rhizome with numerous knotty tubers.

Habitat: Ponds, lakes, and slow-moving streams.

Distribution: Generally throughout the area, but *N. odorata* is found more toward the coastal plain while *N. tuberosa* is less common and found south to Maryland.

Edible parts: Young leaves, flowerbuds, seeds, tubers.

Food uses: Cooked greens, cooked vegetable, flour, potato substitute.

Precautions: Do not collect from polluted water.

Preparation: Collect the young leaves in the spring and prepare as a cooked green. The flower buds are collected in the summer and used as a cooked vegetable. The dried seeds can be ground into flour or made as a cooked vegetable. Tubers from *N. tuberosa* appear as swellings on the rhizome and are prepared as a potato substitute.

Recipes:

Tubers and Greens

2 cups water-lily tubers (washed)	2 cups dandelion leaves
3 tablespoons oil	3 strips bacon (fried and broken)
4 leeks (chopped)	salt and pepper to taste

Boil water-lily tubers in water for 20 minutes. Cool, peel, and quarter. Sauté leeks in oil until lightly brown. Add dandelion leaves. Cook until wilted. Add tubers and bacon and cook until warm. Salt and pepper to taste.

Water Lily Oriental Style

3 cups water-lily flowerbuds (washed)	½ cup pineapple juice
	½ cup almonds (chopped)
1 cup water	salt and pepper to taste
1 tablespoon cider vinegar	1 Jerusalem artichoke (peeled and sliced)
1 tablespoon ground ginger	
2 tablespoons soy sauce	boiled rice

Boil water-lily flowerbuds in water for 10 minutes. Drain. If buds are large, halve or quarter. Combine all ingredients except rice and simmer for 15 minutes. Serve over rice.

Remarks: *Nymphaea* refers to the nymphs of Greek mythology who were very beautiful and lived in the water. *Tuberosa* refers to the tubers, and *odorata* means odor or fragrant. The white water lilies are commonly planted as ornamentals in most of the world. They can be used as flower clocks, with *N. tuberosa* opening from 8:00 A.M. to 3:00 P.M. and *N. odorata* from 7:00 A.M. to 1:00 P.M. The petioles and flower stalks have large air passages in them. In some lakes the water lilies grow so abundantly that they hinder boaters, swimmers, and fishermen and are considered to be "weeds." To control the "weeds," the lake level can be lowered in the fall, which results in the winter freezing of the rhizomes. Herbicides may also be used or pathways can be cut through the massive colonies by hand or machine. In some books the genus name may be listed as *Castalia*.

STRAWBERRY
(Field strawberry, Wild
   strawberry)

Fragaria virginiana Duchesne
Rosaceae

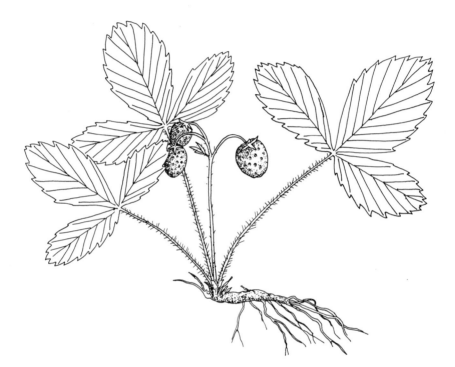

Characteristics: These three- to six-inch perennial herbs spread by runners, which form colonies. The compound leaves are composed of three coarsely toothed leaflets. The alternate leaves have hairy petioles. Up to twelve separate flowers form a flat cluster at the end of the flower stalk. The flowers have five white petals, five green sepals, and numerous stamens and pistils. The red fruit is much smaller than the cultivated strawberry. Flowering occurs from April to June.
Habitat: Relatively dry fields, pastures, waste areas, railroad tracks, and open woodlands.
Distribution: Throughout the area.

Edible parts: Fruit and leaves.

Food uses: Fresh fruit, tea, jam, jelly, pie, shortcake.

Precautions: Partially wilted leaves used for tea have been reported to cause some stomach problems.

Preparation: Wash fruits in cold water. Remove calyx and pedicel. Dry on towels. Use fresh or dried leaves to make tea. Fruits are used to make jams, jellies, pies, or shortcakes, or are eaten fresh.

Recipes:

Wild Strawberry Salad

1 quart wild strawberries	½ cup walnut meats (ground)
½ cup sugar	1 quart whipped cream
10 canned peach halves	

Combine sugar and strawberries. Fill peach halves with strawberries. Sprinkle ground walnuts on strawberries. Cover with whipped cream.

Strawberry Muffins

1 cup strawberries (cleaned and washed	⅔ cup milk
¼ cup shortening	2 cups flour
⅓ cup sugar	½ teaspoon salt
2 eggs (beaten)	3 teaspoons baking powder

Combine shortening and sugar. Add beaten eggs. Sift together flour, salt, and baking powder. Combine dry mixture, milk, and sugar mixture. Gently fold in strawberries. Grease muffin pans and fill two-thirds full. Bake at 400° F for 25 minutes.

Remarks: *Fragaria* is from the Latin name for strawberry, *fragrum,* which probably refers to the smell of the fruit. The name "strawberry" may derive from the Anglo-Saxon "streowberrie," which refers to a growth form that makes the plant appear to be "strewed" on the ground. Another possible origin of the word may be a reference to the berries being sold on pieces of straw. Wild strawberries are among the sweetest of wild fruits. They are much smaller than cultivated strawberries and much sweeter. The "fruit" of the strawberry is really a multiple fruit consisting of numerous tightly packed smaller fruits known as achenes. These are what we call "seeds." Leaves and fruits are rich in vitamin C. The fruit is also rich in iron, potassium, and calcium. An herbal tea made from dried leaves has been used to counter diarrhea. Linnaeus used the fruits to prevent gout.

WINTERGREEN *Gaultheria procumbens* L.
(Checkerberry, Teaberry) Ericaceae

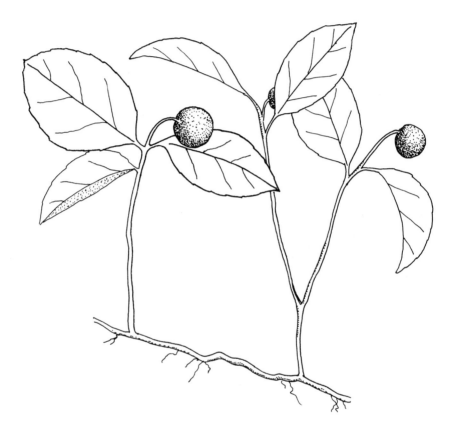

Characteristics: Wintergreen is a creeping perennial that grows from a rhizome to a height of 8 inches. The alternate, simple evergreen leaves are shiny, entire to slightly toothed, and clustered at the tops of the stems. The crushed leaves have the odor of wintergreen. The white five-lobed flowers are usually solitary on a drooping stalk. The fruit is a bright red, mealy berry. Flowering occurs in July and August.
Habitat: Acid soils of dry or moist woods.
Distribution: Throughout the area.

Edible parts: Leaves and fruit.

Food uses: Salad, tea, fruit, jam, pie.

Precautions: Anyone sensitive to aspirin should not eat wintergreen. It contains methyl salicylate, which is closely related to aspirin. Partridgeberry (*Mitchella repens*) closely resembles wintergreen.

Preparation: Wintergreen leaves can be collected throughout the year. Fresh leaves are better than dried. Leaves can be used in salads or tea. Fruits can be eaten raw, made into jams, jellies, and pies, used for tea, or added to pancakes, muffins, or salads. Collect the fruits during the fall and winter.

Recipes:

Wintergreen Pie

4 cups wintergreen berries (washed)	2 tablespoons lemon juice
1½ tablespoons tapioca	3 tablespoons butter
½ cup sugar	2 teaspoons milk
½ cup raisins	½ teaspoon cinnamon
1 piecrust shell and top crust	

Mix wintergreen berries, tapioca, sugar, and raisins. Place in piecrust shell. Sprinkle with lemon juice and dot with butter. Cover with top crust. Cut vents in the crust. Brush piecrust with milk. Sprinkle with cinnamon. Bake for 45 minutes at 375° F or until done.

Wintergreen Muffins

1 cup wintergreen berries (washed)	2 tablespoons sugar
1 cup whole wheat flour	1 egg (beaten)
1 cup white flour	1 cup milk
4 teaspoons baking powder	3 tablespoons vegetable oil
½ teaspoon salt	

Sift together the flours, baking powder, salt, and sugar. Combine egg and milk. Add dry ingredients and oil to milk. Stir. Fold in 1 cup of wintergreen berries. Fill greased muffin cups two-thirds full and bake at 400° F for 25 minutes or until done.

Remarks: The name *Gaultheria* commemorates Jean-François Gaultier (1708–56), who was a Canadian physician. *Procumbens* describes the creeping growth form of the plant. The common name of wintergreen refers to the plant being green all winter. Technically, wintergreen is a low-growing shrub. The pleasant-smelling oil of wintergreen, once used in medicines, chewing gum, candy, toothpaste, and cough drops, was first obtained from this plant. Twigs of black birch replaced wintergreen as the source of oil of wintergreen, and today most of it is produced synthetically. Medicinally, wintergreen has been used as an antirheumatic and a rubifacient, and to relieve the pain of headaches and toothaches.

PARTRIDGEBERRY   *Mitchella repens* L.
(Twinberry, Checkerberry, Squaw vine)   Rubiaceae

Characteristics: This creeping evergreen grows to about 10 inches high. The stem roots at the nodes and forms large colonies. The ovate leaves are opposite, dark green, and smooth, with a single white line along the midrib. Twin flowers with four white petals occur at the ends of the stems. A single red fruit with eight seeds forms from the fusion of the twin flowers. Flowering occurs from May to July.
Habitat: Moist, cool woods, especially in acid soils under conifers.
Distribution: Found throughout most of the area.

Edible parts: Fruit.

Food uses: Snack, salad.

Precautions: Often confused with wintergreen, which lacks the white line in the middle of the leaf and has the characteristic wintergreen odor.

Preparation: Collect in the late fall and winter. The fruit is dry, seedy, pulpy, and lacks taste. It is used mostly to add color to salads or as a nibble to ward off hunger pains.

Recipes:

Partridgeberry Apple Salad

½ cup partridgeberry fruits	½ cup swiss cheese (shredded)
2 apples (peeled and diced)	½ cup mayonnaise
½ cup pineapple tidbits	leaf lettuce
½ cup white seedless grapes (halved)	2 tablespoons walnuts (chopped)

Except for lettuce and walnuts, mix all ingredients in a bowl. Place servings on individual lettuce leaves. Sprinkle with walnuts.

Pistachio Partridgeberry Salad

1 cup crushed pineapple (drained)	½ cup walnuts (chopped)
½ cup partridgeberries	1 cup mini marshmallows
1 package pistachio instant pudding (3 oz.)	2 cups milk

With electric mixer, beat pudding and milk for 2 minutes. Add remaining ingredients, mix, and then refrigerate.

Remarks: Linnaeus honored his botanical correspondent from Virginia, Dr. John Mitchell, by naming this genus, *Mitchella,* after him. The term *repens* refers to the plant's creeping or prostrate growth form and has the same word derivation as the term repent. Which partridge the common name refers to is unclear. The term partridge is used to describe a number of gallinaceous birds. It probably refers to the ruffed grouse, but the wild turkey and quail are possibilities. By having some flowers with short styles and others with long styles, cross-pollination is guaranteed. The two "eyes" at the bottom of the fruit are the calyx remains of the two fused ovaries. "Squaw vine" refers to the use of this medicinal herb by Indian women to regulate the menstrual cycle and facilitate childbirth.

PURSLANE
(Pusley, Low pigweed)

Portulaca oleracea L.
Portulacaceae

Characteristics: An annual, prostrate herb that forms flat mats about 1 square foot in size and less than 10 inches in height. Stems are shiny, smooth, and often reddish purple. The leaves are fleshy, flat, and broadest nearest the tip. The stems freely branch from a deep, central root. The single flowers have five yellow petals. At maturity, the top portion of the capsule falls away to expose black or dark red seeds. **Habitat:** Common garden weed; vacant lots, waste sites, recently disturbed areas. **Distribution:** Found throughout the area.

Edible parts: Leaves, stems, seeds.

Food uses: Salad, cooked green, pickle, flour, soup.

Precautions: Because it grows so close to the ground, purslane should always be well washed.

Preparation: Collect the stems and leaves in summer and the seeds in the fall. Pinch off tender young leaves and stems and add to a salad or use as cooked greens. Stems can be used with any pickling recipe. Leaves and stems add flavor and serve as a thickener for soups and stews. Dried seeds can be ground into flour.

Recipes:

Purslane Casserole

4 cups cooked purslane (drained)	¾ cup light cream
3 wild leeks	1 cup cracker crumbs
1 cup mushrooms	salt and pepper

Stir-fry chopped leeks and mushrooms together. Place purslane in a casserole dish. Add leeks and mushrooms and salt and pepper to taste. Pour cream over mixture. Top with cracker crumbs. Bake for 25 minutes at 350° F or until firm.

Nonni's Purslane Fritatta

3 strips of bacon	4 slices brick cheese (cut into small
½ cup purslane	pieces)
3 tablespoons onions (chopped)	¼ teaspoon garlic powder
½ cup mushrooms	salt and pepper to taste
6 eggs	

Fry bacon, purslane, onions, and mushrooms in a skillet. Mix eggs, cheese, garlic powder, salt and pepper. Pour egg mixture over fried ingredients and cover. Cook over medium heat. After top and bottom of fritatta are cooked, fold over halfway and serve.

Remarks: Originating in India or Persia, where it has been used for more than two thousand years, purslane is today a prized garden vegetable in much of Europe and Asia. Many North Americans, however, regard purslane as one of the most pesty garden "weeds." Although many people remove this "weed" so that garden vegetables can grow without competition, it is often more nutritious than the vegetables. A 3½-ounce serving of purslane contains only twenty-one calories, but is high in calcium, iron, and vitamin A. On your next trip to Juarez, Mexico, visit the City Market, where purslane is sold as a green vegetable.

LARGE CRANBERRY   *Vaccinium macrocarpon* Ait.
(American cranberry, Sour
   berry)
SMALL CRANBERRY   *Vaccinium oxycoccos* L.
(Sour berry)   Ericaceae

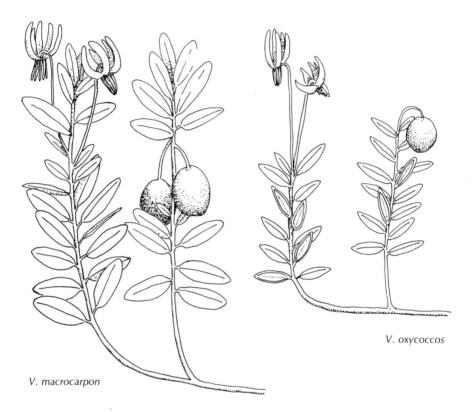

V. oxycoccos

V. macrocarpon

Description: This is a trailing evergreen shrub with slender stems. It is usually less than 1 foot tall. The small, oval, leathery simple leaves are alternate and have a smooth edge. Leaves are dark green above and whitish below. Nodding pink flowers have recurved petals. The bright red, globular berries contain many seeds. *V. oxycoccos,* because of its smaller fruit, is known as small cranberry.

Habitat: Acid areas such as bogs, swamps, shores of lakes; commonly associated with *Sphagnum* moss.

Distribution: *V. oxycoccos* extends south to Pennsylvania and New Jersey and west to northeastern Ohio. *V. macrocarpon* is found further south to North Carolina. Both are found locally in the mountains.

Edible parts: Fruit.

Food uses: Cooked fruit, jelly, jam, cold drink.

Precautions: Often found associated with poison sumac. Collecting on the shelf of a quaking bog could be hazardous.

Preparation: Unbruised fruit can be stored for a long period of time in a cool place. The fruits can be frozen or dried. Too tart to be eaten raw, but those collected late in the season, November or December, are somewhat less tart. Cooking and sugar make the tart berries a delight.

Recipes:

Cranberry Sauce

4 cups cranberries	½ cup orange juice
2 tablespoons butter	2 tablespoons orange rind (grated)
2 cups sugar	2 tablespoons cinnamon
1½ cups water	

Combine cranberries, butter, sugar and water in a saucepan. Boil for about 10 minutes. Stir constantly. Add other ingredients. Boil for 1 minute. Refrigerate.

Cranberry Whip Dessert

1 package orange gelatin	½ cup sugar
1 cup hot water	2 cups cranberries
1 small, unpeeled red apple (cut and cored)	whipped cream

Mix gelatin with hot water until dissolved. Pour gelatin mixture, apple, and sugar in blender. With blender at medium speed, drop in cranberries a few at a time until thickened. Pour into dessert dishes. Chill. Serve with whipped cream.

Remarks: Reportedly the cranberry got its common name from the resemblance of the nodding flowers to the nodding heads of cranes. Cranberries can be picked throughout the winter, and those that are covered by snow remain in especially good shape. *Oxycoccos* is Latin for sour berry. *Macrocarpon* refers to the large fruit. The common market berries are derivatives of *V. macrocarpon* and are grown commercially in New England, New Jersey, Wisconsin, and the Pacific Northwest. Growers collect the berries by flooding the fields and letting the berries come to the surface, where they are skimmed off. Cranberries were probably the first native American fruit eaten in Europe.

SPRING BEAUTY
(Fairy spuds, Groundnut)

Claytonia virginica L.
Portulacaceae

Characteristics: This erect perennial grows to 1 foot tall. A pair of opposite, linear, entire leaves are attached to a frail, succulent stem about halfway up the plant. A loose, terminal raceme bears five to fifteen long-stalked white to pink flowers. The five petals are lined with pink veins. The flowers appear from March to May. Several single leaves may also arise from the same corm that produces the flowering stem.
Habitat: Rich, damp soils in deciduous forests, especially on floodplains.
Distribution: Throughout the area.

Edible parts: Corm.

Food uses: Potato substitute, salad.

Precautions: A great deal of digging is required to get enough corms. Often the deep corms separate from the stems and are difficult to find. Only collect where the plants are in great abundance.

Preparation: Wash the corms in cold water. If the corms are to be baked or boiled, they can be scrubbed with a brush, cooked, and then peeled. If the corms are to be eaten raw in a salad, wash, then peel.

Recipes:

Spring Beauty Stew

2 lb. stewing chicken (cut into pieces)
4 cups water
2 teaspoons salt
½ teaspoon pepper
5 wild leeks (chopped)
¼ cup flour
½ cup water

10 spring-beauty corms (washed and peeled)
1 lb. can tomatoes
2 cups green beans
5 carrots (sliced)
1 cup celery (diced)
1 cup mushrooms (sliced)
1 teaspoon oregano

Cook chicken in water with salt, pepper, and leeks for about 2 hours. Remove chicken skin and cut meat into cubes. Blend flour with ¼ cup of cold water. Add to broth. Add all other ingredients and cook until vegetables are tender.

Spring Beauty–Broccoli Salad

6 slices bacon
2 stalks broccoli
1 medium red onion (sliced)
1 cup raisins

10 spring-beauty corms (boiled and peeled)
1 cup Swiss cheese (cubed)
2 carrots (grated)
1 cup creamy Italian dressing

Fry bacon and crumble. Cut broccoli into small pieces. Layer broccoli, onions, raisins, spring-beauty corms, cheese, carrots, and bacon in a bowl. Pour dressing over and refrigerate for 1 hour. Stir before serving.

Remarks: *Claytonia* commemorates John Clayton (1685–1773), who was a pioneer American botanist. The flavor of the starchy corm resembles the taste of chestnuts. Spring beauty was a commonly used Indian food. The plant is high in vitamins A and C. The "optimal foraging theory" states that organisms forage for food that will provide the greatest amount of energy return for energy expended. On this basis alone, digging for spring-beauty corms would not be energy efficient for the casual edible wild plant forager. Spring beauty is the focus of some cancer research. Age-induced chromosome abnormalities that occur in the somatic cells of spring beauty are being used to study why more malignancies occur in older humans.

Sesuvium maritimum (Walt.) BSP
Aizoaceae

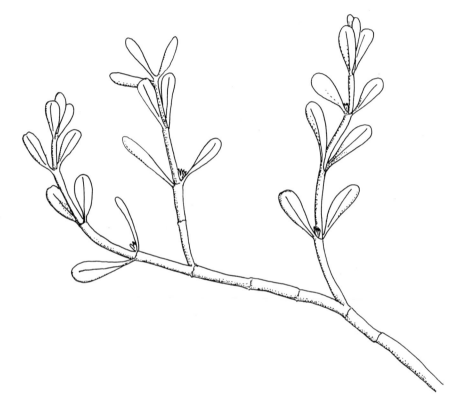

Characteristics: This is a prostrate to slightly ascending succulent annual that grows to 12 inches tall. The opposite, smooth, ovate leaves have an entire margin. Very small purple flowers occur in the leaf axils. The usually solitary, petalless flowers bloom from July to September.
Habitat: Sea beaches.
Distribution: Along the Atlantic coast.

Edible parts: Leaves and stems.
Food uses: Cooked greens, soup.
Precautions: Wash thoroughly to remove sand.
Preparation: Boil in several changes of water to remove saltiness. Collect in early summer.
Recipes:

Sea Purslane Omelet

2 tablespoons butter
¼ cup mushrooms
¼ cup onion (chopped)
1 cup sea-purslane leaves (chopped)
5 eggs (beaten)

¼ cup sharp cheddar cheese (grated)
3 tablespoons milk
pepper to taste

Melt butter in skillet. Add mushrooms, onion, and sea purslane and sauté. Mix eggs, cheese, pepper, and milk. Add to skillet and stir. Cover and cook over low heat.

Sea Purslane Soup

2 cups water
1 cup sea purslane leaves (chopped)
3 cups raw potatoes (diced)
1 teaspoon celery flakes
1 chicken bouillon cube
½ cup celery (chopped)

1 teaspoon parsley flakes
¼ cup onions (chopped)
½ teaspoon pepper
1 teaspoon basil
¼ lb. Velveeta cheese (cubed)
2 cups milk

Boil water and add all ingredients except cheese and milk. Cover and cook until tender. Blend in cheese and milk.

Remarks: The genus name *Sesuvium* is one of many whose meaning is unknown. *Maritimum* refers to the ocean or sea, which describes the plant's habitat on sea beaches from New York to Texas and in the West Indies. Aizoaceae is in the carpetweed family and contains a large number of tropical succulents. *Mollugo verticillata* is the carpetweed that we commonly see on moist soil throughout most of temperate North America.

Each scientific name is followed by the citation of authorities. Usually a single letter such as L. will appear. This means that Linnaeus originated the scientific name. *Sesuvium maritimum* (Walt.) BSP means that Britton, Sterns, and Poggenburg (BSP) originated the present scientific name, but Thomas Walter (Walt.) used *maritimum* in a different taxonomic position and first described the species.

SHEEP SORREL
(Red sorrel)

Rumex acetosella L.
Polygonaceae

Characteristics: This annual or perennial herb that grows to 1 foot tall forms basal rosettes that are connected by rhizomes. The alternate, simple arrowhead-shaped leaves have long petioles with a papery sheath at the petiole base. Small reddish flowers are scattered along thin, terminal spikes that appear from June to October.
Habitat: Lawns, gardens, waste places, old fields.
Distribution: Throughout the area.

Edible parts: Young leaves.

Food uses: Salad, cooked greens, drinks, soup.

Precautions: Contains soluble oxalates that may be toxic if eaten in large quantities. Some cases of dermatitis have been reported.

Preparation: Collect the leaves before the plant flowers. A hot tea or cold drink can be made by pouring a quart of boiling water on a handful of washed leaves and letting it steep for 20 minutes. To most people the sour taste is the appealing feature of this plant. For those who do not like the sourness, boiling the leaves in several changes of water will help.

Recipes:

Sheep Sorrel–Cheese Soup

1 cup sheep-sorrel leaves	2 tablespoons flour
2 cups chicken broth	2 cups milk
¾ cup green onions (chopped)	2 cups cheddar cheese (grated)
2 tablespoons butter	1 teaspoon celery flakes
salt and pepper to taste	

Boil sheep sorrel in water for 10 minutes. Discard water. While sheep sorrel is cooking, sauté onions in butter in a large saucepan. Add flour and cook for several minutes. Add broth and sheep sorrel. Cook over medium heat until thick. Stir occasionally. Add milk and cheese and simmer until cheese melts. Pour into bowls and garnish with celery flakes.

Sheep Sorrel Salad

1 cup sheep-sorrel leaves (washed and chopped)	1 tablespoon mustard
2 cups leaf lettuce (washed and chopped)	1 teaspoon garlic salt
	⅓ cup cider vinegar
1 cup spinach (washed and chopped)	½ cup oil
6 slices of bacon (fried and crumbled)	2 tablespoons sugar
	1 teaspoon salt
	½ teaspoon pepper

Combine sheep sorrel, lettuce, spinach, and bacon. In a separate bowl combine the remaining ingredients. Pour dressing over greens immediately before serving.

Remarks: The specific epithet *acetosella* means "slightly acid" and the common name "sorrel" refers to its sour taste. This plant was naturalized from Eurasia and today is often considered a weed throughout North America. It is often used as an indicator species for acid soil. The plant is rich in vitamins A and C and a good source of potassium and phosphorus. Because of the presence of oxalic acid, usually as soluble oxalates, sorrel should be eaten in moderation. Sheep-sorrel soup helped feed hungry Europeans during World War II.

COMMON BLUE VIOLET
(Meadow violet)

Viola papilionacea Pursh
Violaceae

Characteristics: This perennial herb grows to about 1 foot tall. Leaves and flower stalks arise directly from the rhizome. The alternate, simple, heart-shaped leaves have a toothed margin. The irregular flower has five purple petals and a spur at the back of the flower. The lateral petals are bearded. The lowest petal has purplish veins. Flowers occur from April to June.
Habitat: Moist soil in fields and open woods.
Distribution: Throughout the area.

Edible parts: Young leaves, flowers.

Food uses: Salad, tea, candy, syrup, cooked green, soup, jelly.

Precautions: Do not eat the seeds, fruits, or rhizomes of any violet. These parts of the sweet violet (*V. odorata*) have been reported to be harmful. Some foragers have reported cathartic reactions to the leaves of some of the yellow violets. Young leaves and flowers of the purple violets appear to be safe.

Preparation: The young leaves can be used in soups, salads, or as cooked greens. The taste is somewhat bland, so stronger-tasting greens should be added. Making tea from the leaves requires a larger amount than normal for herbal tea. The flowers are used for making syrup, candy, and jelly. Add violet flowers to an ice cube tray for some interesting party ice cubes.

Recipes:

Violet Candy

3 cups blue violet flowers   1 cup granulated sugar
2 egg whites (beaten)

Rinse the flowers in cold water, drain, and dry on a paper towel. Hold the flower with a pair of tweezers and with a toothpick dab the flowers with egg whites. Sprinkle with sugar. Spread the coated violet flowers on waxed paper and dry.

Violet Syrup

1 quart blue violet flowers (washed)   2 teaspoons lemon juice
½ quart boiling water   1 cup sugar

Place violet flowers in jar. Use enough boiling water to cover the flowers. Secure lid to jar and set aside for 24 hours. Strain the liquid and retain 1 cup of extract. Combine violet extract, lemon juice, and sugar. Bring to a boil and pour into hot, sterilized jars.

Remarks: *Viola* is the Latin name for the sweet violet (*V. odorata*). *Papilionacea* means butterflylike. Over 50 species of violets occur in the northeastern United States and over 800 worldwide. Some tropical members of the violet family are trees and shrubs. Much hybridization occurs among the violets. After the showy, spring flowers disappear, cleistogamous flowers appear. These flowers do not have showy petals and do not open. They are self-pollinated and bear seeds freely. Johnny-jump-up (*V. tricolor*) is a violet as is its cultivated variety, the pansy. Violet leaves are rich in vitamins A and C. Violet is the state flower of Illinois, New Jersey, Wisconsin, and Rhode Island. The United States Congress has considered designating it the national flower.

Characteristics: This is a hairy perennial herb that grows to 12 inches tall. A pair of broad-petioled leaves are produced annually from the rhizome. Between the opposite, heart-shaped leaves arises a solitary reddish-brown, fetid flower that usually sits on the ground. The regular flower has no petals, but does have a deep three-lobed calyx, twelve stamens, and a single ovary. Flowering occurs in April and May.

Habitat: Often in colonies in rich, moist, deciduous woods, along flood plains, and at the base of slopes where there is seepage.

Distribution: Throughout the area.

Edible parts: Rhizome.

Food uses: Spice, candy, syrup.

Precautions: Because of its habit of growing in colonies in rather restricted areas, the plant is very vulnerable to local extirpation. Remember to be a conservationist first and an edible-wild-plant enthusiast second.

Preparation: The rhizome can be used fresh or dried. Dry the rhizome in a warm attic, in the sun, or in an oven at 200° F for 4 hours. After drying, the rhizome can be ground. Store in airtight jars. Wild ginger has a different flavor and is not as potent as commercial ginger.

Recipes:

Stir-Fried Veggies

¾ cup soy sauce	½ cup wild onions (chopped)
4 teaspoons ground wild ginger	1 cup watercress leaves
2 teaspoons olive oil	½ cup mushrooms (sliced)
1 cup lamb's-quarters leaves	½ cup broccoli (segmented)
½ cup daylily buds (boiled)	salt and pepper to taste
½ cup cauliflower (segmented)	4 wild leeks (sliced)

Simmer soy sauce and wild ginger. In a large skillet or wok heat olive oil. Add all other ingredients to oil and stir-fry. When vegetables are half done, add soy sauce mixture. Continue to stir-fry until done.

Wild Ginger Candy

4 cups granulated sugar   ½ quart wild ginger rhizomes
2 cups water

Dissolve sugar in warm water. Wash and scrape wild ginger rhizomes. Cut into one-inch pieces. Add rhizomes to sugar water and simmer until tender. Drain. Place rhizomes on waxed paper to dry.

Remarks: The common name of Aristolochiaceae is the birthwort family, which indicates the herbal use of another species of this family (*Aristolochia clematitis*). *Asarum* is from *asaron*, which is the Greek name for European wild ginger. *Canadense* probably refers to the collection site of the plants that were sent to Linnaeus for identification. The plant is well known for its herbal value and was listed in the United States Pharmacopea and National Formulary. Recent research has shown wild ginger to contain two antibiotics that have broad-spectrum activity against bacteria and fungi. Commercial ginger is obtained from a different plant (*Zingiber officinale*). Look for the wild-ginger flower among the dried leaves of the forest floor, but above the humus. Crawling beetles and ants pollinate the plant.

LEEK
(Ramps, Wild onion)

Allium tricoccum Ait.
Liliaceae

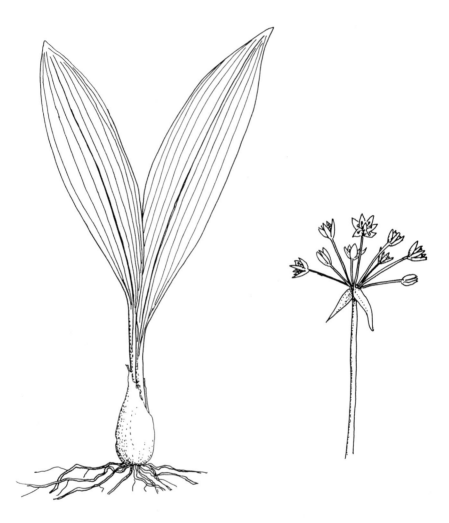

Characteristics: Leeks are perennial, erect, herbaceous plants with 1-foot long leaves arising directly from a white bulb. The flat, lance-shaped, smooth leaves have an entire margin. The leaves occur in early spring and die back before the umbel of white to pink flowers occurs in early to midsummer. All parts of the plant have a distinct onion odor. The fruit is a three-lobed capsule that contains three hard black oval seeds.
Habitat: Rich, moist soil in deciduous woods.
Distribution: Throughout the area.

Edible parts: Leaves, bulb.

Food uses: Salad, seasoning, cooked vegetable, soup.

Precautions: In the spring the leaves of the poisonous death camas and false hellebore resemble those of leek. Always check for the onion odor. Leeks have a very strong flavor and may cause stomach distress for some. Eating raw leeks will result in a breath odor that lingers for several days, while cooked leeks act about the same as onions.

Preparation: Most people use the bulbs rather than the leaves. The bulbs can be collected from early spring to fall, but are stronger in flavor in the fall. The very young leaves should be used. The bulbs can be dried and stored in the same manner as garlic.

Recipes:

Cheesy Leeks

3 cups leek bulbs	½ can mushroom soup
3 tablespoons butter	¾ cup sharp cheese (grated)
3 tablespoons flour	½ cup bread crumbs

Clean and wash leeks. Cut bulbs into thirds. Gently boil leeks in just enough water until tender. Melt butter in skillet. Add flour to melted butter and make a paste. Add mushroom soup, cheese, and leeks. Stir over low heat until thickened. Butter a baking dish. Add mixture to baking dish and cover with bread crumbs. Bake for 25 minutes at 325° F.

Leek Soup

5 leek bulbs	2 tablespoons parsley flakes
3 medium-sized potatoes	salt and pepper to taste
1 cup sheep sorrel	½ cup cheddar cheese (grated)
1 quart chicken broth	

Clean and wash leeks, potatoes, and sheep sorrel. Cut leeks into thirds and cube potatoes. Except for cheese, combine all ingredients and gently boil until potatoes are soft. Ladle hot soup into bowls and sprinkle with cheddar cheese.

Remarks: Ramp festivals are held every spring throughout the southern states. Ham-and-leek dinners are conducted in northern Pennsylvania to coincide with the large influx of trout fisherman. In the Southeastern states, contests are held to see who can eat the greatest number of ramps. Schoolchildren are reported to eat large quantities of leeks so that they will be dismissed from school until the strong odor disappears from their breath. The genus *Allium* also includes onions and garlic. The antibiotic allicin has been isolated from *Allium* and may account for some of the medicinal value associated with *Allium*. Because leeks grow in large colonies, they are easy to collect. Always leave a part of the colony intact for future collecting.

WOOD SORREL (Sheep sorrel)   *Oxalis stricta* L. Oxalidaceae

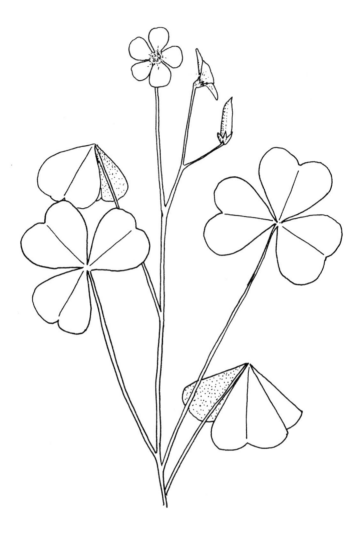

Characteristics: An erect, herbaceous, hairy plant that grows to 15 inches tall. The compound leaves have three heart-shaped leaflets that are folded or droop. The umbellike inflorescences are terminal or arise from the axils of the alternate leaves. Five separate yellow petals and ten stamens characterize the regular flower. The hairy capsule is long, thin, and erect and resembles a miniature okra. Flowers throughout the summer.

Habitat: Various habitats from moist, open woodlands to fields and waste areas.

Distribution: Throughout the area.

Edible parts: Young leaves.
Food uses: Salad, drinks, salad dressing, soup.
Precautions: Calcium absorption is affected by the oxalic acid found in wood sorrel. Kidney failure has also been associated with the consumption of foods with oxalic acid and potassium oxalate. Eat wood sorrel in moderation.
Preparation: The oxalic acid that makes wood sorrel a potentially harmful plant is also responsible for this plant's delightful lemony taste. Add the washed leaves to mixed green salads, soups, or salad dressings. A cold drink is also made from the leaves.
Recipes:

Wood Sorrel Salad Dressing

2 cups wood-sorrel leaves (chopped)	1 teaspoon chives (chopped)
1 cup water	½ teaspoon dill
1 cup sour cream	½ teaspoon salt
3 teaspoons sugar	½ teaspoon pepper

Add wood-sorrel leaves to water. Boil for 10 minutes. Combine sour cream, sugar, chives, dill, and salt and pepper. Puree the wood sorrel liquid and add 5 tablespoons to the sour-cream mixture. Blend thoroughly and refrigerate.

Wood Sorrel Salad

½ cup wood-sorrel leaves	1 tomato (cubed)
1 cup purslane leaves	1 cucumber (sliced)
2 cups spinach (torn)	1 hard-boiled egg (sliced)
1 cup watercress leaves (torn)	¼ cup Parmesan cheese (grated)
1 cup creamy Italian dressing	

Combine all greens in bowl. Add dressing and toss. Lay tomatoes, cucumbers, and hard-boiled eggs on surface. Sprinkle with cheese.

Remarks: *Oxalis* is derived from the Greek word *oxus,* which means sour and refers to the acid taste of the leaves. Sorrel comes from the German word for sour. Wood sorrel is thought to be the shamrock that was used by St. Patrick to explain the Trinity. Oxalic acid can occur as soluble oxalates of sodium or potassium or insoluble calcium oxalates. Only a few plants, such as wood sorrel, rhubarb, and purslane, contain oxalates at high enough levels to be considered dangerous. Among the root crops used by the Incas was a plant that they called oca (*Oxalis tuberosa*). During the past twenty years oca has become quite popular in New Zealand, where it is known by the confusing name of "yam."

COMMON CHICKWEED   *Stellaria media* (L.) Vill.
(Starwort, Stitchwort)   Caryophyllaceae

Characteristics: A weak-stemmed winter annual that grows in dense mats to a height of 15 inches. The small, oval leaves have pointed tips and occur in pairs on the stem. Single small white flowers grow from the end of the stems and are present throughout the year. The five petals are deeply cut and have the appearance of ten petals.
Habitat: Abundant on newly cultivated ground, such as gardens and farmland; also waste ground, meadows, open woods, and along streams.
Distribution: Found throughout the area.

Edible parts: Leaves, stems.

Food uses: Salads, soups, stews, cooked greens, tea.

Precautions: Some people confuse the rosettes of ox-eye daisy and similar plants with chickweed. Mouse-ear chickweed (*Cerastium vulgatum*) may be confused with common chickweed.

Preparation: Tender leaves and stems can be added to salads, soups, and stews or used as cooked greens. Chickweed is available year-round, but late fall to early spring is the best collecting period. Dried leaves are used as tea.

Recipes:

Chickweed Pancakes

2 cups pancake flour	1½ cups water
1 teaspoon baking powder	1 egg
2 cups chickweed leaves (washed and drained)	¼ cup vegetable oil

Blend ingredients and fry as pancakes.

Early Spring Greens

1 quart winter cress leaves (chopped)	1 wild leek (chopped)
1 quart chickweed leaves and stems (chopped)	4 slices bacon (fried and crumbled)
2 tablespoons butter	salt and pepper to taste
	½ cup Parmesan cheese (grated)

Boil the winter cress for 10 minutes. Add chickweed and continue to boil for 5 minutes. Drain greens and add butter while greens are still hot. Stir in bacon, leek, and salt and pepper to taste. Cover with cheese.

Remarks: Most edible-wild-plant enthusiasts can easily find food in midsummer; however, winter is more of a problem. Just remember where you saw chickweed before winter arrived; it will still be there under the snow. Because of its year-round availability, this plant is important as an antiscorbutic. Flowers can be observed in every month of the year. It is called chickweed because chickens and other birds feed on the seeds. The *Stellaria* part of its scientific name refers to the starlike appearance of the flowers. Weight watchers who want to shed a few pounds have been reported to drink chickweed tea. It is a mild laxative and a diuretic. Chickweed is a common late-fall and early-spring garden weed. As with many other "weed" species, chickweed is not native to the United States.

SPATTERDOCK   *Nuphar luteum* (L.) Sibth. and Sm.
 (Yellow water lily,   Nymphaeaceae
   Yellow pond lily)

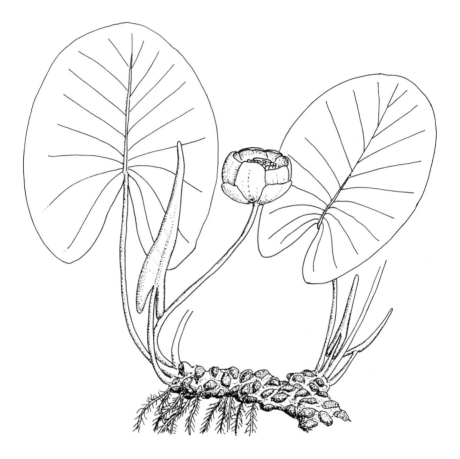

Characteristics: This is an aquatic perennial herb with a very stout rhizome that is densely covered with triangular leaf scars. The large, oval, shiny leaves have a notch cut from the blade. Leaves and flowers are raised about 1 foot above the water. The simple yellow flower grows on a long stalk. A large, yellowish-green stigmatic disk occurs in the center of the flower. The broad, oval fruit contains numerous brown, oval seeds. Flowering occurs throughout the summer.
Habitat: Standing bodies of water and slow-moving streams.
Distribution: Throughout the area.

Edible parts: Seeds, rhizome.
Food uses: Potato, popcorn, flour.
Precautions: Do not collect from contaminated water. Rinse rhizome thoroughly.
Preparation: Collect fruits in late fall when mature. Remove seeds and dry in sun or oven. Seeds can be popped, parched, or ground into flour. The rhizome should be washed, peeled, and boiled in two changes of water. Use the rhizome as you would potatoes, or grind into flour. The rhizome is definitely a survival food only.
Recipes:

Spatterdock Popcorn

1½ tablespoons oil	2 tablespoons butter
½ cup dried spatterdock seeds	1 teaspoon salt
	¼ cup Parmesan cheese (grated)

Pop the spatterdock seeds as you would regular popcorn. If using a hot-air popper, omit the oil. After popping, pour melted butter over popcorn and sprinkle with salt and/or Parmesan cheese. The spatterdock seeds will not pop into the large, white familiar popcorn, but will usually just pop open.

Scalloped Spatterdock

4 six-inch spatterdock rhizomes	½ teaspoon pepper
4 wild leeks (chopped)	1 cup Romano cheese (grated)
1 cup sharp cheese (grated)	4 tablespoons butter
1 garlic clove (chopped)	1 cup milk
1 teaspoon salt	

Wash and peel spatterdock rhizomes. Place in saucepan, cover with water, and add a pinch of salt. Boil for 10 minutes. Discard water. Add fresh water and boil for 20 minutes. Drain and let cool. Slice the rhizomes and place half in casserole dish. Cover with leeks, sharp cheese, garlic, salt, and pepper. Spread the remainder of the spatterdock on top. Cover with grated Romano cheese. Place chunks of butter on top. Pour milk over casserole. Bake for 30 minutes at 400° F. Pour off excess liquid and continue baking until brown.

Remarks: Because of the large quantities of starch in the rhizome, spatterdock is often used as a potato substitute. The Indians collected the rhizomes by walking in shallow water and feeling for the rhizomes with their bare feet. The sepals are large, petallike, and yellow while the petals are minute. Nymphaceae is derived from *nymphe*, the water nymph. *Nuphar* is thought to be of Arabic origin. *Luteum* means yellow.

Cakile edentula (Bigel.) Hook.
Brassicaceae

Characteristics: This herbaceous, succulent annual plant grows to 1 foot tall. The opposite, smooth, ovate leaves have a wavy margin. The regular flower has four petals and four long and two short stamens. The pale purple flower blooms in July and August. The indehiscent fruit is transversely divided into two joints of different sizes and shapes with the upper joint longer. The crushed leaves have a peppery odor.
Habitat: Coastal sands.
Distribution: Atlantic coast and the shores of the Great Lakes.

Edible parts: Stem, leaves, flower buds, young fruits.

Food uses: Cooked vegetable, cooked greens, salad, seasoning, pickles.

Precautions: Rinse carefully to remove all sand. At island sites around the Great Lakes, this plant has limited populations and is vulnerable to overexploitation. Always leave some seeds to maintain this annual's population.

Preparation: The leaves can be used as a cooked green, pickled, in salads, or for seasoning. Use the stems and flower buds as a cooked vegetable. Young fruits can be used for seasoning and pickled.

Recipes:

Sea Rocket Oriental

2 tablespoons soy sauce	1 red pepper (chopped)
1 teaspoon lemon juice	1 medium onion (chopped)
2 teaspoons sugar	¼ cup celery (chopped)
2 teaspoons ground ginger	¼ cup mushrooms (chopped)
2 tablespoons olive oil	¼ cup bamboo shoots
2 cups young sea-rocket fruits	¼ cup water chestnuts
1 cup sea-rocket leaves (chopped)	

Combine soy sauce, lemon juice, sugar, and ginger and set aside. Add olive oil to a wok or large skillet. Heat, then add sea rocket, pepper, onion, celery, mushrooms, bamboo shoots, and water chestnuts. Stir-fry for several minutes over high heat until tender. Stir soy mixture and add to vegetables. Stir-fry for another two minutes.

Sea Rocket Greens

2 quarts sea-rocket leaves   2 tablespoons butter

Wash and rinse sea-rocket leaves. Steam or boil for 8 to 10 minutes. Drain. Add butter and stir.

Remarks: Sea rocket is in the mustard family (Brassicaceae). Previously this family was known as the Cruciferae. The crosslike arrangement of the four petals are aptly described by the term Cruciferae, which means to "bear a cross." In an attempt to uniformly name plant families, taxonomists have agreed to add "-aceae" to the most prominent genus in the family. *Brassica* is the genus of most of our cultivated mustards and is used in the family name of Brassicaceae. Economically important mustards include cabbage, broccoli, cauliflower, rape, kohlrabi, rutabaga, brussel sprouts, turnips, and radish.

Taraxacum officinale Weber.
                                                 Asteraceae

Characteristics: This perennial herb has a large taproot. Basal leaves form a rosette. Leaves are lance-shaped with large irregular teeth that point down to the leaf base. The yellow flower heads occur in the spring and later become fluffy balls of dry fruits. The flower stalk is hollow and has no leaves. Leaves and roots contain a milky sap. Some flowers are present from early spring to late fall. In undisturbed areas the plant may reach a height of 18 inches.
Habitat: Found in fields, lawns, roadsides, waste areas, disturbed sites.
Distribution: Common throughout the area.

Edible parts: Leaves, flowers, roots, flower buds.

Food uses: Salad, cooked greens, coffee, wine, cooked vegetable, fritters.

Precautions: Old leaves are bitter. Avoid lawns that have been sprayed with pesticides or frequented by pets. Some people confuse the leaves with fall dandelion, sow thistle, chicory, and ox-eye daisy. The flowers may be confused with coltsfoot.

Preparation: Collect the young leaves and flower buds in the early spring. Flowers can be collected at any time, but are most abundant in the spring. Roots are best in the fall and early winter, but can be collected year-round. Leaves can be used in salads or as cooked greens; flower buds as cooked vegetables; flowers in fritters and wine; and roots for coffee and as a cooked vegetable.

Recipes:

Dandelion Wine

1 gallon dandelion flowers	3 oranges
1 gallon boiling water	3 pounds brown sugar
3 lemons	2 packages yeast

Wash flowers in cold water. Place flowers in a 2 gallon or larger crock. Cover with 1 gallon boiling water. Cover container and let stand for 3 days. Filter the mixture and save the liquid. Chop lemons and oranges into small pieces. Add chopped lemons and oranges (seeds, skins, and all) and sugar to dandelion liquid in an enamel pot. Cover and boil for 30 minutes. Cool to lukewarm and pour into crock. Add 2 packages of yeast. Cover container and ferment for 3 weeks or until bubbling stops. Always allow for the carbon dioxide to escape because containers can explode. Filter through cheesecloth and pour into bottles. Seal with corks.

Dandelion Coffee

Wash and dry about a quart of dandelion roots. Roast roots in an oven at 300° F until the roots are crisp and dark brown. Coarse-grind the roots. Use about ½ cup of dandelion root coffee in an eight-cup percolator. Add a pinch of salt to the coffee. This brew will be stronger than regular coffee. Some people add chicory roots for a blended coffee flavor.

Remarks: This native of Eurasia is now a cosmopolitan weed in North America. European settlers brought the plant with them to be used for medicinal purposes. The *officinale* part of its scientific name attests to its official recognition as a medicinal herb that was sold in shops or apothecaries. Some of the leaves have large teeth that resemble a lion's canine teeth. The common name of dandelion originates from the French *dents de lion* or teeth of the lion. Dandelion is high in calcium, potassium, vitamin A, thiamine, and riboflavin. The W. S. Wells and Son Company in Maine grows dandelions commercially and sells about 1,000 cases of the canned greens each year. The major problem with growing dandelions commercially is controlling the "weeds." A Dandelion Festival is held in White Sulphur Springs, West Virginia, on the weekend before Memorial Day. Since 1968 the Nature Wonder Weekend has been held annually at North Bend State Park, West Virginia. The first edible wild plant served at the first meeting was dandelion coffee and was prepared by Euell Gibbons. The diuretic characteristic of dandelion is reflected in its American common name of "pee-the-bed" and its French-Canadian name of *pissenlit*.

Suaeda maritima (L.) Dum.
Chenopodiaceae

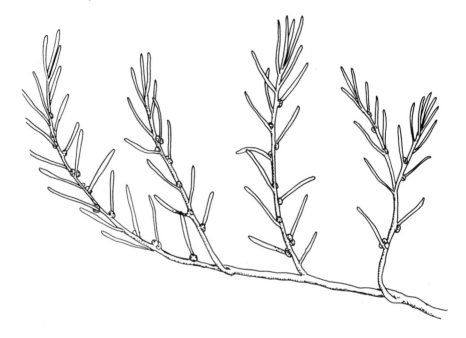

Characteristics: A small prostrate to ascending plant that may grow to 18 inches tall. Numerous linear, fleshy, alternate leaves are gradually reduced to bracts at the inflorescence. The entire, pointed leaf has a whitish bloom. The small, buttonlike greenish flowers have five stamens and a deep five-lobed corolla. Terminal spikes and axillary flowers are present. Flowering occurs from midsummer to early fall.
Habitat: Salt marshes and beaches.
Distribution: May occur south to Virginia, but more northern.

Edible parts: Young stems, leaves.
Food uses: Cooked greens, seasoning, soup.
Precautions: Wash thoroughly with cold water to remove sand and salt.
Preparation: After washing, soak in cold water for 10 minutes in each of two changes of water to remove some of the saltiness. The young stems and leaves are used as a cooked green or in soup. Fresh or dried leaves can be used to season stews and soups.
Recipes:

Sea Blite Soup

2 chicken breasts	2 celery stalks (chopped)
2 quarts water	¼ teaspoon rosemary
1 cup sea-blite leaves (washed and chopped)	¼ teaspoon thyme
	¼ teaspoon parsley flakes
3 carrots (diced)	1 garlic clove (minced)
2 leeks or green onions (chopped)	½ cup Parmesan cheese

Boil the chicken breasts in water for 30 minutes. Remove chicken. Add sea blite, carrots, leeks, celery, garlic, and spices to chicken broth. Remove chicken skin and cut chicken into chunks. Add chicken chunks to broth. Simmer for 45 minutes. Add parmesan cheese and simmer until ready to serve.

Sea Blite Swiss Chard Greens

1 cup sea-blite leaves (washed)	2 green onions (chopped)
2 cups Swiss chard	1 hard-boiled egg
Italian salad dressing	

Boil the sea blite and Swiss chard separately until done. Drain. Combine salad dressing, onions, sea blite, and Swiss chard. Mix well. Slice hard-boiled egg and place on top of greens.

Remarks: Some individuals do not like the salty taste of sea blite. Soaking in cold water and boiling in several changes of water will remove some of the saltiness. Combining it with other greens will also reduce the salty taste. The embryo plant in the seed is spirally coiled. Sea blite may have been introduced from Europe. The specific epithet of *maritima* refers to its habitat of bordering the sea.

COMMON PLANTAIN   *Plantago major* L.
(Soldier's herb)
NARROW-LEAVED PLANTAIN   *Plantago lanceolata* L.
(Rib grass, English plantain)   Plantaginaceae

P. lanceolata   P. major

Characteristics: These perennial herbs have basal leaves that form a rosette. The simple, thick leaves of common plantain are broad and ovate, while narrow-leaved plantain has long, narrow leaves with definite parallel "ribs." The leafless flower stalk has inconspicuous white flowers arranged in a spike. The protruding stamens are most obvious. Narrow-leaved plantain has the flowers clustered at the tip while common plantain has the flowers scattered over most of the flower stalk. Vascular fibers extend from the pulled petiole. The plants flower from June to October. The height of these plants ranges from 6 to 18 inches.
Habitat: Lawns, fields, roadsides, waste areas.
Distribution: Throughout the area.

Edible parts: Young leaves, seeds.

Food uses: Salad, cooked greens, tea, flour, soup.

Precautions: Old leaves are tough and bitter with stringy veins. These are common lawn plants, so avoid picking where pesticide spraying has occurred or pets have relieved themselves.

Preparation: The young leaves can be mixed with other greens in a salad. Steam or boil the leaves to make a cooked green. The leaves can be used as a marginal tea. It has been reported that the dried seeds can be ground into a flour.

Recipes:

Cream of Plantain Soup

4 wild leeks (chopped)	½ quart young plantain leaves
1 garlic clove (minced)	½ cup mushrooms (sliced)
2 teaspoons butter	1 cup evaporated milk
1 tablespoon cornstarch	1 teaspoon parsley flakes
2 cups chicken broth	salt and pepper to taste

In a large saucepan, sauté leeks and garlic in butter. Sprinkle cornstarch over leeks and garlic. Add chicken broth. Cook plantain leaves in water until tender. Drain and cool. Puree plantain in blender. Add pureed plantain and all other ingredients to broth. Heat to boiling. Simmer until thickened. Pour into bowls and sprinkle with parsley flakes.

Plantain–Broccoli Salad

1 cup plantain leaves (chopped)	1 green onion (chopped)
1 head broccoli (broken into small pieces)	3 celery stalks (chopped)
	3 carrots (grated)
¼ pound bacon (cooked and crumbled)	1 cup mayonnaise
	½ lb. sharp cheese (cubed)

Mix all ingredients and chill before serving.

Remarks: *Plantago* is the ancient Roman name for this plant. It is probably derived from "platus," which means flat or plane, and may refer to the large flat leaves of common plantain. The genus of sycamore or plane tree is *Platanus* and is derived from the same word. Common plantain leaves are often used as food for pet rabbits. A native of Eurasia, the common names of "Englishman's foot" and "white man's foot" refer to its presence in the New World where Europeans had passed.

Medical studies show that the plant can be used to cure and stop the itch of poison ivy. Soldier's herb refers to the military use of the plant as an antiseptic, astringent, and poultice. Plantain is used as a common name for plants from several families: robin's plantain (composite), rattlesnake plantain (orchid), and tropical plantain (banana). The use of the name plantain for several unrelated plant species points out the importance of using scientific names. *P. psyllium* is the source of psyllium seeds, whose mucilaginous seed coats are used as a laxative.

WATERCRESS
(Scurvy grass)

Nasturtium officinale R. Br.
Brassicaceae

1–2'

Characteristics: A perennial herb that may be submersed, floating, erect to 18 inches, or prostrate on mud. The weak stems are easily broken and produce a large mass of thin white roots. The alternate, pinnately compound leaves have three to nine leaflets with the terminal leaflet usually the largest. The flower is characterized by four white petals that are arranged in a cross and six stamens (2 short and 4 long). The narrow, slender fruits have a beak. Flowering occurs from April to October.
Habitat: Clear, quiet, shallow waters of springs and brooks.
Distribution: Throughout the area.

Edible parts: Young leaves and stems.

Food uses: Salad, cooked greens, seasoning, soups.

Precautions: Parasitic diseases are commonly reported for watercress eaters who live in areas devoid of proper sanitary sewage facilities. The parasites are contained in human feces and are transmitted through snails. Consuming uncooked watercress that contains snail feces completes the parasites's life cycle.

Preparation: Young growth can be collected throughout the year by pinching or cutting with a knife or scissors. Collect from unpolluted water. Plants may be disinfected by soaking in water with iodide purifying tablets and washing in potable water.

Recipes:

Betty's Cream of Watercress Soup

⅓ cup green onions (minced)	5½ cups chicken broth
3 tablespoons butter	3 egg yolks
4 cups packed watercress leaves (washed)	½ cup whipping cream
3 tablespoons flour	½ teaspoon salt

Sauté onions in butter until translucent. Add watercress and cook slowly until wilted. Sprinkle in flour and stir over moderate heat for 3 minutes. Combine with boiling chicken broth. Add salt. Puree. Combine egg yolks and whipping cream. Gradually combine both liquids. Simmer for a few minutes to cook egg yolk. Garnish with watercress leaves.

Watercress Salad

1 cup tightly packed watercress leaves (washed)	1 green onion or chives
1 cup cabbage	½ cup violet leaves

Finely chop all ingredients and combine. For the dressing combine ½ cup sour cream, ¼ cup lemon juice, and salt to taste.

Remarks: *Nasturtium* means "nose twister" and refers to the pungent odor of this plant. *Officinale* indicates its official recognition as a medicinal plant available in shops or apothecaries. The cultivated, flowering plant with the common name of nasturtium (*Tropaeolum majus*) is not the same plant as watercress. The plant is rich in minerals as well as vitamins A, B2, C, D, and E. Settlers brought the plant to America chiefly for its effectiveness in preventing scurvy. The Greeks and Romans considered it brain food, and a Greek proverb states "Eat cress and learn more wit." A native of Eurasia, the plant now grows in almost every state and most countries. Watercress is grown commercially. It is available in the grocery store produce section, canned as a cooked green, or in vegetable drinks such as V8 juice. The radishlike taste makes it appealing in soups and salads, on pizza, or between two slices of bread as a watercress sandwich.

Fascioliasis is a disease caused by the infestation of parasitic worms known as liver flukes. Humans are mainly infected with liver flukes by eating raw watercress that harbors a developmental stage of the flukes. These flukes are deposited on the watercress by snails. Infected sheep, cattle, and humans pass the fluke back onto the snails.

COLTSFOOT
(Foalsfoot, Coughwort)

Tussilago farfara L.
Asteraceae

1–2′

Characteristics: The flower stalk has reddish scales. The flower at the top of the stalk has numerous yellow rays in layers similar to dandelion blossoms. The leaves that appear after the flowers have died are large and broad and downy on the underside. The leaves are rounded at first, but later become somewhat heart-shaped. Flowers occur from March to June. The plant ranges in height from 6 to 18 inches.

Habitat: Waste places, roadsides, railroad shoulders.

Distribution: Found throughout the general area, but in limited areas south of Pennsylvania.

Edible parts: Leaves.

Food uses: Candy, tea, seasoning.

Precautions: This plant commonly occurs in waste areas that may be contaminated with various pollutants. Carefully select the sites from which this plant is collected. The flowers may be confused with dandelion.

Preparations: Collect fresh, young leaves from May to August. Wash thoroughly.

Recipes:

Coltsfoot Candy

2 cups coltsfoot leaves   4 cups sugar
2 cups water

Boil coltsfoot leaves in water. Remove leaves. Add sugar. Boil remaining extract until the resulting syrup forms a hard ball when dropped in cold water. Pour onto a cookie sheet. Allow to set. Eat as a hard candy.

Seasoning

Place leaves in a sunny area to dry. After leaves are dried, burn leaves and use residue as a salt substitute.

Remarks: Coltsfoot is a well-known medicinal herb. A tea is used for colds and the leaves are smoked for respiratory ailments. During the Middle Ages, a painting of coltsfoot on a doorstep was used to identify apothecaries. The first part of the scientific name (tussi) means cough, and refers to its value as a cough remedy. Several cough medicines on the market today use "tussin" in their brand names. The appearance of the flowers before the growth of the leaves has resulted in the common name "son before father." Recent studies show that the young flowers produce a high incidence of liver cancer in rats. The common names of coltsfoot and foalsfoot derive from the resemblance of the leaves to the hoof of a young horse. Those patches of yellow flowers that occur along roadsides in the early spring are probably coltsfoot and not dandelion. Coltsfoot is one of the early flowering plants and is regarded as a "sign of spring."

PENNYCRESS

1–2'

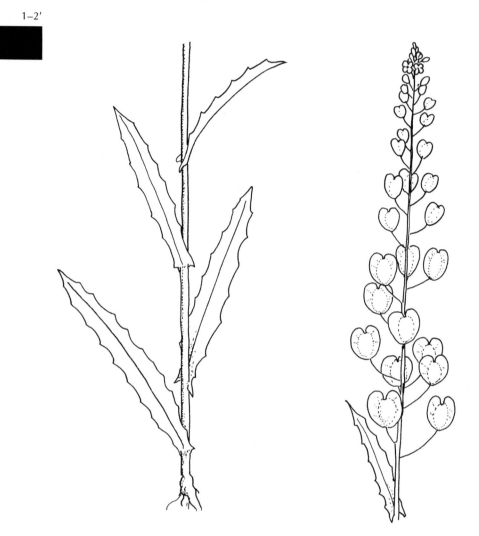

Characteristics: This is an erect, smooth annual plant that reaches a height of 20 inches with mostly entire, alternate lance-shaped leaves. Basal leaves wither before the appearance of the white flower. Flowers occur in racemes. Each flower has four petals that are arranged in a cross. The flattened, nearly circular fruits have a deep notch at the tip. Flowering occurs from April to June.
Habitat: Waste areas, fields, disturbed sites.
Distribution: Throughout the region.

Edible parts: Young, basal leaves and seed pods.

Food uses: Salad, cooked greens, seasoning.

Precautions: Use only tender, young basal leaves. Use seed pods sparingly, for they may cause gastric distress. May be confused with the peppergrasses (*Lepidium* spp.).

Preparation: Boil leaves in two changes of water for cooked greens. Use leaves sparingly in salad to add taste. Dry seed pods and grind for use as pepper substitute.

Recipes:

Pennycress Salad Dressing

6 tablespoons olive oil
3 tablespoons wine vinegar
½ teaspoon salt or to taste

1 teaspoon ground pennycress seed pods

Combine ingredients in small jar and shake. Store in refrigerator.

Double-Cooked Potatoes

2 medium potatoes
½ cup young pennycress leaves
2 teaspoons butter

salt to taste
½ cup cheddar cheese (grated)

Bake potatoes until soft. Cut potatoes in half. Scoop out potato, but save skins. Boil pennycress in two changes of water. Drain. Place potatoes, butter, and pennycress in bowl and mix until smooth. Salt to taste. Put potato mixture into potato skins. Add cheddar cheese to top of potatoes. Place on cookie sheet and bake at 300° F for 5 minutes.

Remarks: Pennycress is another of the many mustards used as an edible wild plant. The cress portion of the common name indicates that it is a mustard. This European native is popular in many parts of the world and commonly cultivated in Europe. *Thlaspi* is the Greek name for cress. The term *arvensis* refers to its common occurrence in cultivated fields. Leaves of pennycress are slightly bitter and should be used sparingly and with milder-tasting plants. The peppergrasses have similar seed pods, but lack the deep notch.

CHEESES
(Mallow, Cheese-weed)

Malva neglecta Wallr.
Malvaceae

1–2'

Characteristics: This annual or biennial is usually a sprawling plant that covers about a square yard and may also reach a height of 2 feet. The round or heart-shaped leaves have a scalloped margin with small teeth and a relatively long petiole to 6 inches. The leaves are alternate. White to pinkish, five-parted flowers occur throughout the summer. The fruit is flat and round.
Habitat: Gardens, waste areas, poorly maintained lawns, roadsides, around buildings.
Distribution: Throughout the area.

Edible parts: Young leaves, green fruits, roots.

Food uses: Confection, salad, nibble, soup, cooked greens, pickles.

Precautions: Pesticides may be a problem with plants collected from lawns and gardens. The mucilage of the leaves and fruits are distasteful to some people, while others find the cooked greens to be edible, but not very flavorful.

Preparation: Use the young leaves and fruits as a soup thickener like okra. A confection can be made from the roots or fruits. Green fruits are eaten as a nibble. The young leaves can be prepared as a cooked green. The fruits and young leaves are added to salads. The green fruits can be pickled.

Recipes:

Cheesy Cheeses Soup

1 cup onion (chopped)	¼ teaspoon garlic powder
2 tablespoons vegetable oil	3 cups milk
1 quart young cheeses leaves	1 chicken bouillon cube
(chopped)	1 cup Parmesan cheese (grated)
salt and pepper to taste	2 slices provolone cheese

Stir-fry onions in oil until light brown. In a saucepan combine cheeses, salt, pepper, garlic, milk, bouillon cube, and fried onions. Heat to just below boiling, cover and simmer for 10 minutes. Stir in Parmesan cheese and simmer for 5 minutes. Pour into two bowls and top with a slice of provolone cheese. If cheese does not adequately melt, place bowls in an oven for a few minutes.

Cheeses Confection

2 cups green cheeses fruits   ½ cup sugar

Clean and chop the fruits. Place the fruits in a saucepan and cover with water. Slowly boil until the liquid becomes thickened. Strain out debris. Cool the thickened liquid. Beat while slowly adding the sugar until frothy and the desired sweetness is obtained. Can be used as a confection, meringue, or whipped cream.

Remarks: This plant is a native of Eurasia and North Africa. Cheeses is in the same family as marshmallow, but the marshmallow is in a different genus (*Althaea*). The arrangement of the fruit in a ring resembles a wheel of cheese and accounts for the common name of cheeses. The mucilage, which is offensive to some people, is the ingredient that makes the plant medicinally valuable for use as a skin softener.

MAYAPPLE
(American mandrake, Wild
lemon, Umbrella plant)

1–2'

Podophyllum peltatum L.
Berberidaceae

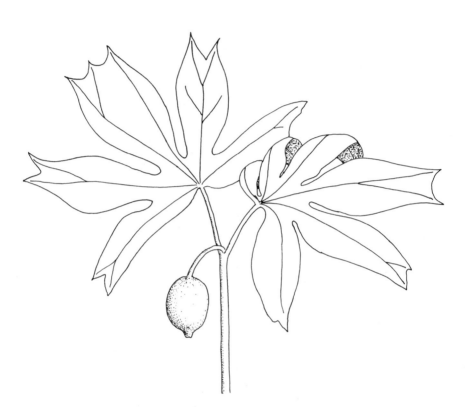

Characteristics: Large umbrellalike leaves that occur singly or in pairs characterize this 1–2-foot plant. The leaves have coarsely toothed lobes. The leaf stalk attaches to the center of the leaf. In May, a single, large, waxy white flower is found at the branching point of the pair of leaves. The egg-shaped fruit is green at first, but when mature is yellow and resembles a lemon. Flowers in May and June.
Habitat: Rich deciduous woodlands, flood plains, moist meadows.
Distribution: Found throughout the area.

Edible parts: Fruit.

Food uses: Fruit, jelly, beverage.

Precautions: Only the ripe fruits are edible. All other parts, including the immature fruit, are poisonous. Collect the soft, ripe yellow mayapple fruits in the fall when the deciduous trees are losing their leaves.

Preparation: The mature fruit can be eaten raw or made into a jam or jelly. The juice can be added to lemonade or other fruit juices to make a punch. The musky taste is offensive to some people. Cooking eliminates the musky flavor.

Recipes:

Mayapple Jam

5½ cups ripe mayapple fruits (chopped)	7 cups sugar
	1 package pectin
½ cup water	dash of salt
½ cup lemon juice	

Combine mayapples, water, and lemon juice. Bring to a boil, cover, lower heat, and simmer for 20 minutes. Stir often. Add sugar and bring to boil. Boil hard for 3 minutes. Stir often. Add pectin and salt and boil for 1 minute. Stir and skim off foam. Ladle into hot, sterilized jars and seal with paraffin.

Mayapple Punch

3 cups ripe mayapple fruits (washed, drained, crushed)	1 cup sugar
	1 quart ginger ale
3 pieces of gingerroot	

Place mayapples and gingerroot in saucepan, cover with water, and slowly bring to a boil. Simmer for 25 minutes. Add sugar. Set aside to cool, but stir occasionally. Pour into sieve and press pulp through mesh. Spoon into cups and fill cups with ginger ale. Stir and serve.

Remarks: Although the plant is called mayapple, in this region the fruit appears in June and ripens in the fall. Podophyllin is obtained from the plant and used in some medicines. Peltatine is a mayapple-derived compound that is being used in cancer research. The plant usually occurs as a "colony." These "colonies" are actually a single plant that is interconnected by a rhizome system. Only the stems that have two leaves bear a flower. Mammals like to eat mayapples and often get to the fruits first. To avoid this problem, collect the fruits in late summer while they are still green. Then store them in sawdust, where they can ripen and animals will not find them.

WILD ONION

Allium spp.
Liliaceae

1–2′

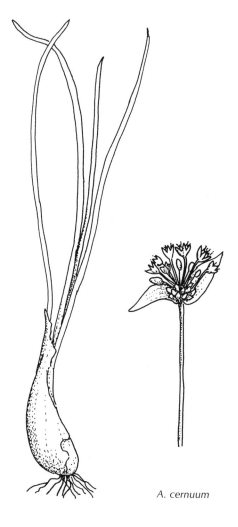

A. cernuum

Characteristics: These are biennial or perennial herbs that grow to 2 feet tall. The grasslike leaves may be flat or round and arise from an onion-scented bulb. Flowers occur in umbels and may vary from white to pink or may be replaced by bulblets. The flowers mainly appear in May and June and later form capsules with black seeds.
Habitat: At least ten species of wild onions occur in the area. They differ in habitat. Most are found in the dry, rocky soils of woodlands. Some are found on moist floodplains while others that have "escaped" from cultivation are found in lawns, fields, and roadsides.
Distribution: Various species can be found throughout the area.

Edible parts: Leaves, bulbs, bulblets.

Food uses: Cooked greens, salad, seasoning, soup.

Precautions: Death camas (*Ziadenus* spp.) includes about twenty species of poisonous plants that occur in North America. They resemble wild onions in appearance, but lack the onion odor.

Preparation: Collect the leaves in the spring and use as scallions. Bulbs can be collected throughout the year, but are stronger in the fall. Bulblets are used mainly for seasoning and are collected in the summer.

Recipes:

Wild Onion Soup

10 wild-onion bulbs (sliced)	1 teaspoon salt
¼ cup butter	½ teaspoon pepper
1 cup watercress (chopped)	1 tablespoon parsley
2 tablespoons flour	2 teaspoons Worcestershire sauce
4 cups beef broth	

In a saucepan sauté onions in butter. Add watercress when onions are translucent. Continue to sauté until watercress is wilted. Sprinkle flour on watercress. Stir. Add beef broth, salt and pepper, parsley, and Worcestershire sauce. Simmer for 30 minutes.

Creamed Wild Onions

1 can cream of mushroom soup	20 wild-onion bulbs (sliced)
1 teaspoon parsley	½ cup carrots (sliced and boiled)
1 teaspoon thyme	½ cup celery (sliced and boiled)
½ teaspoon paprika	½ cup bread crumbs
salt and pepper to taste	1 tablespoon butter

Combine soup, parsley, thyme, paprika, and salt and pepper. Pour into casserole dish. Sprinkle with onions, then carrots, celery, and bread crumbs. Dot with butter. Bake at 400° F for 30 minutes or until bread crumbs are brown.

Remarks: In addition to the wild species, there are many cultivated members of *Allium*: scallions, shallots, garden onions, garlic, leeks, and chives. The word *Allium* is the ancient Latin name for garlic. Chicago is derived from the word "shikato," which refers to the place where onions grow. The field garlic (*A. vineale*) often becomes a noxious weed in lawns and pastures. Cows that forage on onions will produce a sour-tasting milk. Many cultures used members of *Allium* for medicinal purposes. Folklore has long promoted garlic as having medicinal value. Allicin, which has been isolated from garlic, has been found to be a powerful antibacterial agent and to have chemotherapeutic value in treating cancerous tumors. A new anticlotting chemical has been synthesized from garlic. The Society of the Stinking Rose is an organization of garlic enthusiasts.

SHEPHERD'S PURSE
(Shepherd's bag, Pepper plant)

Capsella bursa-pastoris (L.) Medic.
Brassicaceae

1–2′

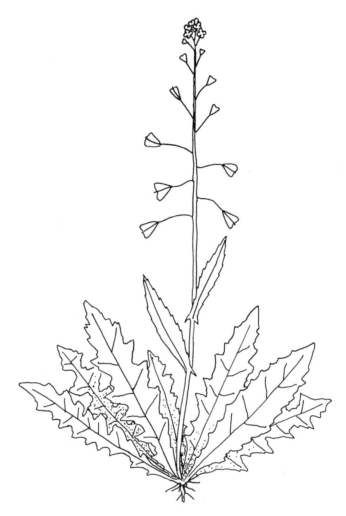

Characteristics: These annual or biennial, sparingly branched plants grow to 2 feet tall. The erect stem arises from a rosette composed of oblong leaves that are deeply lobed to toothed. The alternate leaves on the erect stem are smaller than the rosette leaves and slender and clasping. The white flowers have four petals that are arranged in a cross. Flowers are primarily produced in April and May. Fruits are heart-shaped to triangular and slightly flattened, with a notched tip.
Habitat: Lawns, gardens, waste areas.
Distribution: Throughout the area.

Edible parts: Young leaves, seed pods.

Food uses: Salad, cooked greens, seasoning, soup.

Precautions: Commonly found in waste areas where pollutants may be present.

Preparation: Collect leaves before the plant flowers. Cook leaves in at least one change of water when preparing as cooked greens. Raw leaves have a peppery taste and should be used sparingly in salads. Dry the seed pods and grind to use as a pepper substitute.

Recipes:

Shepherd's Purse Cream Soup

3 cups shepherd's purse leaves (washed)	½ cup butter
	½ cup flour
1 cup water	1 quart milk
¼ cup celery (chopped)	½ teaspoon salt
½ cup onion (chopped)	½ teaspoon garlic powder

Cook shepherd's purse in water. Drain and puree in blender. In a saucepan sauté onions and celery in butter. Add flour and stir. Add milk and cook over medium heat until smooth. Add shepherd's purse, salt, and garlic powder. Simmer for 15 minutes.

Mock Hamburgers

8 ounces lentils	½ cup mushrooms (sliced)
1 cup shepherd's purse leaves (chopped)	1 teaspoon salt
	1 egg
1 tablespoon barbecue sauce	1 cup flour
1 cup bread crumbs	

Boil lentils in water until soft. Drain. Mash lentils. While lentils are cooking, boil shepherd's purse leaves in two changes of water. Drain. Combine all ingredients except flour and mix thoroughly. Form mixture into patties. If consistency is not thick enough to hold patties together, add more bread crumbs. Coat patties with flour. Fry in cooking oil until done.

Remarks: *Capsella* is from the Latin and means "little box," which describes the fruit or seed pod. The seed pods are also thought to resemble the purses (*bursa*) carried by shepherds (*pastoris*) and account for the specific epithet of *bursa-pastoris*. Some of the earliest research on plant embryology was conducted with this plant. Botany textbooks usually always cite Mabel Shaffner's work on *Capsella* embryogenesis. This European immigrant is found throughout the United States, and most people consider it a weed rather than a valuable edible wild plant. As a medicinal, the plant is used as an astringent for hemorrhoids, as a treatment for diarrhea, and as a curative for uterine hemorrhages.

LARGE-FLOWERED   *Trillium grandiflorum* (Michx.) Salisb.
   TRILLIUM   Liliaceae
(White trillium)

1–2′

Characteristics: This erect, herbaceous perennial plant grows to almost 2 feet tall. A whorl of three broad leaves are found below the large white flower. Three large, showy white petals that turn pink with age alternate with three lower, shorter green sepals. A single flower terminates the single stem. The flower has six stamens and three stigmas. The plant arises from a tuber.
Habitat: Rich, moist usually deciduous woods.
Distribution: Throughout the area.

Edible parts: Young leaves.

Food uses: Salad, cooked greens.

Precautions: The leaves become bitter with age. Some people find the leaves difficult to digest. Only pick the plant where it is legal to do so and only where especially abundant.

Preparation: Collect the young, expanding leaves. Soak in cold water.

Recipes:

Steamed Trillium

6 cups trillium leaves	¼ teaspoon salt
2 wild-leek bulbs	½ cup water
4 teaspoons olive oil	

Wash and cut up trillium leaves. Clean and wash leeks and mince. Heat oil in skillet. Add leeks to hot oil and sauté. Combine leeks, salt, and water in a saucepan. As water begins to boil, add trillium and mix. Cover pot and steam for 10 minutes or until leaves are tender.

Trillium Salad

1 orange	¼ cup raisins
½ grapefruit	¼ cup walnuts
1 apple	sweet-and-sour dressing
4 cups trillium leaves (washed)	

Cut sections from oranges and grapefruit into ½ inch pieces. Peel apple and cut into small sections. Tear trillium leaves. Toss all salad ingredients in salad bowl. Add sweet-and-sour dressing to taste.

Remarks: In several states this plant is categorized as protected, in need of preservation, or vulnerable. It is reported to take at least six years for a tuber to grow large enough for a plant to produce its first bloom. Picking the aerial portion of the plant removes the photosynthesizing organs and obviously has some effect on the survival of the tuber. Examination of the major characteristics shows that most parts of the plant are in threes and account for the name *Trillium. Grandiflorum* describes the large flower. Eastern North American Indians used a tea from the root to facilitate childbirth and also to regulate menstruation. Ants are major agents in seed dispersal.

RED CLOVER
WHITE CLOVER

Trifolium pratense L.
Trifolium repens L.
Fabaceae

1–2'

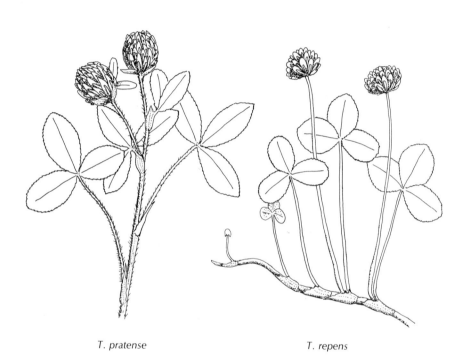

T. pratense

T. repens

Characteristics: These perennial herbs have flowers in dense compact heads. The alternate, compound leaves bear stipules. The three leaflets often have white chevrons on the upper surface. Red clover is an erect plant, more robust, grows to a height of 2 feet, and has reddish-purple flowers. White clover has creeping stems that may cover an area of one square yard. The white to pinkish-tipped flowers have long peduncles and the leaves have long petioles.

Habitat: Cultivated, roadsides, fields, waste areas, lawns.

Distribution: Throughout the area.

Edible parts: Young leaves, flowers, seeds.

Food uses: Tea, flour, cooked greens, salad, fritters, wine.

Precautions: May be confused with other herbs with three leaflets such as black medic, wild indigo, sweet clover, and wood sorrel. Young leaves and flowers are not very digestible when eaten raw and may cause bloating. White clover contains a cyanogenic glycoside that yields hydrocyanic acid. This acid causes asphyxiation at the cellular level.

Preparation: Young leaves and flowers should be cooked for 10 minutes to make them more digestible. The flowers are used for tea, wine, and fritters. Flowers and seeds can be ground into flour. The young leaves and flowers are used in salads, but are not considered choice items.

Recipes:

Clover Tea

Gather the flower heads at peak bloom. Spread the flowers on a cookie sheet and dry in a warm, dry area out of the sun. When the flowers are brittle to the touch, chop or place in a blender. Store in dry jars and seal. Place one tablespoon of dry flowers in a cup and cover with boiling water. Remove the debris by straining. Although clover can be used alone, most people prefer to combine it with other ingredients, such as spearmint, peppermint, or cinnamon sticks.

Clover Blossom Fritters

1 cup all-purpose flour	salt and pepper to taste
1 egg	½ teaspoon garlic powder
1 tablespoon melted butter	1 teaspoon baking powder
1 cup milk	2 cups washed red clover blossoms

Combine flour, egg, butter, milk, salt and pepper, garlic powder, and baking powder. Stir thoroughly to make batter. Heat enough vegetable oil in a heavy skillet to completely cover the blossoms. Drop clover blossoms into batter and cover completely. When oil is crackling hot, drop coated blossoms into oil and deep-fry until golden brown.

Remarks: Most of our clovers originated in Eurasia. Only the proboscis of the bumblebee is long enough to take the nectar from the red-clover flower and at the same time pollinate the pistil. Clovers are often planted with other legumes and grasses and cut for hay, but red clover is preferred. Legumes have bacteria on their roots that can fix nitrogen and thus fertilize the ground. Some consider white clover to be the true shamrock that was used by St. Patrick to illustrate the Doctrine of the Trinity. Other possibilities for shamrock include black medic, hop clover, and wood sorrel. *Trifolium* refers to three leaves, but the three "leaves" are really leaflets that compose one compound leaf. *Repens* refers to the creeping characteristic of white clover while *pratense* indicates the meadow habitat of red clover. After pollination white clover flowers fold downward.

GROUND-CHERRY
(Lantern-plant, Husk tomato)

Physalis spp.
Solanaceae

1–2'

P. sublabrata

Characteristics: These are herbaceous plants and include annuals and perennials with simple, alternate leaves. The yellow, funnel-shaped flower has a five-lobed calyx and corolla and often a dark center. The flowers hang singly from the nodes. Various species will flower from April to October. The calyx enlarges to form the lantern, which includes a single, many-seeded berry. The color of the fruit ranges from orange to purple when ripe.

Habitat: Fields, disturbed areas, old railroad beds, waste areas, farmyards.

Distribution: Throughout the area, but less abundant northward through New York.

Edible parts: Mature fruit.

Food uses: Jam, jelly, preserves, pies.

Precautions: Except for the ripe fruit, all parts of the plant, including the unripe green fruit, are considered poisonous.

Preparation: Collect in the late summer or fall when the fruit is ripe and the husk begins to dry.

Recipes:

Ground-cherry Jam

4 cups ground-cherries (crushed)	6 cups sugar
½ cup water	1 teaspoon cinnamon
1 tablespoon lemon juice	1 package pectin

Mix ground-cherries, water, and lemon. Bring to a boil and stir. Add sugar and cinnamon and bring to a hard boil for 1 minute. Stir constantly. Remove from heat, add pectin, stir, and skim off foam. Ladle into hot, sterilized jars and seal with paraffin.

Ground-cherry Pie

4 cups ground-cherries (crushed)	1 teaspoon nutmeg
1½ cups sugar	1 piecrust shell and top crust
½ cup flour	2 tablespoons butter
1 teaspoon lemon	

Combine ground-cherries, sugar, flour, lemon, and nutmeg. Pour into unbaked pie shell and dot with butter. Cover with piecrust and cut vents in crust. Bake for 40 minutes at 400° F or until brown.

Remarks: The South American (*P. peruviana*) and the European (*P. alkekengi*) are commonly cultivated and used indoors as dry flower decorations. Ground-cherry is not related to the cherries, but is a member of the nightshade family that includes tomato, potato, tobacco, deadly nightshade, and jimsonweed. All or most parts of these plants are poisonous. The plant grows close to the ground and the fruit resembles a cherry, which accounts for the common name. *Physalis* is derived from the Greek *physa,* which means bladder and refers to the inflated calyx. The Chinese lantern is an ornamental *Physalis* with a larger, bright red bladder.

GLASSWORT
(Samphire, Saltwort)

Salicornia europea L.
Chenopodiaceae

1–2'

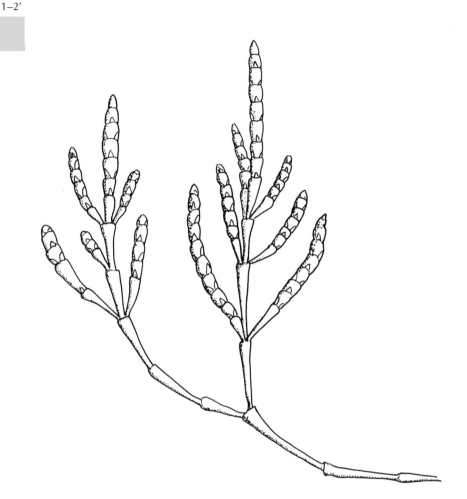

Characteristics: This plant appears to have leafless stems. The leaves, however, are reduced to minute, opposite scalelike structures. The succulent jointed stems are usually branched near the base. It grows to a height of 2 feet. The annual is a bright green in the summer, but in the fall takes on various hues of red. It usually grows erect, but some plants are sprawling. Tiny green flowers are hidden in the joints and are present from August to October.
Habitat: Salt lands along the coast; often on tidal flats.
Distribution: Along the Atlantic coast.

Edible parts: Young stem tips.
Food uses: Salad, pickles.
Precautions: The salty taste may be offensive to some individuals.
Preparation: Add stems to salads or pickles. Collect tips from mid-spring to autumn.
Recipes:

Pickled Glasswort

15 pounds glasswort stem tips	10 cups distilled white vinegar
small onions	5 pounds granulated sugar
garlic cloves	8-ounce pouch pickle mix

Boil stems in unsalted water for 5 minutes. Drain. Place 1 onion and 1 garlic clove in bottom of each hot, sterilized quart jar. Immediately pack glasswort into jars. Combine vinegar, sugar, and pickle mix. Bring mixture to boil. Stir constantly until sugar is dissolved. Pour pickling liquid into jars to ½ inch from top. Cap jars and place in boiling water for 15 minutes. Tighten lids. Store for 1 month.

Cheesy Glasswort

2 cups glasswort stem tips	½ cup brick cheese (grated)
2 tablespoons butter	

Boil glasswort for 5 minutes. Drain. Add butter and stir until melted. Sprinkle with cheese. Place in oven at 300° F for 5 minutes.

Remarks: *Salicornia* is derived from the Latin words *sal* and *cornia,* which mean salt and horn. The term aptly describes the hornlike branches of this salt-marsh herb. Glasswort is reported to live in soils that have more than 2 percent salt. This halophyte is therefore used as an indicator plant for salty soils that are incapable of supporting agricultural crops. Pintail ducks eat the seeds and geese feed on the fleshy branches. Economically the Chenopodiaceae are of minor importance. Garden beets, spinach, and Swiss chard are members of this family known for their agricultural value, while glasswort, orache, and especially lamb's-quarters are valued as edible wild plants.

GALINSOGA
(French weed,
Quick weed)

1–2′

Galinsoga quadriradiata Ruiz and Ravon
Asteraceae

Characteristics: This is an erect annual herb that grows to 2 feet high. The stem is hairy and forked with simple, opposite leaves that are toothed and have three principal veins. The flower heads resemble minute daisies and are composed of five white, three-lobed rays and a yellow central disk. Flowers are present from May to October.
Habitat: Gardens, waste areas, roadsides, disturbed areas.
Distribution: Widespread throughout the area.

Edible parts: Leaves.

Food uses: Cooked greens, soup.

Precautions: Because of its habitat locations, it may be exposed to roadside sprays, salt, lead, etc.

Preparation: Collect young plants before flowering. Galinsoga should be boiled in at least one change of water.

Recipes:

Galinsoga Cheese Soup

1 onion (chopped)	1 cup galinsoga (chopped and
1 garlic clove (chopped)	boiled)
4 tablespoons flour	salt and pepper to taste
3 cups milk	1 cup cheddar cheese (grated)

Stir-fry onion and garlic in oil. Slowly add flour and brown. Add milk. Stir until thick. Add galinsoga and salt and pepper to taste. Cover and simmer for 20 minutes. Stir in cheese until melted.

Galinsoga Casserole

2 cups galinsoga (chopped)	salt and pepper
1 can cream of mushroom soup	1 cup crushed potato chips
1 tablespoon onion (minced)	

Boil galinsoga for 10 minutes. Drain. Combine mushroom soup, minced onion, and galinsoga in a casserole dish. Add salt and pepper to taste. Top with crushed potato chips. Bake at 300° F for 30 minutes.

Remarks: A weed has been defined as a plant for which we have no use or a plant that grows in a place where we don't want it to grow. Gardeners consider galinsoga to be a weed. Wild-plant foragers, however, have plenty of use for this edible plant. Galinsoga is also a victim of its size. The small daisylike flower is very pretty, and if it grew to the size of a daisy it would be included in flower gardens instead of being considered a "weed." The genus name of *Galinsoga* commemorates the eighteenth-century Spanish doctor Mariano Martinez Galinsoga. The classical name of the Asteraceae family is Compositae, which refers to their composite or head type of inflorescence.

INDIAN CUCUMBER ROOT
(Indian cucumber)

Medeola virginiana L.
Liliaceae

1–2'

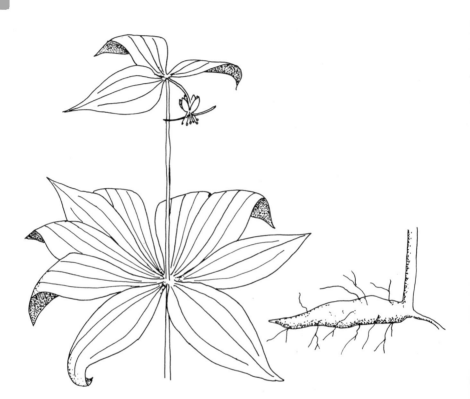

Characteristics: This herbaceous perennial with a single, unbranched erect stem grows to a height of 2½ feet. A whorl of five to eleven leaves appears about halfway up the stem while a smaller terminal whorl has three to four leaves. The dangling greenish-yellow flowers occur in May and June and later form dark purple berries. The white rhizome is 1 to 3 inches long.
Habitat: Rich, moist woods; often associated with hemlock.
Distribution: Throughout the area.

Edible parts: Rhizome.

Food uses: Raw, salad, pickles, cooked vegetable.

Precautions: Because the plant usually occurs in small localized populations and harvesting the rhizome kills the plant, prudence should be used when collecting.

Preparation: The rhizome is fairly clean when removed from the soil, but wash in cold water. Some people peel the rhizome.

Recipes:

Indian Cucumber Root Salad

6 medium potatoes (boiled)	1 cup celery (chopped)
1 cup sliced Indian cucumber root	2 tablespoons fresh parsley
1 small onion (chopped)	favorite salad dressing

Peel and cube potatoes while warm. Except for salad dressing, add remaining ingredients and toss. Add salad dressing and toss.

Indian Cucumber Root Pickles

1 cup Indian cucumber root (washed and sliced)
1 large Spanish onion (cut into chunks)
2 tablespoons salt

Brine:

¾ cup white vinegar	1 teaspoon dill seed
¾ cup sugar	½ teaspoon mustard seed
1 teaspoon celery seed	½ teaspoon turmeric

Mix Indian cucumber root and onion and sprinkle with salt. Add enough water to cover. Let stand for ½ hour. Combine brine ingredients. Drain Indian cucumber root and onion mixture and add to brine. Heat slowly until brine is hot. Pour into 2 canning jars and refrigerate.

Remarks: A native plant of North America. The genus name *Medeola* is derived from the name of the Greek enchantress Medea. This is the only species in this genus. The flower usually dangles between the leaves in the upper whorl and may not be observed immediately. The styles of the pistil are quite long. The cucumber-shaped rhizome also has a cucumber flavor.

WINTER CRESS
(Yellow rocket, Wild mustard)

Barbarea vulgaris R. Br.
Brassicaceae

2–3'

Characteristics: A biennial or winter annual that initially forms a rosette but later bolts and forms an erect herbaceous plant to 30 inches tall. The long-stalked lowest leaves are deeply lobed with a large terminal lobe. Upper leaves are toothed, sessile, and somewhat clasp the stem. The seed pods are long and narrow. It overwinters as a rosette. There are four long and two short stamens. Bright yellow flowers with four separate petals occur from April to June.

Habitat: Moist waste ground, roadsides, gardens, fallow fields.

Distribution: Throughout the area.

Edible parts: Leaves of the winter rosette, flower buds.

Food uses: Salad, cooked greens, cooked vegetable.

Precautions: Avoid collecting from fallow fields and roadsides that have been sprayed with pesticides or other contaminants. Recent research has shown that winter cress may affect normal kidney function.

Preparation: Pick the leaves from the rosette throughout the winter up to flowering. Can be used sparingly in salads or as cooked greens. If the bitterness is objectional, boil in several changes of water. The buds can be used as a broccoli dish.

Recipes:

Winter Cress Soup

¾ cup green onions (chopped)	2 cups winter cress leaves (chopped)
2 tablespoons butter	2 cups milk
2 tablespoons flour	salt and pepper to taste
2 cups chicken broth	

In a large saucepan, sauté onions in butter. Add flour and cook for several minutes until thick. Add chicken broth. Add winter cress and simmer for 10 minutes. Add milk and salt and pepper. Simmer for 5 minutes.

Winter Cress Au Gratin

1 pound winter cress flower buds	salt and pepper to taste
⅓ cup onion (chopped)	¼ cup Parmesan cheese
3 tablespoons butter	1 teaspoon paprika
2 tablespoons flour	
½ cup sharp cheddar cheese (shredded)	

Lightly boil winter cress for 5 minutes. Drain and save liquid. Sauté onions in butter until brown. Add flour and 1 cup of winter cress liquid. Stir constantly. Stir in cheddar cheese until melted. Add salt and pepper to taste. Pour some of the sauce into a baking dish. Add winter cress flowerbuds and cover with remaining sauce. Sprinkle with Parmesan cheese and paprika. Broil for 5 minutes or until light brown.

Remarks: *Barbarea* refers to St. Barbara's feast day on December 4. It is unclear whether *Barbarea* was used because of the planting of winter cress seeds on that day or because these were the only greens available on that day. *Vulgaris* refers to the common occurrence of the plant. Winter cress is high in vitamin C and is often called scurvy grass because of its use in preventing this disease. This exotic plant was introduced from Europe, but is now naturalized throughout the northeastern United States. Because of its availability throughout the winter, this plant was highly valued as a cooked green before modern transportation made most greens available throughout the year.

OX-EYE DAISY
(White daisy)

Leucanthemum vulgare Lam.
Asteraceae

2–3'

Characteristics: This herbaceous, rhizomatous perennial grows to 30 inches tall. Irregularly lobed, narrow alternate simple leaves are scattered on a smooth stem that grows from an overwintering rosette. Flowers appear in 2-inch heads. The white ray flowers number from fifteen to thirty while the central disk is yellow and usually depressed in the center. Flowering occurs from May to October.
Habitat: Fields, meadows, roadsides, and waste areas.
Distribution: Throughout the area.

Edible parts: Young leaves.

Food uses: Salad, cooked greens, soup.

Precautions: Only eat the young leaves from the overwintering rosette. Some people are allergic to the flower.

Preparation: Pick young leaves in the spring and wash in cold water. Mix with milder-tasting greens.

Recipes:

Ox-eye Daisy Salad

3 cups ox-eye daisy leaves (washed and torn)

2 eggs (boiled and sliced)

6 spring beauty corms (peeled and sliced)

6 slices crisp bacon (crumbled)

Dressing:

1 cup salad oil

¾ cup sugar

1 teaspoon celery salt

1 tablespoon Worcestershire sauce

1 medium onion (finely chopped)

¼ cup cider vinegar

1 teaspoon salt

Mix dressing ingredients in blender. Pour dressing over salad and toss.

Cream of Greens Soup

1 medium onion (chopped)

2 tablespoons butter

2 cups ox-eye daisy leaves (chopped)

2 cups winter-cress leaves (chopped)

½ cup flour

1 cup water

3 cups milk

½ teaspoon pepper

1 teaspoon garlic powder

2 teaspoons Áccent

½ cup provolone cheese (grated)

In large saucepan sauté onions in butter. Add chopped leaves and cook gently for 5 minutes. Combine flour and water. Add flour mixture to greens. Stir and gradually add milk. Add seasonings and simmer for 10 minutes. Serve with a sprinkling of cheese.

Remarks: Previously this plant was classified in the genus *Chrysanthemum*. As scientists accumulated more information about this plant, it was felt that it should be removed from this genus and placed in a separate genus. *Leucanthemum* means white flower and *vulgare* refers to its common occurrence. A native of Eurasia, the "common white flower" is naturalized throughout most of temperate North America. Placing the flower of ox-eye daisy under your bed pillow is said to ensure dreams of a loved one. When pulling the individual ray flowers and reciting "He/she loves me, he/she loves me not," always start with "He/she loves me," for there is usually an uneven number of ray flowers. The "flower" is really a bouquet of about a hundred individual ray and disk flowers. The name daisy is thought to be a corruption of "day's eye" and refers to the closing of the flower at night. Ox-eye refers to the resemblance of the flower to the eye of an ox.

CHICORY
(Blue sailors, Ragged soldiers)

Cichorium intybus L.
Asteraceae

2–3'

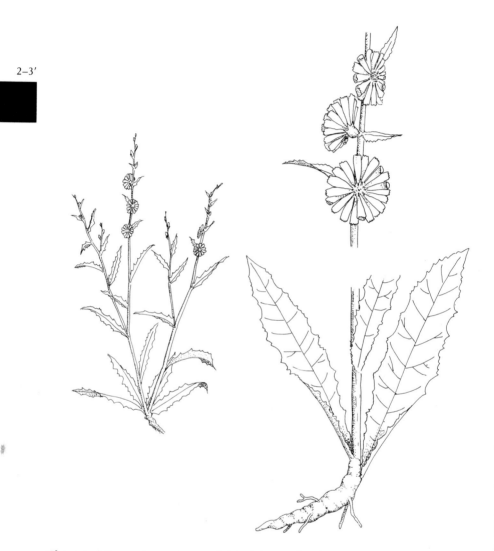

Characteristics: This erect perennial herb is usually about 3 feet tall. It has a long taproot. The leaves have deeply toothed margins. Flowers resemble dandelion flowers in form and are usually blue, but may be white or pink. Petal tips are square with notches that make them appear ragged. Flowers are stalkless, found along the upper stem, and occur from May to October. It is freely branched, almost leafless, and has a milky sap.

Habitat: Roadsides, waste areas, fields.

Distribution: Found throughout the area.

Edible parts: Young leaves, roots, young shoots.

Food uses: Coffee, salad, cooked greens.

Precautions: Basal leaves may be confused with dandelion. Collect only young leaves because the older leaves are bitter.

Preparations: Dig roots just after flowering ceases to early spring. Use ground roots as coffee substitute or coffee additive. Young leaves can be added to salads or cooked as a potherb. Dig below the first spring leaves and sever the young shoot from the taproot. These whitened, developing leaves make an excellent spring green.

Recipes:

Wilted Greens Salad

2 cups young dandelion leaves	¼ cup cider vinegar
2 cups young chicory leaves	1 tablespoon sugar
6 slices bacon	2 tablespoons water
2 tablespoons bacon drippings	½ teaspoon salt
2 hard-boiled eggs (chopped)	¼ teaspoon pepper
2 tablespoons green onions (chopped)	

Wash and clean dandelion and chicory leaves. Drain. Fry bacon until crisp. Save 2 tablespoons of drippings. Crumble bacon. Tear greens into a bowl. Add eggs and onions to greens. Combine 2 tablespoons bacon drippings, vinegar, sugar, water, salt, and pepper in a saucepan. Heat to almost boiling. Pour over greens. Toss lightly. Garnish with bacon.

Chicory Coffee

Scrub the taproots. Place taproots on a cookie sheet, put in oven, and roast at 300° F until hard, brittle, and brown through the middle. Grind the roots and brew the same as with regular coffee. Chicory is stronger, so use less than you normally would. Try various combinations of chicory, dandelion, and regular coffee.

Remarks: Chicory is the preferred coffee in much of Louisiana and the neighboring states. English and French coffee houses routinely serve this caffeine-free coffee. Chicory was used to extend the coffee supply during the Civil War and the World Wars. New spring rosettes grow from the base of last year's flower stalk. Remember where the plants are located this year in order to get some spring greens next year. Linnaeus used the plant as a part of his floral clock because the flowers opened at 5:00 A.M. and closed at noon. Chicory is a native of Eurasia. Endive is also included in the genus *Cichorium*.

ORACHE
(Spearscale)

Atriplex patula L.
Chenopodiaceae

2–3'

Characteristics: Orache is a 3-foot erect-to-prostrate herbaceous annual. The simple, broadly triangular leaves have the lower teeth pointing outward. The leaves are mostly alternate, but some lower leaves may be opposite. Small green flowers with reddish bracts arise from the leaf axils. The leaves and stems are usually white-mealy. Flowering occurs throughout the summer to early fall.
Habitat: Saline or alkaline soils, waste areas.
Distribution: Throughout the area.

Edible parts: Young leaves and stem tips.

Food uses: Cooked greens, soup, salad.

Precautions: Rinse thoroughly to remove salt. May be confused with lamb's-quarters (*Chenopodium album*). The plant is naturally salty.

Preparation: After rinsing thoroughly, use in any manner that you would use salty spinach.

Recipes:

Orache Wedding Soup

1 cut-up chicken	1 cup carrots (sliced)
2 cups small meatballs	2 cups orache leaves (torn)
1 cup celery (diced)	1 cup Romano cheese (grated)
1 small onion (chopped)	3 eggs (beaten)

Boil chicken by itself. In a separate pot, bring meatballs to a boil, then drain off water. Add meatballs to chicken pot and finish cooking both meats. Add celery, onion, and carrots. Bring orache to a boil in a separate pot. Discard water and add orache to the chicken pot. Add cheese, stir in eggs, and continue cooking for 15 minutes.

Scalloped Orache

½ cup wild leeks or onions (chopped)	1 can cream of mushroom soup
	1 cup cheddar cheese (shredded)
4 cups steamed orache	½ pint sour cream
¼ cup butter	

Sauté leeks in butter. Combine all ingredients and blend well. Turn into greased baking dish. Bake at 350° F for 25 minutes.

Remarks: Although ragweed pollen (*Ambrosia*) is the most allergic pollen in the United States and gets much of the blame for hay fever, many other plants, such as orache, also produce aeroallergens. A mycorrhiza is a symbiotic relationship between a fungus and a plant root. About 95 percent of all plants have mycorrhizae. Included in the small group of plants that do not are aquatic plants, mustards, and the goosefoot family (Chenopodiaceae). A paste is made of the plant leaves to relieve the sting of insect bites. *Atriplex* is the Greek name for this plant. *Patula* refers to the area around Padua, Italy.

ARROWHEAD
(Wapato, Duck Potato,
Swamp Potato)

Sagittaria latifolia Willd.
Alismataceae

2–3′

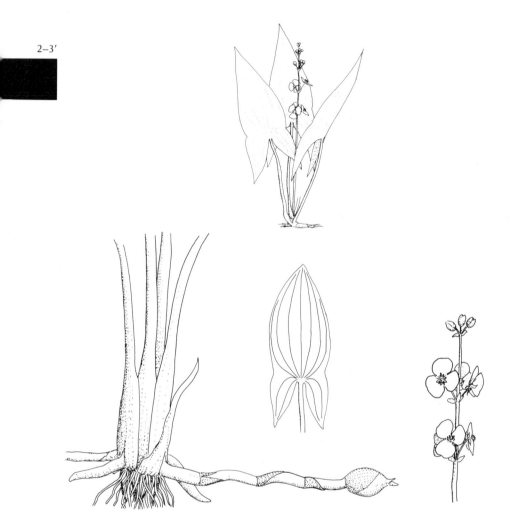

Characteristics: This perennial herb has arrowhead-shaped leaves that are alternately arranged on a rhizome. Tubers occur at the ends of the rhizomes. The height of the plant (up to 3 feet) is primarily due to a very long petiole. The flowers occur in clusters of threes. Each flower has three white petals. Flowering occurs throughout the summer and early fall.

Habitat: Swamps, marshes, slow-moving streams, and along the edges of ponds.

Distribution: Throughout the area.

Edible parts: Tubers.

Food uses: Any potato dishes.

Precautions: Could be dangerous if eaten raw. Collect from unpolluted water. May be confused with arrow arum and pickerelweed.

Preparation: Rhizomes grow from the base of each plant. Follow the rhizomes with your hand. At the end of these long subterranean runners are the tubers or "potatoes." Remove the tubers. Scrub the tubers thoroughly and boil in salted water for 15 minutes. Some people leave the skins intact, but the tubers are probably better if peeled. Fall and early spring are the best times for collecting.

Recipes:

Arrowhead Spread

1 cup arrowhead tubers (diced)	½ cup plain yogurt
½ cup shredded coconut	½ teaspoon mint
2 tablespoons safflower oil	

Blend arrowhead, coconut, and safflower oil in a blender until smooth. Turn mixture into a bowl. Stir in yogurt and mint. Blend well and chill.

Arrowhead Casserole

10 arrowhead tubers	½ pound Velveeta cheese (cubed)
1 green pepper (diced)	¾ cup butter
1 large onion (diced)	½ cup milk
1 cup celery (chopped)	1 cup cornflakes
4 slices bread (cubed)	salt and pepper to taste

Scrub tubers and then boil for 15 minutes. Peel tubers and cube. Combine tubers, pepper, onion, celery, bread, and cheese in a casserole dish. Melt butter and pour over top. Sprinkle milk over surface. Cover with crumbled cornflakes. Bake uncovered at 350° F for 40–45 minutes.

Remarks: In Asia, Orientals cultivate the arrowhead along the edges of rice paddies. American Chinese, especially in California, continue to cultivate this plant. Arrowhead was a favorite of North American Indians. Lewis and Clark described how Indian squaws waded in the water and dug the tubers with their toes. The tubers floated to the surface, where they were collected and thrown into a canoe. Lewis and Clark relied on the tubers for food as they explored the Northwest. The tubers are high in starch and phosphorus. *Sagittaria* is derived from the Latin word *sagitta*, which means an arrow, and *latifolia* means broad leaves. This plant definitely has broad, arrow-shaped leaves.

OSWEGO TEA
(Bee balm, Bergamot)

Monarda didyma L.
Lamiaceae

2–3'

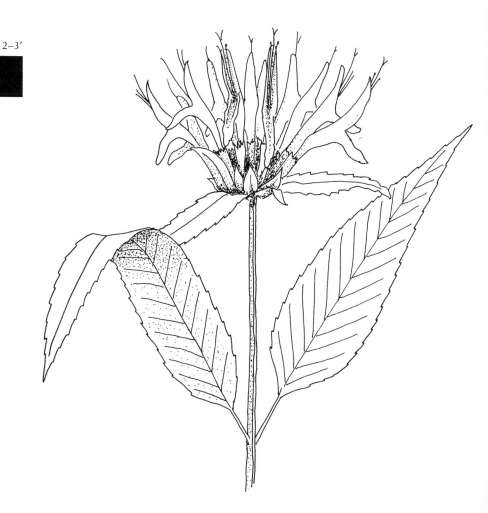

Characteristics: This herbaceous perennial plant is usually about 3 feet tall. The square stem bears opposite ovate-to-lanceolate toothed leaves. The irregular, two-lipped bright red flowers are arranged in ragged headlike clusters. Flowering occurs from July to September. There is a mint odor to crushed leaves.
Habitat: Moist woods and stream banks.
Distribution: Widely distributed throughout the area.

Edible parts: Leaves and flower heads.
Food uses: Tea, seasoning, salad, jelly, candy.
Precautions: Some people find the taste too sweet.
Preparation: Dried leaves and flower heads are stored in air-tight jars in a dark place. Fresh leaves and flower heads are more commonly used, with leaves being preferred.
Recipes:

Oswego Tea Jelly

1 quart Oswego-tea leaves	3 cups sugar
3 cups water	1 package pectin

Wash leaves in cold water and drain. Pour boiling water over leaves. After 5 minutes strain and retain liquid. Add sugar and bring to a boil. Stir constantly. Add pectin and bring to a rolling boil. Boil 1 minute. Skim off foam, ladle into hot, sterilized jars, and seal with paraffin. If mint green color is desired, add 4 drops of food coloring.

Candied Oswego Tea Leaves

1 cup granulated sugar	1 quart Oswego-tea leaves (washed)
½ cup water	1 cup superfine granulated sugar

Combine sugar and water. Boil until mixture thickens and a drop from a spoon forms a thread. Cool to room temperature. Hold leaves by petiole and dip in sugar solution and then lightly in superfine sugar. Place on wax paper and allow to dry.

Remarks: The genus name *Monarda* honors the Spanish botanist Nicholas Monardes. The term *didyma* means pair and refers to the two stamens. This plant was used by the Oswego Indians. In protest of the tea tax imposed by the British government, American Colonists refused to purchase tea from the British East India Company. Instead the Colonists drank smuggled Dutch tea and the native Oswego tea. Bee-balm refers to an ointment made to soothe bee stings. The flowers are attractive to hummingbirds, bees, and several species of butterflies. Other members of this genus, such as *M. fistulosa* and *M. media*, are also edible. Bergamot oil is usually obtained from *M. fistulosa*. The leaves are reported to be high in vitamins A and C. The common name of bergamot refers to its citruslike scent, which resembles bergamot oranges.

PEPPERMINT
(Pepper, White mint)

Mentha piperita L.
Lamiaceae

2–3'

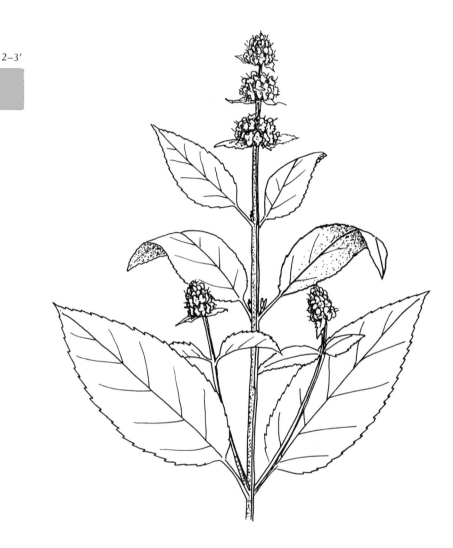

Characteristics: Peppermint is a perennial herb that grows up to 3 feet tall. The square stem bears opposite, ovate leaves that are sharply toothed. The pink to pale-violet flowers are arranged in terminal spikes. The tubular, irregular flowers have five lobes that enclose four stamens. A peppermint odor and peppery taste characterize the leaves.
Habitat: Wet places such as roadside ditches, wet fields, and stream banks.
Distribution: Throughout the area.

Edible parts: Leaves.

Food uses: Salad, tea, seasoning, jam, jelly, candy.

Precautions: The taste may vary a great deal from one population to another.

Preparation: Select the younger leaves near the tip of the plant and rinse in water. Fresh or dried leaves can be used. Peppermint has a strong taste and should be mixed with other greens in a salad. Store dried leaves in a tightly covered jar. Leaves can be used to season fish and some red meat dishes.

Recipes:

Candied Peppermint Leaves

1 quart peppermint leaves   1 cup superfine granulated sugar
3 egg whites

Rinse peppermint leaves in cold water, then air-dry on a towel. Beat egg whites until thickened. Dip peppermint leaves in egg whites and then sugar. Place coated leaves on a cookie sheet covered with wax paper. Place cookie sheet in oven that has been preheated to 200° F. Remove from oven after 30 minutes. Cool and store in air-tight jars.

Peppermint Salad Dressing

½ cup olive oil   2 teaspoons lemon juice
¼ cup tarragon vinegar   1 teaspoon salt
½ teaspoon pepper   1 teaspoon basil
½ cup peppermint (finely chopped)

Combine ingredients and chill before serving.

Remarks: *Piperita* means pepper-scented. Peppermint probably originated through the hybridization of spearmint and another mint. Because of its ability to hybridize, the peppermint flavor may vary widely, and it may resemble spearmint in appearance. Brought to the colonies from Europe by the early settlers, this plant is now widely established throughout the area. Herbal uses of this plant include tea to relieve stomach and bowel pains and to treat nausea. Peppermint oil is used to flavor candy, toothpaste, chewing gum, and ice cream. Some individuals perfume their homes by gently boiling peppermint leaves or using the crushed, dried leaves in a sachet. The mint family (Lamiaceae) was previously known as Labiatae.

SPEARMINT
(Garden mint)

Mentha spicata L.
Lamiaceae

2–3'

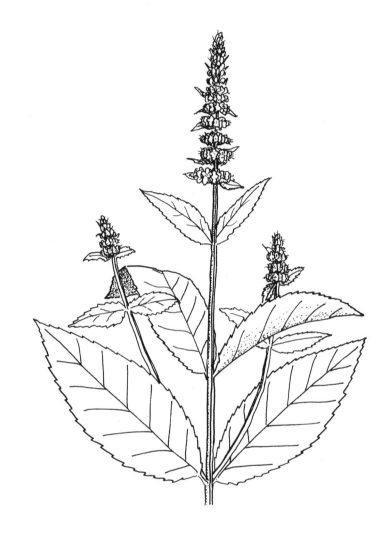

Characteristics: This erect perennial grows to 2 feet tall. The opposite, simple, ovate, toothed leaves often have a hairy midrib. Stems are smooth and square. The plant spreads mainly by rhizomes and stolons. Crushed leaves have a strong odor of spearmint. The pink-to-violet flowers occur in spikes that are terminal and from leaf axils. Flowering occurs during midsummer.
Habitat: Fertile, moist soil; often along ditches.
Distribution: Throughout the area.

Edible parts: Leaves.

Food uses: Tea, candy, jelly, flavoring, salad.

Precautions: Spearmint oil can cause dermatitis. Peppermint closely resembles spearmint and is probably a hybrid of spearmint and *M. aquatica*. Because of hybridization, spearmint may show a great amount of variation in odor and taste.

Preparation: If using fresh leaves, wash in cold water. For storing dry leaves, cut the stems and wash in cold water. Shake off excess water, tie in bundles, and hang upside down in a dry place such as an attic. After the leaves are dry, separate the leaves from the stem and store the leaves in airtight glass jars.

Recipes:

Mint Sauce

¼ cup water	pinch of salt
½ cup honey	½ cup fresh spearmint leaves
¼ cup cider vinegar	(chopped)

Mix water, honey, vinegar, and salt and heat until warm. Pour over spearmint leaves and let stand for ½ hour.

Spearmint Salad Dressing

1 tablespoon spearmint leaves (finely chopped)	½ teaspoon salt
	⅛ teaspoon pepper
¼ cup tarragon vinegar	½ cup olive oil
1 teaspoon onion (minced)	

Combine ingredients and mix in blender for several minutes.

Remarks: *Mentha* is derived from either the classical Greek name for mint (*minthe*) or the Latin name (*menta*). *Spicata* refers to the spike inflorescence. The previous name used for the mint family was Labiatae, which referred to the two-lipped appearance of the flowers. A labium is a lip. Spearmint is a native of Europe, but was brought to North America by early colonists who valued it as a medicinal. Spearmint and peppermint are well known for their carminative properties. Spearmint is used as a flavoring in medicines, toothpaste, chewing gum, and candy. Other products make use of its fragrance: disinfectants, candles, bath salts, and potpourris. The plant is easily established in flower gardens, but its habit of rapid vegetative growth soon changes its relative value from wildflower to "weed." Mint oil from some *Mentha* contains 90 percent menthol, which is used in mentholated cigarettes.

DAYLILY

Hemerocallis fulva (L.) L.
Liliaceae

2–3'

Characteristics: This is a perennial plant with basal leaves that are long and swordlike. The roots form a tangle of elongated tubers. Two- to three-foot high stalks support funnellike unspotted, orange flowers. Flowering occurs in June and July.
Habitat: Escaped from gardens and old homesites, roadsides, edges of fields, culverts, and ditches.
Distribution: Found throughout the area, but usually in localized populations.

98

Edible parts: Flower buds, flowers, tubers, young shoots.

Food uses: Salad, cooked vegetable, asparagus, fritters, soup, seasoning.

Precautions: Daylilies do not agree with everyone. Cases of poisoning have been reported from the midwestern United States. Do not eat the raw plant. May be confused with iris and daffodil.

Preparation: Add the young shoots to salads or prepare like asparagus. Young flower buds can be cooked like green beans. Fritters are made from the flowers. Tubers can be added to salads or prepared as potatoes. Dried flowers are used as a soup thickener and for seasoning.

Recipes:

Daylily Oriental

3½ cups daylily flower buds (rinsed and drained)
1 cup water
1 tablespoon cider vinegar
½ cup almonds (sliced)
2 tablespoons soy sauce
salt to taste
hot boiled rice to serve 6

Combine daylily buds and water in saucepan. Bring to boil and simmer for 20 minutes. Drain off most of water, leaving about 2 tablespoons. Add vinegar, nuts, soy sauce, and salt. Stir and cook for 5 minutes. Serve over rice.

Daylily Fritters

1½ cups flour
2 teaspoons baking powder
dash of garlic salt
salt and pepper to taste
¾ cup milk
2 eggs
½ teaspoon basil
¼ cup Parmesan cheese
10 daylily flowers

Sift together flour, baking powder, and garlic salt. In another bowl beat milk and eggs together. Combine mixtures with basil and cheese until smooth. Wash flowers, clip off stems, and pull out stamens and pistil. Pat dry with paper towels. Dip blossoms into batter and deep-fry until golden brown. Place fritters on paper towels and salt and pepper to taste.

Remarks: *Hemerocallis* means "one day beauty" and refers to the one day that the flower is open. *Fulva* refers to the tawny orange color. Asians have used the plant for food for centuries and use practically all parts of the plant. The daylily rarely produces seeds; its main form of reproduction is from rhizomes. A yellow dye can be extracted from the flowers. As a monocot, daylily has flowering parts in multiples of three.

LAMB'S-QUARTERS
(Goosefoot, Pigweed)

Chenopodium album L.
Chenopodiaceae

2–3'

Characteristics: This much-branched annual grows from 2 to 4 feet tall. Stems and leaves are often white and mealy. Older plants turn reddish. The lower, broad, toothed leaves resemble a goose foot. The upper leaves are alternate, entire, and narrow. The small green flowers are in dense spikes, but are inconspicuous.
Habitat: Waste areas; disturbed soils such as gardens, farmland, construction sites.
Distribution: Widely distributed throughout the area.

Edible parts: Leaves, seeds.

Food uses: Cooked greens, cereal, flour, salad, soups.

Precautions: This plant is often found on waste sites, and care should be taken to be sure the area is free of contaminants. Lamb's-quarters contains oxalic acid, which tends to bind with calcium. It is also known to accumulate toxic levels of nitrate.

Preparation: Entire young plants that are less than 10 inches in height can be used. On old plants, pinch off the tender stem tips. Leaves can be used in salads, soups, and as cooked greens. Flour can be made from the seeds. A hot breakfast cereal can be made by boiling the seeds until soft.

Recipes:

Lamb's-Quarters Cream Soup

1 quart lamb's-quarters (washed)	½ cup celery (chopped thin)
3 garlic cloves (chopped)	5 cups chicken broth
2 tablespoons butter	1½ cups heavy cream
2 potatoes (peeled and cubed)	salt and pepper to taste

Sauté lamb's quarters and garlic in butter for several minutes in a large saucepan. Add potatoes, celery, and chicken broth and boil for 30 minutes. Puree and return to medium heat. Stir in heavy cream and salt and pepper.

Lamb's-Quarters Supreme

3 tablespoons olive oil	2 boiled potatoes (cubed)
1 cup onions or wild leeks (sliced)	2 teaspoons lemon juice
4 cups lamb's-quarters (washed and drained)	6 slices crisp bacon (crumbled)
	salt and pepper to taste
½ cup parsley (chopped)	
1 teaspoon rosemary	

Fry onions, lamb's-quarters, parsley, and rosemary in oil for 10 minutes over medium heat. Add potatoes and cook for five minutes. Stir occasionally. Stir in lemon juice and salt and pepper. Place in serving dish. Sprinkle bacon on surface.

Remarks: Many people rate this plant as the best of the cooked greens. Spinach is also in this family, but it cannot match lamb's-quarters for flavor and nutrients. Lamb's-quarters exceeds spinach in protein, calcium, phosphorus, thiamine, riboflavin, niacin, vitamin A, and vitamin C. The genus name *Chenopodium* refers to the resemblance of the leaves to a goose (*chen*) foot (*pod*). *Album* means white and refers to the white, mealy appearance of the leaves. A single plant can produce 100,000 seeds, which may remain dormant in the soil for up to forty years. This plant was once thought to be a native of Eurasia, but it has been found among sixteenth-century seeds stored by American Blackfoot Indians. Quinoa (*Chenopodium quinoa*) was used as a grain crop by the Incas. This cousin of lamb's-quarters is one of the richest sources of protein among the grain crops. It also has high levels of the amino acids lysine and methionine.

STINGING NETTLE
(Nettle, Seven-minute itch)

Urtica dioca L.
Urticaceae

3–4'

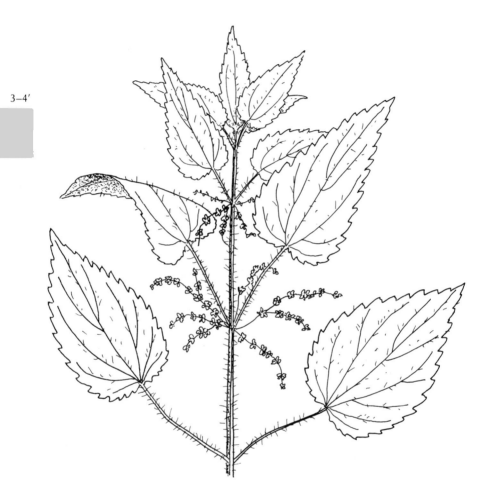

Characteristics: This plant is an upright herbaceous perennial from 2 to 4 feet tall. The four-sided hollow stem bears simple, opposite, ovate leaves that have a toothed margin. Bristly, stinging hairs are found on the stem and leaves. Green to cream-colored flower clusters are produced in the upper leaf axils from June to September.
Habitat: Moist, fertile soils on flood plains, roadside ditches, trailsides.
Distribution: Throughout the area south to Virginia.

102

Edible parts: Young shoots and tender tips of plants.

Food uses: Cooked greens, tea, soup.

Precautions: Wear leather gloves to collect this plant. Many cases of severe dermatitis have been reported. A boy from New Castle, Pennsylvania, had nettles rubbed on his stomach and had a swollen navel and abdomen for three weeks.

Preparation: The stinging irritant is destroyed by boiling the plant in water for 5 minutes. Contrary to the usual rules for making tea, boil the leaves and shoots in water for 10 minutes. The leaves and shoots can be dried for later use in soups or tea. Collect before the plant flowers. Best to collect when plants are about 6 inches tall.

Recipes:

Nettle Casserole

½ cup onion (chopped)	2 cups nettle shoots (boiled and drained)
½ cup celery (chopped)	
¼ cup margarine	3½ cups water
½ cup mushrooms (sliced)	2 cups cooked rice
1 can cream of chicken soup	½ cup cheddar cheese (shredded)

Sauté onion, celery, and mushrooms in margarine. When done, add to chicken soup, nettle, water, and rice. Stir over medium heat until creamy. Put in casserole dish and sprinkle cheese on top. Bake for 40 minutes at 350° F.

Cream of Nettle Toast

2 cups nettle (chopped)	salt to taste
1 can cream of mushroom soup	toasted bread
½ cup light cream	2 hard-boiled eggs

Boil nettles for 15 minutes. Drain and combine nettles with soup, cream, and salt. Stir over medium heat for 10 minutes. Spread on toast. Crumble eggs and sprinkle on top.

Remarks: *Urtica* is the Latin name for nettle. *Dioca* refers to dioecious, which means there are male and female plants. During World War I the plant provided fiber for making fabrics for tents, clothing, and wagon covers. Other uses include dye, paper, rope, and fishing nets. Nettle is also a diuretic, and is used as a hair rinse and in commercial hair growth preparations. The stinging hairs do not sting, but the hypodermiclike mechanism is activated by brushing against the hairs. Plants that have been suggested to relieve the "seven-minute itch" and reduce the cluster of white swollen areas are jewelweed, plantain, yarrow, and dock. Stinging nettle is high in iron, protein, and vitamins A and C. In "The Wild Swans" by Hans Christian Andersen, Eliza has to make green flax from stinging nettles and weave the material into eleven shirts in order to change her eleven brothers from swans back to princes. With her fingers bloody and swollen from the nettles, Eliza manages to complete all but the sleeve of the eleventh shirt by the deadline. Her brothers put them on and are immediately changed from swans into princes, but her youngest brother has a swan's wing instead of an arm.

GOOSEBERRY
(Dogberry, Pasture gooseberry)

Ribes cynosbati L.
Saxifragaceae

3–4'

Characteristics: This is a low, bushy deciduous shrub that grows to 4 feet high. The alternate, maplelike leaves have three to five blunt lobes and coarse teeth. Leaves are clustered on short lateral branches. Usually one to three spines occur at the nodes, and scattered prickles may occur along the internode. Small greenish-white flowers occur in May and June and are followed by bristly, round, red-purple fruits that often occur in small clusters. The remains of the calyx form a brownish projection at the bottom of each berry.
Habitat: Moist woods and fields.
Distribution: Frequently in forested areas throughout the region.

Edible parts: Fruit.

Food uses: Fresh or dried fruit, jelly, desserts, fruit sauce.

Precautions: Be careful of the bristles, spines, and prickles. Pick only ripe fruit.

Preparation: Wash and rub or peel the fruit to remove bristles. Cooking also removes bristles. To dry, spread in a thin layer on a cookie sheet, then place in sun or in oven at 200° F until dry.

Recipes:

Gooseberry Preserves

4 cups gooseberries   3 cups sugar
½ cup pineapple juice

Place gooseberries in large pan. Add pineapple juice and bring to a boil. Stir well. Add sugar and stir constantly. Boil about 20 minutes and keep stirring. Remove from heat, pour into hot, sterilized jars, and seal with paraffin.

Gooseberry Pie

¼ cup butter or margarine	3 tablespoons evaporated milk
1 cup brown sugar	¼ teaspoon vanilla
2 eggs	1 pie shell and top crust
2½ cups ripe gooseberries	

Cream butter and brown sugar. Beat eggs and stir in. Add milk, gooseberries, and vanilla. Put mixture into unbaked pie shell. Add top crust. Bake at 425° F for 15 minutes or until pie is brown on top.

Remarks: The name gooseberry has nothing to do with geese, but instead is a corruption of the French *groise,* which translates as hairy. Gooseberries and wild currants are closely related and are classified in the same genus (*Ribes*). Most currants can be distinguished from gooseberries by the lack of spines on the stems. Gooseberries are widely cultivated in Europe and North America. Indians removed the bristles from the fruit by singeing them over hot coals. Gooseberry spines were used as fish hooks, probes for boils and blisters, and needles for tattooing. Because gooseberries are rich in pectin, the use of commercial pectin is unnecessary when making jams or jellies. The black currant from Europe and most of the American currants are carriers of the fungus that causes white-pine blister rust. These plants have been eradicated from many areas where white pine grows.

PICKERELWEED
(Tuckahoe)

Pontederia cordata L.
Pontederiaceae

3–4'

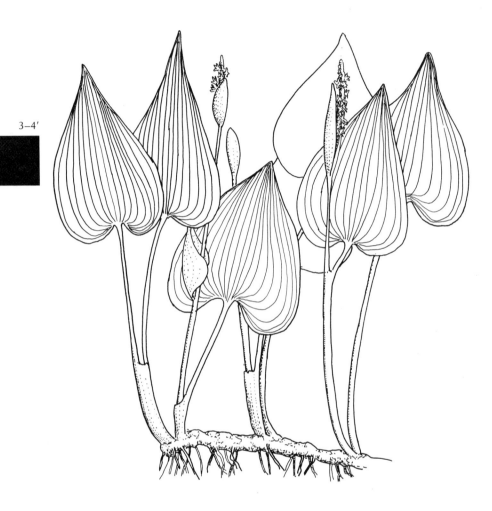

Characteristics: Pickerelweed is an erect perennial herb that reaches a height of 4 feet. Large, usually arrowhead-shaped leaves occur in clumps from a rhizome. The leaves are thick, dark green, and entire. The flower stalk is spikelike with blue flowers, slightly taller than the leaves, and arises from the long leaf petiole. There are six petals and six stamens to each flower. This colonial plant flowers throughout the summer.
Habitat: Shallow water of marshes, ponds, lakes, and slow-moving streams.
Distribution: Throughout most of the area.

Edible parts: Young leaves, seeds.

Food uses: Salad, cooked greens, snack, flour.

Precautions: Avoid collecting the plant from polluted water. May be confused with *Sagittaria latifolia* and *Peltandra virginica*.

Preparation: Use young leaves in salads or as a boiled or steamed vegetable. Seeds can be eaten as a snack or roasted and ground into flour. Collect the young leaves before they are fully open in early summer. Seeds ripen in late summer and early fall.

Recipes:

Pickerelweed Nibbles

1 cup pickerelweed fruits   ¾ teaspoon salt
1 tablespoon butter

Remove the outer skin of the fruit by either rubbing and then winnowing or soaking fruits in hot water and then removing skins. Add dry seeds to melted butter and salt. Spread seeds on an ungreased cookie sheet and roast for 45 minutes at 250° F.

Pickerelweed Omelette

¼ cup chives   ¼ cup milk
¼ cup mushrooms   6 eggs (beaten)
2 wild leek bulbs (diced)   salt and pepper to taste
2 tablespoons butter   ¼ cup cheddar cheese (grated)
½ cup young pickerelweed leaves
   (chopped)

Sauté chives, mushrooms, and leeks in butter in a large skillet until brown. Mix pickerelweed, milk, eggs, and salt and pepper in a separate bowl and then add to skillet ingredients. Mix quickly, cover with lid, and cook for several minutes over medium heat. Remove lid and sprinkle cheese on top. Cover and cook for another minute. Slide omelette from skillet by using a large spatula.

Remarks: Linnaeus honored the botanist Guilo Pontedera by naming the genus (*Pontederia*) after him. Although the leaves are shaped more like an arrowhead, the term *cordata* means "heart-shaped." Northern pike, which are also called pickerel in Canada, and true pickerel are commonly found among these plants and reflect the common name of pickerelweed.

DOCK
(Curled dock, Yellow dock)
(Sour dock, Bitter dock, Broad-leaved dock)

Rumex crispus L.
Rumex obtusifolius L.
Polygonaceae

3–4′

R. crispus   ' R. obtusifolius

Characteristics: These erect perennials grow to 4 feet high. Only basal leaves are found in the early spring. Basal leaves may differ in shape from the aerial leaves. The erect stem has alternate leaves with sheathing stipules at their bases. Small greenish to brown flowers mature into reddish-brown fruits. Each of the three angles of the fruit extends into a flattened wing. *R. crispus* has long, narrow leaves with a wavy margin. The leaves of *R. obtusifolius* are more ovate, without a wavy margin, and often with reddish veins.
Habitat: Disturbed soil, fields, roadsides, waste places, gardens.
Distribution: Throughout the area.

Edible parts: Young leaves, seeds.

Foods uses: Salad, cooked greens, flour, gruel.

Precautions: Consuming large quantities of dock has been reported to cause an upset stomach. May be confused with other plants that form a rosette. As indicated by the common name, the plant is somewhat bitter, but with a hint of lemon flavor.

Preparation: Collect the leaves in the early spring before the flower stalk appears. The leaves are used in salads and as cooked greens. The seeds are collected in late summer and fall and ground into flour or gruel. If the bitterness of the cooked green is too offensive, boil in several changes of water.

Recipes:

Dock Clam Soup

1 large onion	2 cups canned clams
4 tablespoons butter or margarine	2 cups milk
2 cups young dock leaves (shredded)	pepper

Brown onion in butter or margarine. Add two cups of dock leaves to pan and stir for several minutes until leaves are wilted. Add clams and milk. Bring to a slow simmer for about 1 minute. Dust with pepper.

Spring Salad Delight

1 cup dandelion leaves	1 green onion (chopped)
2 tablespoons sheep sorrel	salt and pepper
1 cup dock leaves	oil and vinegar
2 tablespoons violet leaves	violet flowers
1 cup blackberry shoots	

Combine dandelion, sheep sorrel, dock, violets, blackberry shoots, and onion, and lightly toss. Season with salt, pepper, oil, and vinegar. Garnish with violet flowers.

Remarks: Docks are rich in vitamins A and C. Because of the bitterness, vinegar is often omitted from salads with bitter dock. The plants are natives of Europe, but naturalized in much of the United States. *Crispus* refers to the curly nature of the curled dock leaf while *obtusifolius* refers to the large leaves of bitter dock. The family name Polygonaceae translates to "many-jointed" and refers to the stipule-encased "joints" of the stem. The seeds of curled dock can be ground and used as a tobacco substitute. The dried flower stalks are often used in dried flower arrangements. The bitterness in dock is caused by oxalic acid, which binds with calcium and keeps the body from absorbing it. Therefore, plants with large amounts of oxalic acid, such as dock, sheep sorrel, wood sorrel, Swiss chard, lamb's-quarters, beet tops, and spinach, should be eaten in moderation.

SOW THISTLE
(Spiny-leaved sow thistle)

Sonchus asper (L.) Hill.
Asteraceae

3–4'

Characteristics: This annual herbaceous plant grows to 4 feet tall. The alternate, toothed, ovate, spiny leaves have rounded auricles that clasp the smooth stem. The simple leaves occur in a basal position and also on the erect stem. Seeds and stems have a milky sap. More than 100 yellow ray flowers compose the flower head, which is relatively small and arranged in a flat-topped inflorescence. Flowers occur from July to October.

Habitat: Waste places, gardens, fallow fields.

Distribution: Throughout the area.

Edible parts: Young leaves.

Food uses: Cooked greens, salad, soup.

Precautions: Leaves become bitter with age and therefore should be collected in the spring. Some instances of nitrate accumulation have been reported. Wear gloves to collect. The young plant may be confused with blue lettuce and thistles.

Preparation: If using in a salad, use scissors to remove the spiny prickles from the leaves. Mix with other blander greens in a salad. For cooked greens, boil in one change of salted water.

Recipes:

Sow Thistle Salad

1 cup seasoned bread cubes	½ head lettuce (torn)
1 wild leek (chopped)	1 cup Italian dressing
3 tablespoons vegetable oil	2 hard-boiled eggs (sliced)
1 quart young sow-thistle leaves	½ cup Parmesan cheese (grated)

Brown bread cubes and leek in vegetable oil. Cool. Wash and remove spines from sow-thistle leaves. Tear the leaves and combine lettuce, sow thistle, and bread cube-leek mixture. Toss and add dressing. Place in salad dishes and top with egg slices and cheese.

Sow Thistle Soup

1 cup young sow-thistle leaves (chopped)	2 carrots (grated)
	1 teaspoon celery salt
2 quarts chicken broth	1 garlic clove (minced)
1 medium onion (chopped)	1 teaspoon basil
1 cup spinach (chopped)	salt and pepper to taste
1 cup whole kernel corn	

Combine ingredients and bring to boil. Cook over medium heat until done.

Remarks: *Sonchus* is the ancient Greek name for this plant. *Asper* means very rough and refers to the spiny leaves. The plant is a native of Europe, where it has been a popular food, but it is now naturalized throughout most of temperate North America. Thistle is from the Anglo-Saxon word for tearer. Common family names include sunflower, composite, and aster. Composite refers to the head type of inflorescence, which is a mass or composite of many individual flowers. A previously used name for this family is Compositae. *Sonchus*, like dandelion, is a composite with only ray flowers. Sunflowers, however, have ray and disk flowers organized into a composite inflorescence. Tansy has only disk flowers.

SWEET FERN
(Wild tea)

Comptonia peregrina (L.) Coult.
Myricaceae

3–4'

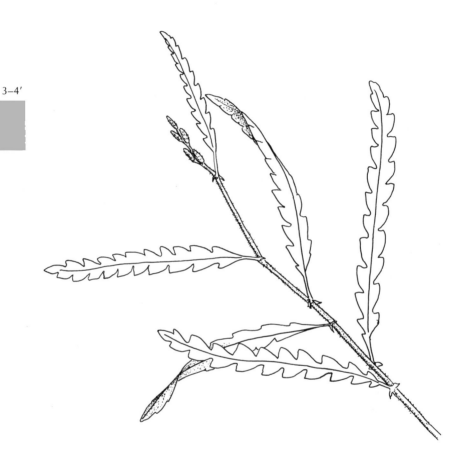

Characteristics: Sweet fern is a much-branched shrub that grows to 4 feet tall. The alternate, simple, linear leaves with a lobed margin give a fanlike appearance. Leaves have yellow resin dots and are aromatic. The unisexual flowers appear from April to June. Small nuts are present from September to October.
Habitat: Dry, sandy soils in clearings and woodlands.
Distribution: Throughout the area.

Edible parts: Leaves.

Food uses: Tea, seasoning.

Precautions: Often found along the wooded edges of pipelines that may be contaminated with herbicides.

Preparation: Fresh or dried leaves may be used. Select young, unblemished leaves. Older leaves tend to dry at the margins and are not as flavorful. Use one teaspoon of dry or 2 teaspoons of fresh leaves to make tea.

Recipes:

Baked Fish ZEC Style

2 fish fillets	1 small onion (sliced)
2 sweet fern leaves	salt and pepper to taste
2 teaspoons butter	

Place fish fillets on heavy aluminum foil. Cover fish with other ingredients. Fold aluminum foil to make a sealed package. Cover aluminum foil package with hot coals. Cook for 8 minutes. If a wood fire is impractical, cook over the charcoal grill. Cook on one side for 5 minutes; then turn and cook for 3 minutes.

Sweet Fern Jello

2 teaspoons sweet fern leaves	1 cup cold water
1 cup boiling water	1 banana (sliced)
1 package lemon-flavored gelatin	

Pour boiling water over sweet fern leaves. Steep for 5 minutes. Remove leaves. Bring sweet fern tea to a boil and add to gelatin. Stir until dissolved. Add cold water and stir. Refrigerate until slightly thickened. Add banana. Refrigerate.

Remarks: Some scientists include sweet fern in the same genus as bayberry and give it the scientific name *Myrica asplenifolia*. *Asplenifolia* means spleen leaf and probably refers to the resemblance of the long, thin leaf to the human spleen. *Peregrina* means foreign or exotic. Dried leaves are burned as an insect repellent. A strong tea made from the leaves has been used as a skin wash for poison ivy. Sweet fern is a producer of aeroallergens. Leaves and flowers have been used to make a tea for the control of diarrhea. Sweet fern has flowers and therefore is botanically not a fern.

MARSHMALLOW

Althaea officinalis L.
Malvaceae

3–4'

Characteristics: This perennial herb grows to 4 feet tall. The alternate, simple, velvety leaves are widest at the base and irregularly and coarsely toothed. Five pink, showy petals and a bushy column of stamens characterize the flower. Flower clusters arise from the upper leaf axils from July to September. Fruit is a flattened disc. There is a large, whitish mucilaginous root.

Habitat: Salt marshes and some localized fresh-water areas.

Distribution: Mainly scattered along the coast from Virginia to Connecticut.

Edible parts: Young leaves, flower buds, roots.

Food uses: Candy, cooked vegetable, soup thickener, pickle.

Precaution: Wash in several changes of water to remove marsh debris and surface slime.

Preparation: Use the young leaves as a soup thickener. Flower buds are pickled. Roots are used for a vegetable or candy.

Recipes:

Fried Marshmallow Roots

1 quart marshmallow roots   1 medium onion (chopped)
butter   salt and pepper to taste

Wash the roots in several changes of water. Peel roots and slice crosswise. Boil root slices until soft. Strain roots and place on paper towels until fairly dry. Fry onions in butter in frying pan, then add roots. Salt and pepper to taste.

Marshmallow Candy

1 quart marshmallow roots   cake sprinkles
½ cup granulated sugar

Wash the roots in several changes of water. Peel roots and slice crosswise. Place roots in saucepan and just cover with water. Boil for 30 minutes. Strain off roots and keep liquid. Gently boil liquid and add granulated sugar. Keep boiling until liquid becomes thick. Remove from heat. Cool. Beat mixture until foamy. Drop by spoonfuls onto waxed paper and place in refrigerator to cool. Dust with cake sprinkles.

Remarks: Mallow is derived from the Greek word *malakos,* which means soft and refers to the velvety leaves. *Althaea* is also Greek and refers to its healing properties. Plants officially recognized for medicinal value are often given the specific epithet *officinalis.* The plant is used as an herbal medicine to cure coughs, sore throats, and ailments of the stomach, intestine, and urinary tract. It is also used as a poultice and as a skin lotion. The original confectionery was more like a paste and originally used as a medicinal. The white ball-like confection that we know as a "marshmallow" is a further development of this root-derived paste. The Romans considered it a delicacy. Today's "marshmallows" are not made from marshmallow roots, but instead are composed of egg albumen, starch, gum, syrup, and flavorings. Marshmallow is a native of Europe, but is naturalized along the East Coast.

JEWELWEED
(Touch-me-not, Snapweed)

Impatiens capensis Meerb.
Impatiens pallida Nutt.
Balsaminaceae

3–4'

I. capensis

Characteristics: These annuals with smooth succulent stems grow to 5 feet tall. The simple leaves are alternate and have a wavy margin. A swollen area that is a lighter green marks the area where the petiole is attached to the almost translucent stem. The spotted jewelweed (*I. capensis*) has an orange-yellow flower that is thickly spotted with reddish-brown. The pale jewelweed (*I. pallida*) flower is pale yellow and may have some reddish-brown spots. The drooping flowers are saclike and resemble a cornucopia. The fruit is a capsule that explodes upon touching.
Habitat: Jewelweeds usually form dense patches in shaded areas. They occur in moist deciduous forests, near springs and wet meadows, and on flood plains.
Distribution: Found inland throughout the area. Spotted jewelweed is more common.

Edible parts: Young shoots and fruits.

Food uses: Cooked greens, nibble, soup.

Precautions: Jewelweed shoots must be cooked. The edibility of jewelweed is suspect. The young jewelweed can be easily confused with the numerous nondescript herbaceous seedlings that appear at the same time.

Preparation: Collect the plant when less than 6 inches tall. When the seeds are ripe and brown, they can be eaten as a nibble or snack. Capturing the seeds as they explode from the capsule is a challenge. The seeds have a walnut taste and should be eaten in moderation.

Recipes:

Cream of Cheddar Jewelweed Soup

4 cups jewelweed shoots	½ cup flour
½ cup butter	3 quarts milk
¾ cup wild leeks or chives	3 teaspoons salt
(chopped)	2 oz. cheddar cheese (shredded)

Cook jewelweed shoots in at least two changes of boiling water. Drain, cook, and puree. Sauté leeks in butter. Blend in flour and stir in milk and cook until smooth. Add jewelweed and salt. Heat to boiling. Serve with a sprinkling of cheese.

Jewelweed Delight

4 cups jewelweed shoots	1 tablespoon olive oil
1 egg (beaten)	1 teaspoon garlic salt
¾ cup bread crumbs	½ cup cheddar cheese (shredded)

Wash and chop jewelweed. Boil in two changes of water. Drain. Mix jewelweed, egg, bread crumbs, oil, and garlic salt. Place mixture into well-greased baking dish. Top with cheese. Bake at 200° F for 25 minutes.

Remarks: The name jewelweed may refer to the silver drops of dew or rain found on the leaves or the silvery sheen observed on leaves that are placed underwater. Touch-me-not refers to the ripened capsule's ability to shoot its seeds when touched. The genus name (*Impatiens*) refers to the impatient characteristic of the ripe capsule. *Capensis* refers to the Cape of Good Hope. *Pallida* means pale and is descriptive of the pale yellow color of the flower. The juice of the crushed stem and leaves has been used to counteract the effects of urushiol, which is the poison ivy allergen. The juice has also been used to relieve the itching caused by insect bites and stinging nettle and as a treatment for athlete's foot. There are some records of animal poisoning. Spotted jewelweed is also know as *I. biflora*.

MILKWEED
(Common milkweed)

Asclepias syriaca L.
Asclepiadaceae

3–4'

Characteristics: This perennial herb grows to 6 feet tall. The simple, thick, opposite, ovate leaves have an entire to wavy margin. The hairy stem is usually unbranched and gray-green. All parts of the plant have a sticky, milky sap. Pink flowers occur in dense, rounded umbels from leaf axils. The fruit is an elongated, warty follicle that contains many seeds. Each seed has a tuft of soft white hairs. It flowers in July and August.

Habitat: Dry soil, old fields, roadsides, cultivated fields.

Distribution: Throughout the area.

Edible parts: Young shoots, flower buds, flowers, young pods.

Food uses: Vegetable, fritter, cooked greens.

Precautions: Some milkweeds such as butterfly weed (*A. tubersoa*) and swamp milkweed (*A. incarnata*) are poisonous. May be confused with the dogbanes (*Apocynum* spp.). Livestock have been poisoned by eating the mature plant.

Preparation: The plant is bitter and should be boiled in two or three changes of water. The flowers are less bitter, but should be boiled at least once. Collect the young shoots when 6–8 inches tall. The flower buds can be used as a broccoli substitute and the young shoots for asparagus.

Recipes:

Fried Milkweed Pod Fritters

10 young milkweed pods	¼ cup cooking oil
1 cup flour	salt to taste
1 cup cornmeal	

Boil milkweed pods for 5 minutes in each of three changes of water. Drain pods and cool. Split pods lengthwise. Combine flour and cornmeal. Roll pods in flour and cornmeal mixture. Fry pods in hot oil until brown. Drain pods on paper towels. Add salt to taste.

Milkweed Buds Au Gratin

2 cups milkweed buds	salt to taste
2 tablespoons butter	Romano cheese (grated)

Boil milkweed buds gently for 2 minutes in two changes of water. In the third change of water, cook for 5 minutes. Drain well. Add butter while still hot and stir. Salt to taste. Cover with cheese.

Remarks: Milkweed is named for the white sap. *Asclepias* refers to the Greek god of medicine and *syriaca* to Syria. Linnaeus thought the plant came from the Middle East, but it is a native of North America. Some milkweeds contain cardiac glycosides and a toxic resin. The cardiac glycosides affect the heart muscles, and toxic resins are among the most violent poisons. The cardiac glycosides, which are not found in common milkweed, are poisonous to some insects. A few insects, such as the monarch butterfly, are immune to the poison. Birds that eat the monarch, however, find the poison to be an emetic, and the birds soon learn to avoid these unpalatable orange and black butterflies. (The palatable orange and back viceroy butterfly is a mimic of the monarch.) During World War II the fluff of milkweed seeds was used in life preservers.

SWEET FLAG
(Calamus)

Acorus calamus L.
Araceae

3–4′

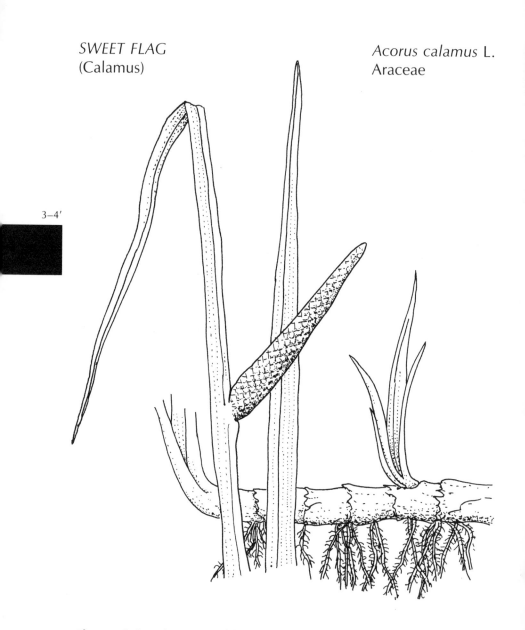

Characteristics: This perennial herb has erect, swordlike leaves that can grow to 6 feet tall, but are usually from 2 to 4 feet in height. The yellowish-green leaves, with the midrib usually off-center, arise in a clump from the rhizome. Leaves and rhizomes are aromatic. Numerous yellow flowers form a long, tapering spadix that emerges at an angle from the leaflike flower stalk. The spathe extends above the spadix and is about twice as long as the flower stalk. It flowers from May to August.
Habitat: Shallow water of marshes, swamps, ponds, streams, and lakes.
Distribution: Throughout the area.

Edible parts: Rhizome, young shoots.
Food uses: Candy, salad.
Precautions: *Iris* spp. (flag) is poisonous and can be mistaken for sweet flag. *Iris* has showy blue or yellow flowers and dark green leaves and lacks the spicy odor. The Food and Drug Administration has classified sweet flag as unsafe and oil of calamus as a carcinogen.
Preparation: Collect young shoots in the spring when 6–12 inches tall. Retain the white inner leaves. Rhizomes can be collected throughout the year.
Recipes:

Sweet Flag Salad

1 cup young sweet-flag shoots (chopped)
½ cucumber (sliced)
3 cups leaf lettuce (torn)
2 green onions (chopped)
½ cup blue violet flowers
Italian dressing to taste

Combine solid ingredients and toss. Add dressing and toss lightly.

Candied Sweet Flag

10 six-inch sweet-flag rhizomes   5 cups sugar
3 cups water

Wash and peel sweet-flag rhizomes. Cut into 1-inch pieces. Boil rhizomes for 20 minutes in each of four changes of water. Drain and set aside. Dissolve sugar in water. Heat to make a syrup. Add sweet-flag rhizomes to syrup and boil for 30 minutes. Drain and dry on wax paper.

Remarks: *Acorus* probably originated from the Greek word *akoras,* which is a name that was used for some plants with aromatic roots. *Calamus* means reed. Sweet flag has been used for centuries in Asia as an herbal medicine. On the basis of the number of medicinal uses attributed to a single plant, sweet flag ranked number one among the American Indians. The plant was such a valuable item to them that it became a medium of exchange. Medicinal uses include indigestion, flatulence, toothache, coughs, and fever. Calamus is mentioned in the Bible several times. Sweet flag has been used as an aid to help smokers stop smoking. Chewing on the rhizome is thought to overwhelm the desire for tobacco. Asarone, which is present in sweet flag, is chemically similar to mescaline and has hallucinogenic properties.

AMARANTH
(Pigweed, Redroot)

Amaranthus hybridus L.
Amaranthus retroflexus L.
Amaranthaceae

3–4'

A. hybridus

A. retroflexus

Characteristics: Species of *Amaranthus* are typically coarse, hairy annuals. These species are usually 2 to 4 feet tall, but may grow to 6 feet. The dull green leaves are alternate, ovate to lance-shaped, and long-stalked. The greenish flowers are densely crowded into narrow spikes or borne along the stem and often are not recognizable as flowers. Flowering occurs from August to October. Older plants have a red root.
Habitat: Recently disturbed soils, such as gardens, farmland, construction sites, and waste areas.
Distribution: Common and widespread throughout the area.

Edible parts: Leaves, seeds.

Food uses: Salad, cooked greens, flour, cereal, soups.

Precautions: Leaves from plants grown in soils with excess nitrate should be eaten in moderation. Amaranth is an accumulator of nitrates. After digestion, nitrates are converted into nitrites, which are more toxic than nitrates. Nitrite replaces oxygen in hemoglobin and causes a disease called methemoglobinemia. Toxicity to these compounds has been reported in ruminants and children. Nitrates are also a potential source of the carcinogen nitrosamine.

Recipes:

Amaranth Oriental

2 quarts green amaranth leaves (washed and drained)
6 slices bacon (fried and crumbled)
4 tablespoons cider vinegar
1 cup boiled rice
3 tablespoons soy sauce
1 can unsweetened pineapple (drained)
salt and pepper to taste

Boil greens for 15 minutes in enough water to barely cover. Drain, reserving one quarter of the liquid. Return to heat and add bacon, vinegar, rice, soy sauce, pineapple, and salt and pepper. Simmer until tender or about 20 minutes. Serve hot.

Amaranth Cheese Soup

3 tablespoons cooking oil
1 onion (chopped)
1 garlic clove (chopped)
2 tablespoons flour
3 cups milk
1 quart young amaranth leaves (washed)
salt and pepper to taste
4 slices bacon (crumbled)
1 cup cheddar cheese (grated)

Sauté onions and garlic in cooking oil. When translucent, add flour. Stir. Slowly add milk and stir. Add amaranth and salt and pepper. Cover and simmer for 15 minutes. Stir in bacon and cheese and serve when cheese is melted.

Remarks: The name *Amaranthus* is derived from the Greek word meaning unfading and refers to the flower's ability to retain color after drying. The globe amaranth (*Gomphrena globosa*) is commonly planted in flower gardens for use as a dried flower. The Aztecs used *Amaranthus hypochondriacus* as a source of flour. In Aztec rituals, amaranth flour was mixed with human blood and formed into communion cakes that resembled Aztec gods. The conquering Spanish stopped this practice and forced the Aztecs to grow wheat instead of amaranth. High in protein, minerals, and vitamins A and C, amaranth has been rediscovered and is being projected as a grain of the future. American Amaranth, Inc., is a Minnesota-based firm that is looking for new amaranth growers. Unlike other grains, amaranth is rich in the essential amino acid lysine. A confection made from popped amaranth seeds and honey or molasses is popular in Mexico. Amaranth lacks gluten and must be mixed with wheat flour to make yeast-leavened breads.

BURDOCK
(Cardoni, Gobo, Bardona)

Arctium lappa L.
Arctium minus Schk.
Asteraceae

4–6'

A. *minus*

Characteristics: A biennial that produces large, rough, heart-shaped basal leaves (elephant ears) the first year and a bushy flower stalk the second year. After pollination, the lavender-to-white flowers become the familiar brown burs which stick to clothes and pets. Flowering occurs from July to October. The leaf stalk has a groove on its upperside. The first-year plant is about 2 to 3 feet tall while the second-year plant will range from 3 to 5 feet for *A. minus* and 5 to 9 feet for *A. lappa*.

Habitat: Waste areas, roadsides, around barns and abandoned buildings, railroads.

Distribution: Common burdock (*A. minus*) is found throughout the area. Great burdock (*A. lappa*) is found throughout the area, but sparingly.

124

Edible parts: Leaves, leaf stalks, roots, stems.
Food uses: Cooked vegetable, cooked greens, salad, nibble.
Precautions: Might be confused with rhubarb. Be careful to collect from uncontaminated sites.
Preparation: Collect stems and leaf stalks before flowers open. Use only very young leaves. Peel the inedible rind from the leaf stalk and stem. Collect roots from the first-year plant. Roots, stems, and leaf stalks can be used as a cooked vegetable; stems, leaf stalks, and leaves as salads; leaves as cooked greens; and the peeled leaf stalk and stem as nibbles. A little sodium bicarbonate added to the first of two changes of water for the cooked greens and vegetables will help to break down the fibers. Changing the water removes some bitterness.
Recipes:

Fried Cardoni

1½ cups flour	¾ cup milk
2 teaspoons baking powder	2 eggs
dash of salt and pepper	10 young burdock leaf stalks (cut
½ teaspoon garlic powder	into 3-inch pieces)
1 teaspoon parsley flakes	shortening or oil for deep-frying

Sift together flour, baking powder, salt, pepper, and garlic powder. Add parsley flakes. In another bowl beat milk and eggs together. Combine mixtures until smooth. Wash burdock leaf stalks. Boil leaf stalks in water until soft, then drain. Dip leaf stalks in batter and deep-fry in shortening or oil until brown. Drain on paper towels. Add salt if necessary.

Burdock Root Patties

4 cups burdock roots (sliced)	3 tablespoons butter
½ teaspoon salt	1 egg (well beaten)
¾ cup onions, wild leeks, or chives	¼ cup parsley (chopped)
(chopped)	1 cup bread crumbs

Put burdock roots and salt in pan and cover with water. Bring to a boil and simmer for 25 minutes or until roots are tender. Drain and mash roots. Sauté onions in butter until golden. Mix onions, roots, egg, and parsley. Stir in bread crumbs. Form into patties and fry in oil until browned on both sides.

Remarks: A native of Eurasia, burdock is now established throughout the area. Although the common names of burdock and dock (*Rumex* spp.) are similar, these plants are not closely related. Romans protected their money by storing it in the center of giant balls made of pitch, nettles, and burdock burs. Using the Doctrine of Signatures, seed pods were eaten to help things "stick in your mind." Raw stems have been used as an aphrodisiac.

ASPARAGUS
(Asparagus fern)

Asparagus officinalis L.
Liliaceae

4–6'

Characteristics: Wild asparagus looks like commercial asparagus, but is thinner. The perennial herb has feathery, soft fernlike green branchlets. Leaves are reduced to inconspicuous scales pressed against the stem. Small greenish-white flowers occur in May and June. Height varies from 4 to 6 feet.

Habitat: Roadsides, fields, fence rows, and disturbed sites. Sometimes found along salt marshes.

Distribution: Throughout the region.

Edible parts: Young shoots.

Food uses: Cooked vegetable, soup.

Precautions: Older stems are tough. Other plant parts are mildly toxic. Eating large quantities of asparagus produces a mild laxative effect and also acts as a diuretic.

Preparation: Wash young shoots and peel scales and tough parts. Collect in May and early June while stalks are 6 to 12 inches tall.

Recipes:

Asparagus Quiche

20 young asparagus shoots	3 eggs
1 cup lean ham (diced)	½ teaspoon ginger
½ pound mushrooms (sliced)	½ teaspoon nutmeg
9 inch piecrust	1 tablespoon parsley flakes
1 cup Swiss cheese (shredded)	3 tablespoons pimento (diced)
1 cup evaporated milk	salt and pepper to taste

Chop the asparagus shoots into ½-inch pieces. Sauté ham and mushrooms for 5 minutes. Bake piecrust for 6 minutes at 425° F. Spoon asparagus, mushrooms, and ham into piecrust. Top with cheese. In a small bowl, mix the remaining ingredients. Pour into pie shell. Bake at 350° F for 30 minutes.

Asparagus on Toast

12 five-inch asparagus spears	Hollandaise sauce
½ teaspoon salt	Parmesan cheese
4 slices toasted bread	

Steam asparagus in salted water for 15–20 minutes. Drain. Arrange asparagus on toast. Cover asparagus with Hollandaise sauce. Sprinkle cheese on sauce.

Remarks: A native of Europe, asparagus was introduced to the United States by early settlers. The plants may be bisexual, but are commonly unisexual. Male plants are reported to produce a greater yield than female plants. Some people tie the spears into bundles when cooking. *Asparagus* is derived from the Greek word *asparasso*, which means "to rip" and refers to the sharp scales along the stem.

BULL THISTLE
(Hog thistle)

Cirsium vulgare (Savi) Tenore
Asteraceae

4–6′

Characteristics: This biennial herb forms a spring rosette of leaves the first year that resembles a prickly dandelion. The second year, from June to October, the plant produces a 6-foot flower stalk with a purple flower head that resembles a shaving brush. Spiny-winged stems support alternate, spiny, deeply cut leaves. Below the flowers are spine-tipped bracts. The mature seed head appears as a ball of fluffy down.

Habitat: Roadsides, fields, pastures, and disturbed sites.

Distribution: Widely established throughout the area.

Edible parts: Young leaves, young stems, roots
Food uses: Cooked vegetable, salad, cooked greens.
Precautions: Be careful of the spines. The plant is somewhat bitter.
Preparation: Cut spines from young leaves and peel the stems. Rinse in cold water. Stems can be used as a cooked vegetable or salad. Leaves are used in salads and as cooked greens. Roots are used in cooked vegetable dishes. Boiling in a change of water removes the bitter taste.
Recipes:

Thistle Salad Dressing

1 cup thistle stems (peeled and cooked)	1 clove garlic
	1 small onion (chopped)
½ cup vegetable oil	salt and pepper to taste
¾ cup olive oil	5 egg yolks (hard-boiled)
¼ cup wine vinegar	10 black olives (chopped)

Pour all ingredients into blender and mix at medium speed until smooth. Store in refrigerator.

Bull Thistle Fritters

8 four-inch bull-thistle stems	2 eggs (beaten)
1 cup flour	⅔ cup milk
1 teaspoon baking powder	1 teaspoon salad oil
¼ teaspoon salt	¼ teaspoon lemon juice

Clean and peel thistle stems. Boil in water until soft. Drain. Add milk, salad oil, and lemon to beaten eggs. Sift flour, baking powder, and salt together. Add dry ingredients to egg mixture and stir. Dip thistle stems in batter and deep-fry until golden brown.

Remarks: The name thistle means "something sharp." *Vulgare* means common. Because of the effort required to collect and prepare thistle and its flat taste, this plant is considered by many as a survival food rather than a gourmet item. The plant is a native of Eurasia and was probably introduced to North America via the agricultural seed of the early settlers. The down of the thistle is used by the goldfinch in building its nest. Thistle seeds are high in oil and, especially in the winter, are eaten by finches. Other thistles, such as Canada thistle (*C. arvense*), are also edible.

BULRUSH
(Great bulrush, Soft-stem bulrush)

Scirpus validus Vahl.
Cyperaceae

4–6'

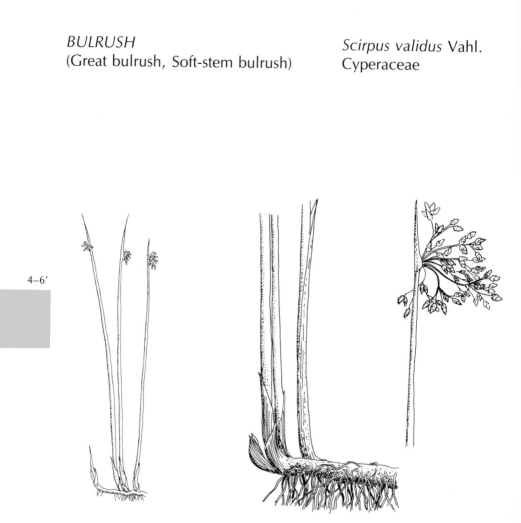

Characteristics: This erect perennial herb grows to 9 feet tall and reproduces by rhizomes. The reduced flowers are not showy and later form seedlike fruits. Flowers and fruits occur in clusters near the top of the stem. The rounded stems are un-branched, pithy, upright, stiff, and pointed.
Habitat: Brackish or fresh-water marshes, shallow water of lakes, and slow-moving streams.
Distribution: Throughout the area.

Edible parts: Young shoots, pollen, seeds, rhizomes.

Food uses: Flour, cooked vegetable, salad, syrup, sugar.

Precautions: Young shoots are preferred to older stems, which are palatable but tough. Do not collect from polluted water.

Preparation: Pollen, ground seeds, and pounded, dried rhizomes can be made into flour. Boiling the young rhizome produces a sweet syrup or sugar. Young rhizomes and early shoots can be peeled and eaten raw. Pollen is used as a flour additive. Use sliced rhizomes in salads or cook as a vegetable.

Recipes:

Stir-fried Bulrush

1 cup bulrush shoots (chopped)	2 tablespoons soy sauce
2 tablespoons vegetable oil	½ teaspoon garlic powder
1 cup bulrush rhizome (chopped)	salt and pepper to taste
1 cup onion (chopped)	

Heat oil in frying pan. Sauté vegetables for 5 minutes. Add soy sauce, garlic powder, and salt and pepper.

Bulrush Bread

1½ cup bulrush flour	1 package yeast
1 teaspoon salt	¼ cup lukewarm water
1 cup boiling water	2 cups all-purpose flour
2 tablespoons soft butter	

Bulrush flour may be obtained from pollen or rhizomes. For rhizome flour, wash rhizomes thoroughly and scrape off roots. Dry in oven under low heat overnight. Peel the dried rhizome and remove fibers. Pulverize the remaining pulp by pounding or use a blender. Combine bulrush flour, salt, and boiling water. Blend well. Add butter to dough and blend. Mix yeast, sugar, and lukewarm water. Add 1 cup of all-purpose flour to bulrush dough. Add yeast mixture to dough. Mix thoroughly. Make ball of dough, place in bowl, cover with towel, and place in warm area for 30 minutes. Place dough on lightly floured surface. Punch down dough. Cover with remaining cup of all-purpose flour and knead for 5 minutes. Form dough into loaf, place in greased bread pan, and let rise for 40 minutes or until double in size. Bake at 375° F for 45 minutes or until brown.

Remarks: Old stems were used by the Indians for weaving into baskets and mats. It was an important food for the Indians because parts of the plant are available year-round. Bulrush primarily reproduces by rhizomes which grow horizontally from the parent plant. Seeds and rhizomes are a favorite food of some ducks. Muskrats eat the leaves and rhizomes. *Scirpus* is the Latin name for bulrush. The bulrushes mentioned in the Bible were probably *Cyperus papyrus* and not *Scirpus*.

RED RASPBERRY   *Rubus strigosus* Michx.
BLACK RASPBERRY   *Rubus occidentalis* L.
                                 Rosaceae

4–6'

R. occidentalis

Characteristics: The raspberries are erect to arching perennials that grow to 6 feet tall. The round stems have a white, waxy covering. The picked fruit has a cone-shaped cavity. The alternate, palmately compound leaves have three to five ovate, toothed leaflets that are whitish beneath. The flowers are composed of five sepals, five white petals, and numerous stamens and pistils. Flowers appear from May to July. Red raspberry has a red fruit and straight rather weak bristles. Black raspberry has a black fruit and straight, curved, or hooked spines.
Habitat: Dry or moist woods, thickets, fields, and roadsides.
Distribution: Throughout the area.

Edible parts: Young shoots, leaves, fruits.
Food uses: Fruit, salad, tea, cold drink, jams, jelly, pies, wine.
Precautions: Use only ripe fruits.
Preparation: Fruits can be used for jellies, jams, pie, wine, or muffins, or eaten raw. The young shoots can be added to salads. Dried or fresh leaves can be used for tea or a cold drink. The fruits freeze nicely.
Recipes:

Black Raspberry Pie

2 tablespoons tapioca	1 teaspoon lemon juice
2 tablespoons warm water	1 pie shell and top crust
4 cups black raspberries (cleaned and washed)	2 tablespoons butter
	2 tablespoons milk
⅔ cup sugar	

Dissolve tapioca in warm water. Mix raspberries, sugar, tapioca, and lemon juice. Pour berry mixture into pie shell. Dot with butter. Cover with top crust. Lightly brush milk on piecrust and sprinkle with sugar. Punch holes in top crust with fork. Bake at 425° F for 10 minutes; then at 375° F for 45 minutes or until cooked.

Red Raspberry Chewy

3 cups red raspberries (cleaned and washed)	2 tablespoons sugar

Combine sugar and raspberries and bring to boil. Cool. Puree in blender or food processor. Pour onto Teflon cookie sheet or waxed paper on non-Teflon cookie sheet. Place in sun, food dehydrator, or oven at lowest setting. Allow to dry until chewy has a leather consistency. Peel off and store in jars or plastic bags in refrigerator.

Comments: *Rubus* refers to the red-colored fruits of some members of this genus. *Occidentalis* means western while *strigosus* refers to the strigose hairs or bristles of red raspberry. In taxonomy individuals who tend to broadly define the word "species" are called "lumpers" while those who narrowly define it are "splitters." Britton and Brown described 24 *Rubus* species for the Northeastern United States and adjacent Canada, while Bailey distinguished more than 400. Raspberries are technically classified as shrubs. From a perennial base, biennial stems emerge. First-year stems (primocanes) do not flower, but second-year stems (floricanes) flower and produce fruits. Raspberry means "the rough berry"; rasp means to rub with something rough. The berries are rich in calcium, phosphorus, and vitamin C. Among the medicinal uses of red raspberry: as an astringent, in the treatment of diarrhea, to relieve painful menstruation, and to facilitate childbirth.

EVENING PRIMROSE
(Morning primrose, Rock rose)

Oenothera biennis L.
Onagraceae

4–6'

Characteristics: A hairy biennial plant that produces a rosette of leaves the first year and a flower stalk the second year that may reach a height of 6 feet. The reddish-stemmed flower stalk is densely covered with long, lance-shaped leaves that are arranged alternately. The yellow flowers occur in a cluster at the end of the flower stalk. Flowering occurs throughout the summer. The tubular flowers have four petals and a four-parted stigma. Four reflexed yellow sepals occur at the base of the petals.
Habitat: Dry, open soil of waste places, fields, roadsides.
Distribution: Found throughout the area.

Edible parts: Young leaves, roots.

Food uses: Cooked vegetable, cooked greens, salad, soups, stews.

Precautions: Collect parts from one-year-old plants in early spring. The plant is very peppery and requires cooking in several changes of water. Because of the amount of boiling required to reduce the peppery taste, this plant is considered more of a survival food. Leaves for salads should be used sparingly.

Preparation: The taproot of the first-year plant is used as a cooked vegetable or added to soups or stews for flavoring. The leaves are cooked as greens or added raw to salads of bland greens.

Recipes:

Evening Primrose Patties

1 cup evening primrose roots	¼ cup honey
1 egg	1 tablespoon melted margarine
½ teaspoon garlic salt	all-purpose flour
1 small onion (diced)	2 tablespoons olive oil

Peel and chop roots. Boil roots in two changes of water. Mash roots and combine with egg, garlic salt, onion, honey, and margarine. Gradually add flour and mix until the consistency of cookie dough is obtained. Form the dough into patties. Fry slowly in oil.

Scalloped Evening Primrose Roots

2 pounds evening primrose roots	1 large onion (sliced)
3 tablespoons butter	½ cup cheddar cheese (grated)
1 teaspoon garlic salt	

Peel the primrose roots and cut into small pieces. Grease a casserole dish with vegetable oil. Spread half the primrose pieces on the bottom of the dish. Layer half the butter, salt, onions, and cheese. Cover with the remaining primrose roots and top with remaining butter, salt, onions, and cheese. Bake at 300° F for 30–40 minutes or until done.

Remarks: Many edible herbaceous plants are alien species that have been introduced into the United States from Europe. The evening primrose, however, is a North American native that has been introduced to Europe. The flowers open near sunset and their odor attracts moths, which bring about pollination. Some members of *Oenothera,* such as sundrops, bloom during the day. The dried flower stalk, with its capsules that resemble flowers, remains erect through the winter and is often added to dried flower arrangements. The peppery taste increases the need for liquids and probably accounts for the genus name of *Oenothera,* which means "wine imbibing." *Biennis* refers to the biennial nature of the plant, but it may also be a short-term perennial. Evening primrose oil is reported to have medicinal value in treating eczema and premenstrual syndrome. Next to human milk, the oil is the richest source of GLA (gamma-linolenic acid) yet discovered. GLA affects prostaglandin production, which in turn affects many body functions. The Food and Drug Administration is investigating the health claims for evening primrose oil.

OSTRICH FERN

Matteuccia struthiopteris (L.) Todaro
Polypodiaceae

4–6'

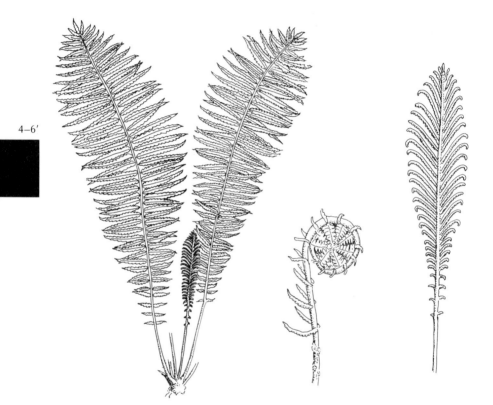

Characteristics: A large fern with sterile, deciduous fronds that grow to 7 feet tall. Sterile fronds are pinnate-pinnatifid with at least twenty pairs each of pinnae and segments. The cluster of sterile fronds that emerge from the erect, scaly rhizome appear vaselike. In the center are the much shorter fertile fronds. The 2-foot fertile fronds are dark brown and resemble coarse feathers.
Habitat: Swamps, moist woods, stream banks, and river islands in near-neutral soil.
Distribution: Scattered throughout the area.

Edible parts: Fiddleheads of sterile frond.

Food uses: Salad, cooked vegetable, soup.

Precautions: The fiddlehead is the tightly coiled growth stage of the frond. Do not collect either the mature frond or the fiddlehead of the fertile frond. Be sure that you can distinguish the fiddlehead stage of the ostrich fern from the other fern fiddleheads.

Preparation: Scrape off brown scales. Rinse in cold water and dry on paper towels. Collect the fiddleheads in early spring.

Recipes:

Ostrich Fern Soup

1 quart water	1 can beef broth
1 teaspoon salt	1 small onion (minced)
4 cups ostrich fern fiddleheads	1 garlic clove (minced)
(washed)	salt and pepper to taste
1 can cream of mushroom soup	1 teaspoon parsley flakes
2 cups milk	

Bring water to boil and add 1 teaspoon salt and fiddleheads. Boil for 10 minutes. Remove from heat, drain, and rinse fiddleheads in cold water. Combine mushroom soup and milk in saucepan. Bring to slow boil. Add fiddleheads, beef broth, onion, and garlic. Cook for 20 minutes over low heat. Pour soup into a blender to liquidize the solids. Add salt and pepper to taste. Reheat soup. Pour in bowls and sprinkle parsley on top.

Cashew—Ostrich Fern Fiddleheads

2 teaspoons butter	3 teaspoons lemon juice
2 cups ostrich fern fiddleheads	3 teaspoons chives (chopped)
(washed)	½ cup cashew nuts (chopped)
3 teaspoons white wine	salt and pepper to taste
3 teaspoons water	paprika

Melt butter in saucepan and add fiddleheads, wine, and water. Cover and cook at medium heat for 15 minutes. Add lemon, chives, cashew nuts, and salt and pepper to taste. Mix thoroughly and cook over low heat for 5 minutes. Sprinkle with paprika.

Remarks: *Matteuccia* commemorates the Italian physicist Carlo Matteucci. The common name refers to the featherlike plumes of the sterile fronds. After the sterile fronds die back in the fall, the fertile fronds still remain. They resemble the fertile fronds of sensitive fern (*Onoclea sensibilis*). The term fiddlehead refers to the resemblance of the young sterile frond to the head of a violin. Fiddleheads are also called crosiers. All ferns have fiddleheads, but only the ostrich fern is known to be edible. Bracken fern (*Pteridium aquilinum*) is often listed as an edible fern, but it is known to contain several toxic substances and should be avoided. Bracken fern not only contains thiaminase, which destroys thiamine and results in a vitamin B1 deficiency, but also has carcinogenic and mutagenic properties. The Four Seasons restaurant in New York City serves 300 pounds of ostrich fern fiddleheads a week in the spring. A house specialty is a soft shell crab-fiddlehead dish. Canned ostrich-fern fiddleheads can be purchased in some stores throughout the year and in New England farmers' markets in June.

WILD LETTUCE
(Prickly lettuce, Blue lettuce)

Lactuca spp.
Asteraceae

4–6'

L. canadensis

Characteristics: These mostly annual or biennial herbaceous plants grow to 7 feet tall. The simple, alternate, mostly toothed leaves have stiff hairs on the midrib of the lower leaf surface. Stem and leaves have a milky sap. The upper stem is much-branched with numerous yellow or blue flower heads that each contain fewer than 50 ray flowers. Flowering occurs from June to October.
Habitat: Open woods, waste areas, fields.
Distribution: Throughout the area.

138

Edible parts: Young leaves, flower buds.

Food uses: Salad, cooked greens, vegetable.

Precautions: May be confused with sow thistle. Some people have reported an upset stomach after eating an excessive amount. Do not use mature stems or leaves. Just as with garden lettuce, milkiness and bitterness increase with the age of the plant.

Preparation: Collect leaves when the plant is 6 to 8 inches tall. Young leaves or flower buds can be used in salads or as a cooked green. Boiling in several changes of water will reduce the bitterness.

Recipes:

Wilted Wild Lettuce

2 cups young wild lettuce leaves (chopped)	½ teaspoon pepper
	4 slices bacon
2 cups leaf lettuce (torn)	¼ cup vinegar
2 green onions (chopped)	1 tablespoon sugar
1 teaspoon salt	

Combine lettuce, onions, and salt and pepper. Fry bacon until crisp. Save drippings. Crumble bacon when cool. Combine vinegar, sugar, and bacon drippings and bring to a boil. Pour over lettuce and toss lightly. Sprinkle bacon on top.

Vegetable Casserole

1 cup wild lettuce flower buds	2 eggs (beaten)
1 bunch broccoli	1¼ cups crushed soda crackers
1 can creamed corn	salt and pepper to taste
1 can whole-kernel corn (drained)	6 slices American cheese
½ cup milk	1 cup crumbled cornflakes
1 tablespoon sugar	

In separate pans boil wild lettuce and broccoli for 5 minutes. Drain. Combine wild lettuce, broccoli, corn, milk, sugar, eggs, soda crackers, and salt and pepper. Pour into casserole dish. Top with American cheese and cover with cornflakes. Bake at 350° F for 1 hour.

Remarks: *Lactuca* is the ancient Latin name and is derived from *lac,* which means milk and refers to the milky sap. Garden lettuce (*L. sativa*) may be found as an escaped plant. The leaves and flowers of wild lettuce resemble the closely related dandelion. Wild lettuce flowerheads, however, are smaller than dandelion flowerheads, and wild lettuce has an erect stem. The young plants of *L. scariola* are toxic to cattle. Several species of *Lactuca* are grown in France, and the extracted lactucarium is used as a mild sedative in cough mixtures. Lactucarium is known as lettuce opium.

COMMON BARBERRY
(European barberry)

Berberis vulgaris L.
Berberidaceae

4–6'

Characteristics: This shrub can grow to 10 feet, but is usually from 3 to 5 feet tall. It has dense arching branches. The three-parted spines occur at the base of alternate, simple leaves. The wedge-shaped leaves have fine teeth. Small yellow flowers occur in the spring and later develop into red berries. The roots have yellow wood.

Habitat: Thickets, old fields, roadsides, waste places, and cultivated areas near houses.

Distribution: Generally escaped, but also planted as an ornamental throughout the area. Less common southward into West Virginia.

Edible parts: Fruit.

Food uses: Cooked fruit, jam, cold drinks.

Precautions: The plant contains the alkaloid herberine. The chemical is used as a broad-spectrum antibiotic against bacteria and fungi, but also has a negative physiological impact on humans. Therefore eat the fruits in moderation. The plant is very spiny; gloves may be in order. The fruit is somewhat sour.

Preparation: Collect in the fall when the fruits are bright red. Rinse in cold water. Dry on towels. The fruit contains enough pectin for jam. Mix the juice with other fruit juices to make a cold drink.

Recipes:

Barberry-Apple Jelly

4 cups barberry fruit	3 cups water
4 apples (quartered with seeds removed)	sugar

Simmer berries and apples in water until the fruit is soft. Strain through cheesecloth or jelly bag. Bring juice to a boil. Stir in an equal amount of sugar and continue to boil until 2 drops come together on a metal spoon or a jelly thermometer reads 200° F. Pour into hot, sterilized jars and seal with paraffin.

Barberry Sauce

2 cups barberry fruit	1 cup molasses
¾ cup honey	

Combine ingredients in a saucepan. Simmer until fruit is soft. Sieve to remove pulp. Boil liquid until about half has evaporated. Serve as dessert topping or on pancakes.

Remarks: Barberries are commonly planted as an ornamental hedge. They are also often planted around homes to attract birds. Many bird species eat the fruits through the winter. A yellow dye is made from the root bark and used to dye baskets, fabrics, and skins. Since barberry is an alternate host for the fungus that causes wheat rust, the plant has been eradicated from most of the wheat belt. However, Japanese barberry is not an alternate host to the wheat-rust fungus. Barberry spines are modified leaves in which the normal leaf tissues have been replaced by a thick-walled tissue called sclerenchyma. *Berberis* is derived from *berberys,* which is the Arabic name of the plant.

CLEAVERS
(Bedstraw, Catchweed)

Galium aparine L.
Rubiaceae

4–6'

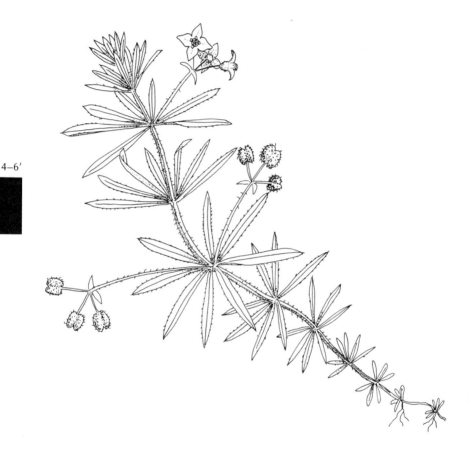

Characteristics: This annual grows to 5 feet long. Slender, weak, square stems ramble on the ground or climb on other plants. Stiff hairs on the stems and leaves enable the plant to cling to clothing. Lance-shaped leaves with hairs on the margin are in whorls of six to eight. Three to five small white flowers arise from the leaf axils and appear from May to July.
Habitat: Fields, thickets, rich moist soils in deciduous forests, flood plains, usually on damp ground and in the shade.
Distribution: Throughout the area.

Edible parts: Young shoots, fruit.

Food uses: Salad, cooked greens, coffee, soup.

Precautions: Often grows near poison ivy. Several plant species are known by the common name of bedstraw.

Preparation: Young shoots can be prepared as cooked greens or cooked and added to salads. A noncaffeine coffee substitute can be made from the fruits.

Recipes:

Cheesy Cleavers Soup

1 cup onion (chopped)	salt and pepper to taste
3 tablespoons vegetable oil	1 tablespoon garlic powder
4 tablespoons flour	1 cup sharp cheddar cheese
3 cups milk	(shredded)
4 cups cleavers shoots	

Stir-fry onion in vegetable oil. When almost done, add flour and milk. Stir until thickened. Add cleavers, salt, pepper, and garlic, then cover and simmer for 20 minutes. Remove cover, add cheese, and stir until melted.

Cleavers Omelet

3 tablespoons vegetable oil	½ cup mushrooms
1 cup cleavers shoots	4 eggs
½ cup onions (chopped)	salt and pepper to taste

Stir-fry shoots in vegetable oil for 5 minutes. Add onions and mushrooms and continue stir-frying until onions are nearly brown. Beat eggs and add salt and pepper. Add eggs to stir-fried vegetables. Cook until firm.

Remarks: *Galium* is a large genus with more than 250 species found throughout the world. The fruits are covered with bristles and are disseminated by adhering to the fur of passing animals. In colonial days men who wanted to lose a little weight in preparation for an important date drank a tea made of this diuretic. The name cleavers comes from the plant's ability to adhere or cleave. The dried plant has been used as "bedstraw" in ticks. When a strainer is not available, the material to be strained can be passed through several inches of cleavers. Coffee is in the same family as cleavers. *Galium* is from the Greek word for milk (*gala*) and refers to the use of some bedstraws for curdling milk.

POKE
(Pokeweed, Pokeberry, Inkberry)

Phytolacca americana L.
Phytolaccaceae

4–6′

Characteristics: This smooth, erect perennial herb grows to 10 feet tall, but usually averages 5 to 6 feet. It has alternate, simple, entire ovate leaves and a red stem at maturity. The greenish-to-white flowers with no petals occur in racemes. The white flower color is due to five sepals. The berry is dark purple and juicy. It flowers from July to September.

Habitat: Cultivated fields, fence rows, waste areas, openings in damp forests.

Distribution: Throughout the area.

Edible parts: Young shoots.

Food uses: Cooked greens, soup, pickles.

Precautions: The presence of the toxic triterpene saponins, one of which is phytolaccin, makes all parts of the plant poisonous. The roots and seeds are especially toxic. Gloves should always be worn when handling the plant.

Preparation: Only collect the young shoots that are less than 6 inches tall and have no red on them. Soak in salt water and then boil for 10 minutes in each of two changes of water.

Recipes:

Poke Casserole

20 poke shoots	¼ pound Velveeta cheese
1 stick butter	1 cup Ritz crackers (crushed)

Boil poke shoots in two changes of water. Drain poke. Melt butter and cheese together. Mix poke, cheese mixture, and all but ¼ cup crackers. Pour mixture into greased casserole dish and sprinkle remaining cracker crumbs on top. Bake at 325° F for 15 minutes.

Poke Soup

3 cups poke shoots	¼ teaspoon parsley flakes
⅓ cup flour	1 cup milk
1½ quarts water	salt and pepper to taste
1 wild leek or garlic clove (minced)	2 teaspoons Áccent
3 tablespoons butter	2 cups chicken broth
8 ounces American cheese (shredded)	

Boil poke shoots in two changes of water. Drain poke. Combine flour and ½ cup water into paste and set aside. Boil the rest of the water and add all other ingredients. Boil for 10 minutes. Slowly add flour mixture to soup and boil for another 5 minutes.

Remarks: Poke is a paradox. It is a dangerously poisonous plant, but some individuals highly prize it as an edible. Many colonists kept poke roots in root cellars to provide green shoots throughout the winter. Poke shoots are still gathered in the spring by many rural Appalachian families for "poke salet." On the other hand, numerous documented cases of poke poisonings vary from gastrointestinal cramps to death. Boiling may remove the toxins. On July 11, 1980, however, twenty-one individuals in New Jersey were poisoned by a poke salad that contained young poke leaves that were boiled and reboiled. None of these people died, but they did have headaches, dizziness, and vomiting for up to 48 hours. Poke mitogen is of special concern because it disrupts the production of normal lymphocytes and can enter the bloodstream through minor cuts. Some researchers who handled the plant without wearing gloves developed abnormal lymphocytes and the problem persisted for eight weeks.

In the presidential election of 1844, supporters of James Polk wore leaves and flowers of poke. The name poke comes from the Indian "pocan," which describes the red dye obtained from the berries. *Phytolacca* means crimson plant. The juice from the berries has been used for ink, making it truly an "ink berry."

BLACKBERRY
(Bramble)

Rubus allegheniensis Porter
Rosaceae

4–6'

Characteristics: A perennial 4- to 6-foot shrub that sends up a series of biennial stems. The second-year stems produce flowers with five white petals. From each flower develops a cluster of drupelets known as a blackberry. The palmately compound leaves are alternate and are composed of three to five toothed pointed leaflets. Prickles often occur on the leaf veins, petioles, and stems.
Habitat: Old fields, margins of woodlands, roadsides, and sunny thickets. Commonly found in the early woody communities of old field succession.
Distribution: Found in most of the region.

146

Edible parts: Young shoots, leaves, fruits.

Food uses: Fruit, jelly, jam, tea, cold drinks, salad, wine.

Precautions: Poison ivy and nettles often grow in the same habitat as blackberries. Avoid getting scratched by the prickles.

Preparation: Only collect fruit when it is solid black. Remove the stem and rinse in water. Collect early in the morning. Fruits can be eaten fresh, in milk, or on cereals; made into jams, jellies, or pies, or fermented into wine. The dried leaves can be used for tea or a cold drink. The young shoots are used in salads. Dried berries can be eaten like raisins.

Recipes:

Blackberry Cobbler

4 cups blackberries	dash of salt
3 tablespoons cornstarch	1 cup biscuit mix
1½ cups brown sugar	⅓ cup cream

Pour fresh blackberries into a casserole dish. Mix together cornstarch, sugar, and salt. Sprinkle mixture over berries. Combine biscuit mix and cream and spread over berries. Bake at 350° F for 30 minutes or until browned. Serve with cream.

Blackberry Jam

4 cups blackberries (crushed)	1 teaspoon lemon juice
4 cups sugar	1 package pectin

Pour blackberries into large saucepan and bring to boil. Add sugar and lemon juice. Stir constantly. Boil for 3 minutes. Add pectin. Bring to boil. Remove from heat. Remove foam. Ladle into hot, sterilized jars and seal with paraffin.

Remarks: Blackberries and raspberries are often confused. The stem of the picked blackberry stays attached to the berry while the raspberry stem detaches and leaves a hollow cavity in the fruit. Dewberry is also a *Rubus*. Its fruits greatly resemble blackberries, but are juicier and not as abundant. Dewberry is not an upright plant like blackberry, but instead tends to be viny. Blackberry fruits are not "berries"; they are drupelets. Remember that it is the second-year canes (stems) that produce the flowers and blackberries. The first-year stem (primocane) typically has palmately compound leaves with five leaflets, but second-year stems (floricanes) usually have fewer leaflets.

ROSE

Rosa spp.
Rosaceae

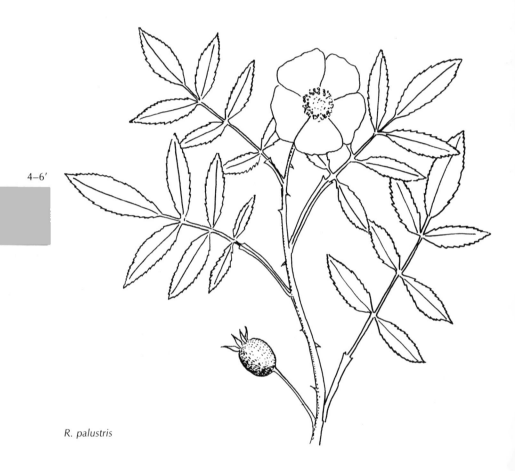

4–6′

R. palustris

Characteristics: Roses are deciduous shrubs or woody vines. The pinnately compound leaves have three to eleven toothed leaflets. Usually large, leafy stipules are attached to the base of the petioles of the alternate leaves. The five petals vary in color, but are usually pink or red. The flowers contain numerous stamens and pistils. The fruits or hips resemble small red apples with the dried remains of five sepals attached to the bottom. Prickles are usually scattered along the stem. At least 10 species of native and escaped roses are found in this region.
Habitat: Disturbed areas, old fields, pastures, roadsides, open woodlands.
Distribution: Throughout the area.

Edible parts: Petals, fruit, leaves.

Food uses: Candy, jelly, salad, tea, pies, wine, jam.

Precautions: Be careful of the prickles. Do not collect from plants that have been sprayed with pesticides. Some people are allergic to rose pollen and rose sap.

Preparation: Rinse petals in cold water and dry on paper towels. Use the petals for tea, jelly, salads, or candy. The leaves are used for tea. The fruits can be used with or without the seeds, but remove the dried flower parts from the fruit. Fruits are used for wine, tea, pies, jam, and jelly, and eaten fresh. Collect the fruits in the fall and early winter.

Recipes:

Rose Hip Jelly

3 quarts rose hips	2 tablespoons lemon juice
5 cups sugar	1 package pectin

Remove dried flower parts from rose hips. Wash in cold water. Cut rose hips in two parts. Boil rose hips for 15 minutes in enough water to cover. Strain through jelly bag. Collect 5 cups of rose hip juice. Combine rose hip juice, sugar, and lemon juice. Bring to a hard boil. Stir. Boil for 1 minute. Add pectin. Skim off foam. Pour into hot, sterilized jars and seal with paraffin.

Rose Hip Cobbler

1 cup flour	¼ teaspoon ginger
½ cup sugar	¾ cup milk
1½ teaspoon baking powder	2 tablespoons melted margarine
1 teaspoon cinnamon	2½ cups rose hips (cleaned and
½ teaspoon nutmeg	washed)

Combine flour, sugar, baking powder, cinnamon, nutmeg, and ginger. Stir in the milk and mix until the batter is smooth. Pour the melted margarine into a 1½ quart baking dish. Pour the batter on top of the margarine. Scatter the rose hips on top of the batter. Bake at 350° F for 40 minutes or until browned.

Remarks: Rose hips contain large amounts of vitamin C and are well known as an antiscorbutic. One cup of rose hips is said to equal the amount of vitamin C in a dozen oranges. Rose-hip powder and tea can be purchased in most health food stores. Some people are allergic to rose pollen and develop the characteristic symptoms of hay fever. Rose oil contains citronellol, which has been reported to cause a contact dermatitis. Rose oil is used for scenting soaps, shampoos, and creams. Teas made from rose hips or leaves do not contain xanthine alkaloids (caffeine). Multiflora rose, a native of eastern Asia, has been highly touted as a living fence and a good food and cover source for wildlife.

At one time the Pennsylvania Game Commission encouraged the planting of this rose and provided them free to cooperative farmers. At present the multiflora rose is listed as a noxious weed in Pennsylvania. Farmers can be fined for having this once highly touted plant growing on their property. The rose is the official flower of the District of Columbia, New York, Iowa, Georgia, and North Dakota.

CATTAIL
(Cat-o'nine-tails)

Typha latifolia L.
Typha angustifolia L.
Typhaceae

6–10'

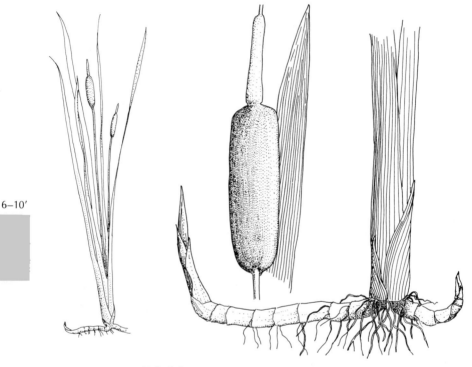

T. latifolia

Characteristics: Leaves are erect and swordlike and grow from a rhizome. Stems are unbranched and tipped by a compact cylindrical head of minute flowers. The lower, female flowers are green, but after seed set turn to the familiar brown color. The smaller head of male flowers is directly above the female head and withers away after releasing the pollen. Flowers appear from May to July. The plant grows from 3 to 12 feet tall.

Habitat: Shallow waters of marshes, swamps, slow-moving streams, and edges of ponds.

Distribution: Nearly cosmopolitan. Narrow-leaved cattail (*T. angustifolia*) is the common species along the coast, while common cattail (*T. latifolia*) is more common inland.

150

Edible parts: Young shoots and stalk, immature female flower head, pollen, rhizome.
Food uses: Flour, vegetable, salad, pickle, cooked greens.
Precautions: The leaves resemble those of the poisonous *Iris*. Droppings from birds, such as redwings, often cover the plants, so be sure to thoroughly wash the plants.
Preparation: Young shoots and stalks collected in the spring and early summer can be used in salads, eaten raw, pickled, or cooked as a vegetable. Immature female flowers (green) can be prepared like corn-on-the-cob. Shake pollen into a paper bag and use with an equal amount of whole grain flour to make pancakes or waffles. Flour can also be made from the rhizome.
Recipes:

Spicy Cattail Shoots

15 young cattail shoots	2 tablespoons parsley
2 teaspoons salt	3 tablespoons vegetable oil
2 tablespoons chives or onions	soy sauce

Peel the outer sheath from the cattail shoots to expose the whitish-green core. Boil the shoot cores in salted water for 15 minutes. Sauté chives, parsley, and shoots in oil. Season to taste with soy sauce.

Cattail Pancakes

1 cup cattail pollen	2 cups milk
1 cup flour	2 teaspoons cinnamon
1 teaspoon baking soda	2 tablespoons melted butter
½ teaspoon salt	

Sift together cattail pollen, flour, baking soda, cinnamon, and salt. Add liquid ingredients to the dry mixture and mix. Set aside for about 10 minutes. Mix and add more milk until desired consistency is obtained. Cook the same as regular pancakes.

Remarks: Many people consider the cattail to be the most versatile edible of our native plants. It is a year-round source of food. More carbohydrates can be obtained from an acre of cattails than from an acre of potatoes, yet few people harvest cattails, and wetlands are rapidly disappearing. The common name comes from the shape of the leaf, which resembles a cat's tail emerging from the marsh. The leaves are used to make chair seats, the cottony seeds are good for pillow stuffing and insulation, and the rhizome fibers can be twisted into a rope. Cattail "fur" can be made by dipping a mature cattail flowerstalk in molding rubber. After drying, the ends are cut off and the flower stalk cut open. Peel the rubber off the stalk and you have cattail "fur."

Rather than digging the entire plant to obtain the young shoots, just grab the innermost leaves and pull. The bottom white portion is what you are after. *Typha* is the Greek name for cattail. *Latifolia* means broad-leaved and *angustifolia* means narrow-leaved. In England *Typha* is commonly called bulrush.

BEACH PLUM

Prunus maritima Marsh.
Rosaceae

6–10'

Characteristics: A sprawling, thornless deciduous shrub that grows from 6 to 8 feet tall. Leaves are oblong, simple, and arranged alternately on the stem. The lower leaf surface is hairy, as are the twigs, buds, and many of the flower parts. The white flowers occur in May before the leaves appear. The fruit has a single seed and is purplish to reddish black.

Habitat: Sandy soils near salt water.

Distribution: Along the Atlantic coast.

152

Edible parts: Fruit.

Food uses: Snack, jelly, jam.

Precautions: The pits contain hydrocyanic acid, which is toxic. Some people do not like the tartness of the fruit.

Preparation: Pick fruit slightly unripe for jelly. Collect from August to October.

Recipes:

Beach Plum and Peach Pie

1½ cups sugar	dash of salt
¼ cup cornstarch	1 teaspoon orange rind (grated)
2 cups pitted beach plums (sliced)	2 tablespoons butter
2 cups pitted peaches (sliced)	1 piecrust shell and top crust

Mix plums, peaches, sugar, cornstarch, and salt together in a large bowl. Pour into piecrust shell. Sprinkle orange rind on top. Dot with butter. Put on top crust. Bake at 400° F for one hour.

Beach Plum Jam

4 cups pitted beach plums (chopped)	2 tablespoons lemon juice
½ cup water	1 package pectin
4 cups sugar	

Place beach plums and water in a large saucepan and bring to a rolling boil. Gradually mix in sugar and stir constantly. Simmer for 20 minutes while still stirring. Add lemon and pectin and bring to a hard boil for 2 minutes. Keep stirring. Remove the foam. Spoon into hot, sterilized jars. Seal immediately with paraffin.

Remarks: Colonists used beach plums to mellow gin because it stretched the liquor supply. Fruit production is spotty and may occur only every three to four years. This may be related to the cold, rainy weather that often occurs during flowering. The bad weather affects the flying insects that are necessary for pollination. Plums, cherries, and peaches are all members of the genus *Prunus* as well as the rose family. *Maritima* translates as pertaining to the sea and refers to the plant's habitat.

GROUNDNUT
(Indian potato, Wild bean)

Apios americana Medic.
Fabaceae

6–10'

Characteristics: Groundnuts are twining perennial vines that climb over other plants and grow to a length of 10 feet. Maroon to brownish-purple flowers occur in clusters in leaf axils. The fragrant flowers resemble bean or pea flowers and the fruits resemble thin bean pods. Flowers are present from June to September. The pinnately compound leaves have five to nine leaflets. The stem has a milky juice and leaves are arranged alternately on the stem. A necklace of golf-ball-sized tuberous thickenings occurs on the rhizomes.
Habitat: Rich, moist soils, especially at edges of thickets and in bottomlands near stream banks.
Distribution: Throughout the area.

Edible parts: Tubers

Food uses: Potato dishes

Precautions: Tubers can be eaten raw, but have a dry taste, and the plant juices leave a coating in the mouth. Resembles other viney legumes that are not edible, such as vetches and sweat pea.

Preparation: Eat raw or cooked; peeled or unpeeled. Use as a potato substitute.

Recipes:

Groundnut and Parsley

12–15 groundnut tubers (peeled)	4 tablespoons butter
salt and pepper	½ cup fresh parsley

Boil the tubers in salted water until done. Drain. Add salt and pepper, butter, and parsley. Mix thoroughly.

Scrumptious Veggies

10 groundnut tubers	1 cup mushrooms
1 small zucchini	1 medium-sized onion
½ sweet pepper	4 tablespoons butter
1 small hot pepper	salt and pepper

Wash, peel, and cut groundnuts into potato-chip slices. Wash, peel, and slice all other vegetables. Place vegetables on a piece of aluminum foil about 1 ft. × 2 ft. Spread butter over vegetables and add salt and pepper to taste. Fold aluminum foil and secure the 3 open sides so that a closed packet is formed. Place packet in hot coals or on top of charcoal grill. Grill on one side for 7 minutes, then turn over and grill for an additional 5 minutes.

Remarks: Eastern American Indians commonly used groundnut and cached it for winter use. The Indians boiled it with meat or corn and also cooked it over hot coals. The Pilgrims relied on groundnut for food during their first winter at Plymouth. Later colonists passed a law forbidding Indians from digging groundnuts on English lands. The native North American groundnut was sent to England for cultivation, but it was not successful as an agricultural crop. The tubers occur only a few inches under the soil and are available year-round. Groundnuts are high in protein compared to potatoes. *Apios* means pear and probably refers to the shape of the tubers.

HAZELNUT
(Filbert, Cobnut, Hazel)

Corylus americana Walt.
Betulaceae

6–10′

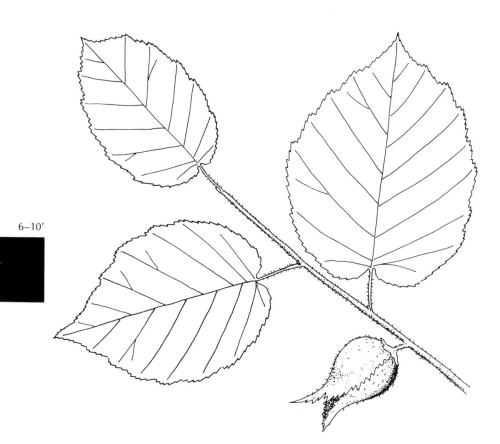

Characteristics: These are deciduous shrubs that grow in dense clumps and to a height of 10 feet. Long yellow catkins are produced in April and May before the leaves appear. The nuts occur in July and ripen in the fall. They are covered by a loose husk that is open at one end. The rough, heart-shaped, alternate leaves have double-toothed margins. The twigs and leaf stalks are covered with stiff brown hairs.
Habitat: Thickets, moist woods and fields, edges of woods.
Distribution: Throughout the area.

Edible parts: Nuts
Food uses: Nuts, flour, candy
Precautions: May be confused with witch hazel.
Preparation: Remove husk and shell. Can be eaten raw or in any recipe calling for nutmeats. The nuts can be pounded or ground into flour.
Recipes:

No-cook Hazelnut Candy

1 egg white	2 teaspoons butter or margarine
2 cups confectioner's sugar	2 cups hazelnuts (finely chopped)

Combine egg white and sugar. Add butter or margarine and blend until smooth and creamy. Mix in 2 cups of finely chopped hazelnuts and form into balls.

Hazelnut Cereal

¼ cup hazelnuts (chopped)	½ cup oatmeal
¼ cup raisins	¼ cup maple syrup

Combine all dry ingredients and mix thoroughly. Can be eaten dry or with milk.

Remarks: It is often difficult to obtain large numbers of hazelnuts because they are also sought by small mammals. North American Indians are reported to have searched for the nut caches of squirrels to obtain a supply of hazelnuts. Most of the commercial filberts (*C. avellana*) come from Europe. Oregon is the chief producer of commercial filberts in the United States. The cobnut is a variety of hazelnut that is popular in England. Although hazelnut is a relatively small shrub, the branches are strong and flexible, and have been used for arrows, baskets, and hoops. Hazelnut is a monoecious plant. This means that it has male (staminate) flowers and female (pistillate) flowers on the same plant. The staminate flowers occur in catkins. The "pussies" of a pussy willow are catkins.

JERUSALEM ARTICHOKE
(Sun choke)

Helianthus tuberosus L.
Asteraceae

6–10′

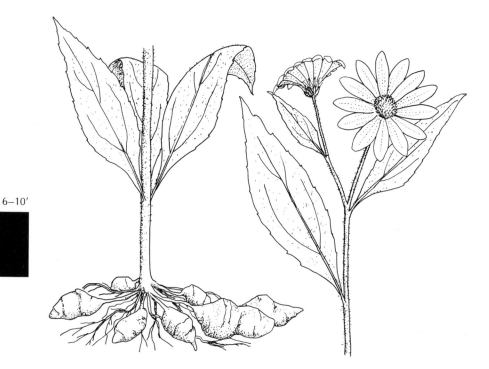

Characteristics: The perennial, herbaceous sunflower grows erect to 10 feet tall and has tuber-bearing rhizomes. The broadly ovate, rough, stiff leaves have long, narrow-winged petioles. The stout, hairy stem has opposite leaves on the lower stem and alternate leaves on the upper stem. The yellow flowers occur from August to October and are found at the tips of the uppermost branches. The ten to twenty yellow ray flowers are notched at the tip.
Habitat: Fields, waste areas, roadsides, damp thickets.
Distribution: Throughout the area.

Edible parts: Tubers.

Food uses: Salad, potato substitute, pickle, coffee substitute.

Precautions: May be confused with other sunflowers. The tubers are often quite knobby and difficult to clean.

Preparation: Collect the tubers in the fall after the plants have died.

Recipes:

Jerusalem Artichoke Pickles

4 quarts Jerusalem artichokes	4 tablespoons whole mixed pickling
1 cup salt	spice
1 gallon water	8 cups white vinegar
2½ cups sugar	small onions
1 tablespoon turmeric	garlic cloves

Scrub, rinse, and drain Jerusalem artichokes. Dissolve salt in 1 gallon water and pour over chokes. Let stand about 18 hours. Rinse and drain. Add sugar, turmeric, and pickling spices to vinegar. Simmer vinegar mixture for 20 minutes. Place 1 onion and 1 garlic clove in the bottom of each hot, sterilized jar. Pack chokes into hot jars. Heat vinegar mixture to boiling and immediately pour over chokes. Seal and place jars in boiling water for 15 minutes.

Scalloped Jerusalem Artichokes

3 pounds Jerusalem artichokes	4 tablespoons flour
½ cup onions (chopped fine)	1½ cups hot milk
1 cup sharp cheddar cheese	salt and pepper
3 tablespoons butter	¾ cup bread crumbs
1 can cream of celery soup	

Wash, peel, and slice chokes into a casserole dish with onions and cheddar cheese. Make several layers. Make sauce by melting butter, stir in celery soup, flour, and milk, and cook until thickened. Salt and pepper to taste. Pour sauce over chokes. Top with bread crumbs. Bake at 350° F for 45 minutes or until done.

Remarks: Jerusalem artichokes are not artichokes, but sunflowers, and are from North America, not Jerusalem. A better common name for these plants is sun chokes, the name used in most grocery stores. Jerusalem may be a corruption of *girasole*, which is Italian for sunflower. The name "artichoke" originated from the habit of people eating the boiled sunflower flower buds with butter in the same manner that artichokes are eaten. *Helianthus* means "sun flower" and refers to the belief that the flowers always face the sun throughout the day. *Tuberosus* refers to the plant's characteristic tubers. In Europe this plant is called Canadian potato. The tuber contains inulin, which is a complex polysaccharide but chemically different from starch. The tubers are reported to be valuable for diabetics and those on a low-starch diet.

COMMON ELDERBERRY
(Elder, Elder blow, Sweet elder)

Sambucus canadensis L.
Caprifoliaceae

6–10′

Characteristics: This deciduous shrub grows to 9 feet tall. The young stems have greenish bark and a large white pith and are scarcely woody. The pinnately compound leaves with five to eleven, but usually seven, leaflets are opposite. The internodes are long and fairly straight. Flowers are white and in dense, flat-topped clusters. Fruits are purple-black. Large, prominent lenticels are on the stem. Flowering occurs in June and July.

Habitat: Moist woods, roadside ditches, thickets, stream banks, edges of marshes.

Distribution: Throughout the area.

Edible parts: Fruits, flowers.

Food uses: Fritters, wine, cold beverages, jelly, jam, baked desserts.

Precautions: Use only flowers and ripe berries since all other parts of the plant and the unripe berries are poisonous. The raw berry is somewhat bitter; cooking sweetens the taste. The red-berried elder (*S. racemosa*) has attractive red fruits, but is not edible.

Preparations: Cut off the stem of the flower or fruit cluster in the field. At home the individual berries can be removed. The flowers are used to make wine and fritters. The fruits are used for wine, cold drinks, jelly, jam, and baked desserts. The fruits can be dried and in the winter used in baked desserts.

Recipes:

Elderberry Wine

3 pounds ripe elderberries	2 pounds sugar
1 pound raisins	1 package dry yeast
4 quarts boiling water	1 slice dry toast

Put elderberries and raisins in a crock and pour boiling water over. Press fruit well with a wooden spoon. Cover and keep for 4 days, stirring daily. Press berries through a fine sieve. Boil juice with sugar in a saucepan for 30 minutes, stirring well. Pour back into crock, and when liquid is lukewarm float the yeast, spread on a piece of toast, on top. Cover with cloth and leave 3 weeks, or until fermentation (bubbling) has stopped. Bottle and cork lightly. After 2 weeks tighten the corks and leave for at least 3 months to mature before using.

Elderberry Deep Dish Pie

1 piecrust shell and top crust	2 cups sugar
2 cups elderberries	2 cups water
juice of ½ lemon	5 tablespoons cornstarch
¼ teaspoon lemon rind (grated)	¼ teaspoon cinnamon

Line deep-dish pie pan with piecrust shell. Add elderberries. Sprinkle with lemon juice and rind. Mix sugar, water, cornstarch, and cinnamon and pour over berries. Place top crust over berries and pinch crust ends together to avoid a spillover. Punch several holes in top crust with a fork. Bake for 30 minutes at 425° F. (Naomi Pugh won the Hazel Wood Commemorative Award and a first place from the National Wild Foods Association for this recipe.)

Remarks: Hollowed elderberry twigs have been used as whistles, pea shooters, flutes, and spiles to tap sugar-maple trees. There have been unconfirmed reports of some toxicity to children who use the stems as pea shooters. Elderberry flower water is used as a skin lotion. The bruised leaves are used as an insect and rodent repellent. Elderberries contain little pectin, so commercial pectin or fruits high in pectin must be added when making jelly.

JAPANESE
KNOTWEED
(Mexican bamboo,
River-weed)

Polygonum cuspidatum Sieb. & Zucc.
Polygonaceae

6–10'

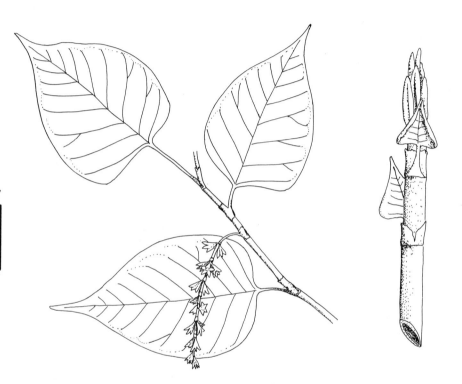

Characteristics: This is a perennial herb that grows to 10 feet tall. Vegetative reproduction from rhizomes results in large colonies. The stems are hollow, smooth, and
covered with green mottling. The alternate, broadly ovate to heart-shaped leaves
have sharply pointed leaf tips. A sheath encloses the stem at each swollen node.
White to greenish-white flowers occur in August and September and arise in clusters
from the upper leaf axils. Fruits are dark brown, triangular, and winged.
Habitat: Vacant lots, areas around buildings, disturbed sites, roadsides, fields.
Distribution: Throughout the area.

Edible parts: Young shoots.

Food uses: Cooked vegetable, jam, salad, pies.

Precautions: May cause photosensitive dermatitis. The tartness may be offensive to some.

Preparation: Collect the asparaguslike shoots that are up to 1 foot in height before they leaf out. Use the shoots as a cooked vegetable or in salads. Young stems up to 2 or 3 feet may be used for jams and pies. Discard the leaves and the skin from the young stems. The stems resemble rhubarb in taste and should be combined with other blander items.

Recipes:

Japanese Knotweed Jam

1 grocery bag of young Japanese knotweed stalks	2 teaspoons lemon peel (grated)
	1 package pectin
½ cup water	2 drops green food coloring
2½ tablespoons lemon juice	4½ cups sugar

Peel Japanese knotweed stalks and chop into ½ inch pieces. Place in a saucepan with water, lemon juice, and lemon peel. Bring to a boil. Add pectin and boil for 1 minute. Add food coloring. Add sugar and bring to a rapid boil for 2 minutes. Pour into hot, sterilized jars and top with paraffin. For an added treat, place ½ teaspoon of Japanese knotweed jam in small cavity in the top of the dough when making bran muffins.

Stir-fried Knotweed

2 tablespoons vegetable oil	1 cup celery (sliced)
1 cup young Japanese knotweed shoots (chopped)	1 cup onion (chopped)
	2 tablespoons soy sauce

Sauté vegetables in hot vegetable oil over moderate heat for 5 minutes. Sprinkle with soy sauce and cook for 2 minutes more.

Remarks: This Asian native was introduced to Europe and North America as an ornamental plant. It easily escapes from cultivation and establishes itself in waste areas. It displaces native-plant communities and soon forms a solid mass of Japanese knotweed. Many consider it to be a noxious weed. It is difficult to eradicate, and even total-kill herbicides have limited success in killing it. In the spring the remains of last year's plants resemble a pile of unorganized bamboo sticks. The red stalks appear in late March and make it one of our earliest wild edibles.

COMMON SUNFLOWER

Helianthus annuus L.
Asteraceae

6–10′

Characteristics: This annual herb grows to 12 feet tall, but is usually from 6 to 8 feet in height. Except for the lowest leaves, the leaves are mostly alternate. The stem and leaves are rough-hairy. The ovate-to-heart-shaped, simple leaves have a toothed margin. Inflorescence is a head with ray and disk flowers. The brownish flattened disk is surrounded by yellow ray flowers. Fruits are produced only from the disk flowers. The fruits are flattened with light and dark gray stripes. It flowers from July to September.

Habitat: Dry soils in waste areas, disturbed fields, roadsides and gardens.

Distribution: Indigenous to the mid- and far west, but cultivated forms readily escape and are found throughout the area.

Edible parts: Seeds.

Food uses: Oil, nuts, flour, gruel.

Precautions: Remember that the flattened, striped structure taken from the sunflower head is the fruit. The seed is inside it.

Preparation: The seeds can be ground into a flour and mixed with wheat flour or used as a gruel. To obtain the oil, crush the fruits and boil, then skim the oil from the surface. Use the oil in recipes calling for vegetable oil. The seeds can be eaten raw, roasted, or added to baked desserts.

Recipes:

Sunflower Zucchini Bread

3 eggs (beaten until foamy)	1 teaspoon baking soda
2 cups sugar	1 teaspoon salt
1 cup vegetable oil	2 teaspoons cinnamon
2 cups zucchini (grated)	1 teaspoon thyme
3 teaspoons vanilla	½ teaspoon ground cloves
3 cups flour	½ cup sunflower seeds (chopped)
¼ teaspoon baking powder	

Combine eggs, sugar, and oil. Add zucchini and vanilla. Combine all dry ingredients. Fold dry ingredients into liquid combination. Pour into two greased bread pans. Bake at 325° F for 1 hour.

Spring Salad Delight

3 cups dandelion leaves	½ cup salad oil
1 cup watercress leaves	½ cup cider vinegar
½ cup common blue violet leaves	¼ cup sugar
½ cup sheep sorrel leaves	1 teaspoon salt
½ cup plantain leaves	½ teaspoon pepper
½ cup wild onions (chopped)	½ cup roasted sunflower seeds

Wash and shred greens. Combine greens and onions and toss. Combine salad oil, vinegar, sugar, and salt and pepper. Pour dressing over greens and toss. Serve in salad bowls and sprinkle with sunflower seeds.

Remarks: *Helianthus* is from the Greek *helios,* sun, and *anthos,* flower. It refers to the belief that the flowers face the sun through the day. The word *annuus* refers to its being an annual. Sunflower oil is not only used as a vegetable oil, but also for soap, hair oil, and shampoo. Farmers use the fruits as cattle and chicken feed. In some parts of Europe, sunflower stalks are used for fuel. Sunflower seeds are becoming increasingly popular as a salad topping or as a snack, and are a popular food item in Russia. Other *Helianthus* species, though they have smaller heads, produce fruits that can be used in the same manner as common sunflower. This plant is rich in protein, oil, minerals, and vitamin D. A native of the mid-United States, the plant is considered by some as America's greatest flower contribution to the world. It has now spread around the world, with its greatest crop use in Peru and Russia.

BLUEBERRY   *Vaccinium angustifolium* Ait.
                                           Vaccinium corymbosum L.
                                           Ericaceae

6–10'

V. corymbosum

Characteristics: These are deciduous colonial shrubs that branch profusely. *V. corymbosum* grows to 15 feet tall, but *V. angustifolium* is much smaller at 1–2 feet. The alternate, simple leaves are smooth on the upper surface, but may have some hair on the lower surface. Bell-shaped, densely clustered white-to-pinkish flowers form the rounded blue berries. Flowers begin to appear in May and ripe fruits are usually present from late June to September.

Habitat: *V. angustifolium* occurs in dry, rocky, or sandy soil while *V. corymbosum* is found in wet soils, swamps, or bogs.

Distribution: *V. corymbosum* occurs throughout the area. *V. angustifolium* is more abundant in the Northeast but does extend south to New Jersey and the mountains of Virginia and West Virginia.

Edible parts: Fruit.

Food uses: Fresh or dried fruit, jelly, jam, wine, syrup, tea.

Precautions: Some members of *Vaccinium*, such as deerberry, are not edible. *V. corymbosum* is often found in ecosystems that are the habitat for timber rattlesnakes, poison sumac, and black bears.

Preparation: Collect from late June to September. Remove stems and rinse in cold water. Spread on a towel to dry. The berries freeze well.

Recipes:

Blueberry Sherbet

2 cups blueberry juice	1 package unflavored gelatin
½ cup honey	2 egg whites (beaten)
1 teaspoon lemon juice	

Combine blueberry juice, honey, and lemon juice in a pan. Heat over medium heat. Add gelatin and stir constantly. Do not boil. When gelatin is dissolved, remove from heat and cool. Stir in egg whites. Beat until mixed. Spread in pan. Freeze.

Blueberry Muffins

2 cups flour	1 egg (beaten)
3 tablespoons sugar	3 tablespoons soft butter
2½ teaspoons baking powder	¾ cup evaporated milk
1 cup blueberries	

Sift together flour, sugar, and baking powder. Stir in blueberries until all berries are coated. Add egg, butter, and milk to the mixture. Stir gently to mix ingredients. Half-fill greased muffin tins with batter. Bake at 375° F for 20 minutes or until done.

Remarks: Wildlife, especially birds, are very fond of blueberries. Commercial growers often keep netting over bushes to protect the crop from foraging birds. The plants occur in colonies from root suckers. The oldest parts of the colony may be hundreds of years old. *V. corymbosum* is a highly variable tetraploid. Many hybrids are found in the southern part of its distribution area, where it interbreeds with several southern blueberry species. Blueberries can also be used as a dye. Blueberry juice can be used as a pH indicator. The blue color of blueberry indicates that it is alkaline. With the addition of some vinegar, the blueberry juice becomes acid and will turn reddish.

REED GRASS
(Phragmites)

Phragmites australis (Cav.) Trin. ex Steud.
Poaceae

6–10'

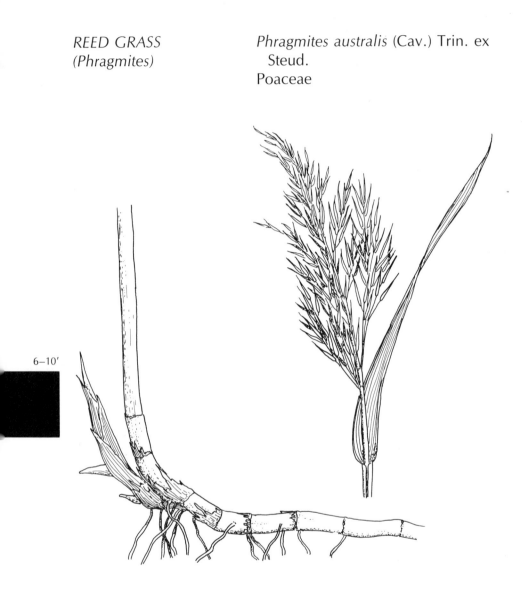

Characteristics: This erect perennial grass grows to 13 feet. Reed grass spreads by rhizomes to form dense colonies. The hollow or pithy stems are jointed. The flat, smooth, narrow leaves are up to 2 feet long. When young, the inflorescence is purple, but it later becomes white and finally brown. The dense clusters of flowers have the appearance of a silky plume.

Habitat: Swamps, ditches, lake shores, brackish marshes.

Distribution: Throughout most of the area, but sparse in the mountains and south of Maryland.

Edible parts: Young shoots, seeds, rhizomes.

Food uses: Flour, pickle, gruel, green vegetables, potato substitute.

Precautions: Often found in roadside ditches that may contain contaminants. May be confused with other grasses.

Preparation: Young shoots can be prepared as a green vegetable or pickled. Flour can be made from the starchy rhizomes or seeds. The rhizomes can also be used as a potato substitute or made into a gruel.

Recipes:

Stir-fried Reed Grass

3 teaspoons vegetable oil	1 can water chestnuts
1 garlic clove (minced)	1 cup chicken broth
1 cup green onions (chopped)	4 tablespoons soy sauce
2 cups young reed-grass shoots	2 tablespoons cornstarch
1 cup mushrooms (sliced)	1 teaspoon ginger
2 cups snow peas	salt and pepper to taste

Heat the oil in a skillet or wok. Add garlic and onions and brown. Wash, drain, and chop reed grass. Add reed grass, mushrooms, peas, and water chestnuts to skillet and stir-fry for 5 minutes. In a bowl, combine chicken broth, soy sauce, cornstarch, ginger, and salt and pepper. Add to skillet and heat for 3 to 5 minutes. Serve with boiled rice.

Reed Grass Salad

3 cups reed-grass rhizomes	2 tablespoons vinegar
1 cup celery (chopped)	2 teaspoons mustard
1 small onion (chopped)	2 tablespoons oil
½ cup cheddar cheese (cubed)	salt and pepper to taste
1 small red pepper (chopped)	

Wash and peel reed-grass rhizomes. Boil or steam rhizomes until tender. Drain and cube. Add all ingredients and stir.

Remarks: Reed grass is commonly found in fresh-water ditches, but it is also tolerant of salt and may occur along brackish marshes. The dried stems are quite sturdy and have been used for arrrows. The stems have also been used to make baskets, and the inflorescences are often used in dry flower arrangements. *Phragmites* is derived from the Greek *phragma,* which means fence and refers to the manner in which these large grasses form a hedgelike growth. The cosmopolitan nature of the plant is reflected by the name *communis,* which means common or general.

BAYBERRRY (Candleberry)   *Myrica pensylvanica* Loisel.
WAX MYRTLE (Candleberry)   *Myrica cerifera* L.
                                 Myricaceae

10–20'

M. pensylvanica   *M. cerifera*

Characteristics: *M. pensylvanica* usually grows as a low, spreading deciduous shrub that forms dense thickets. *M. cerifera* is evergreen and often grows as a small tree up to 40 feet tall in dense thickets. The leaves of these trees are alternate, simple, fragrant, and covered with resin dots. The white fruits are thickly coated with wax. The flowers appear as catkins.

Habitat: *M. pensylvanica* is found on dry hills and sandy shores. *M. cerifera* is found in damp or wet sandy soil.

Distribution: *M. pensylvanica* occurs at a few inland sites as far west as Ohio, but it is mostly found along the Atlantic coast and the shores of Lake Erie. *M. cerifera* is limited to the coastal plain from southern New Jersey southward.

Edible parts: Leaves and fruit.
Food uses: Seasoning, tea.
Precautions: The wax is reported to be slightly narcotic, and in large doses may be an emetic and cause flatulence.
Preparation: Dried leaves can be stored in tightly closed glass jars in a dark cabinet. It can be used as a substitute for bay spice.
Recipes

Bayberry Tea

Pour boiling water on 1 teaspoon of dried leaves or 2 teaspoons of fresh leaves per cup. Steep for several minutes and remove leaves.

Seasoning

Use fresh or dried leaves and, to a lesser extent, the fruits to season soups, stews, roasts, and seafood chowders. Remove the bayberry leaves or fruit from the dish before serving.

Remarks: Since colonial days, the wax boiled from the bayberry fruits has been used for making soaps and candles. The wax from *Myrica* is harder and more brittle than beeswax. It takes about four pounds of fruits to make one pound of wax. Although the bayberry leaf is used in seasoning, it is not the same "bay" leaf found on the supermarket spice shelf. The fruit produced by bayberry is also not a true "berry." Botanically, the "berries" are actually nutlets. The bayberries are among the small group of nonleguminous plants that also have nitrogen-fixing bacteria on their roots. About seventy-five bird species and various mammals eat the seeds and leaves of bayberry. The wax-covered seeds are a favorite food of the myrtle warbler, which was named after this plant. Numerous medicinal applications include remedies for dysentery, sore throat, cold, and fever, along with use as a poultice. Myrtle Beach, South Carolina, is named after the wax myrtle that is common to the area.

SPICEBUSH
(Feverbush, Spicewood, Wild allspice)

Lindera benzoin (L.) Blume
Lauraceae

10–20'

Characteristics: Spicebush is a deciduous, much-branched shrub that may grow to 16 feet tall, but is usually in the range of 6 to 12 feet. Crushed leaves and stems have a spicy aroma. The thin, alternate, simple, obovate leaves have an entire margin. Yellow flowers occur in the early spring before the appearance of leaves. The mature fruit is bright red and contains a single, oval seed.
Habitat: Rich, moist deciduous woods, especially along stream banks.
Distribution: Throughout the area.

172

Edible parts: Young leaves, twigs, fruit, bark.
Food uses: Tea, seasoning.
Precautions: Use the mature fruit.
Preparation: To make substitute allspice, remove the seed from the fruit. Retain the fruit pulp and dry in the sun. Grind the dried fruit pulp. Leaves, twigs, fruits, and bark can be used for seasoning or for a tea. Use fresh or dried.
Recipes:

Spicy Spicebush Tea

5 cups of water	1 cinnamon stick
15 fresh spicebush leaves	maple syrup

Bring water to boil. Place spicebush leaves in teapot and cover with water. Add cinnamon stick. Let steep for 10 minutes. Strain and pour into cups. Add maple syrup as desired.

Spicy Fish

½ cup spicebush tea	1 teaspoon dill
½ pound fish fillets	½ teaspoon paprika
1 teaspoon parsley flakes	½ teaspoon salt

Pour spicebush tea into skillet and add fish fillets. Sprinkle parsley, dill, paprika, and salt on fillets. Cover skillet and cook for 10 minutes.

Remarks: The Laurel family (Lauraceae) is chiefly tropical and includes aromatic trees and shrubs. Sassafras, red bay, and spicebush are classified in the Laurel family, but mountain laurel is not. The genus *Lindera* commemorates the Swedish botanist and physician John Linden (1676–1724). *Benzoin* is the old genus name for this plant and is derived from an Arabic term that means aromatic gum. In some books the scientific name may appear as *Benzoin aestivale*. Since colonial times the plant has been used as a substitute for allspice. The common name of feverbush alludes to its medicinal use by pioneers. The caterpillar that becomes the spicebush butterfly feeds on spicebush leaves.

GREENBRIER (Carrion-flower)   *Smilax herbacea* L.
GREENBRIER (Catbrier)   *Smilax rotundifolia* L.
                                         Smilaceae

10–20′

S. rotundifolia

Characteristics: Greenbriers are climbing perennial vines with green stems and often pairs of tendrils at the base of the leafstalks. The alternate leaves have prominent veins that originate from a common point at the base and terminate at the leaf tip. Leaf margins are entire. Small greenish flowers occur as umbels. Fruits are bluish-black and form a globular structure. *S. herbacea* is not woody, has heart-shaped leaves, but no prickles. The four-sided stems of *S. rotundifolia* have sharp, stout prickles scattered on the stem and round leaves.

Habitat: Thickets, open forests, edge of clearings. *S. herbacea* is often found on riverbanks and wet areas.

Distribution: Generally found throughout the area. *S. rotundifolia* is more abundant and extends through most of Ohio.

Edible parts: Roots, young shoots, tendrils, young stem tips, young leaves.
Food uses: Nibble, salads, cooked greens, jelly, flour, cold drink.
Precautions: Be careful not to confuse greenbrier with other viney plants such as virgin's bower, moonseed, poison ivy, grape, and honeysuckle.
Preparation: Young shoots are cooked like asparagus. Tendrils are used as a nibble. Young leaves, tendrils, and young shoots are prepared as cooked greens or used in salads. A dry powder can be extracted from the roots that can be used in jellies as gelatin, as a soup thickener, or as a cold drink. Use only the uppermost 3–6 inches of the young stem tips.
Recipes:

Greenbrier Potatoes

6 medium-sized potatoes   4 tablespoons butter
1 cup greenbrier stem tips   salt and pepper
½ cup fresh parsley

Peel and cube potatoes. Boil in water until soft. When potatoes are almost cooked, boil greenbrier tips for 2 minutes in a separate pot. Drain potatoes and greenbrier. Combine greenbrier, potatoes, and parsley in a bowl. Add butter and mix thoroughly. Add salt and pepper to taste.

Greenbrier Salad

4 cups young greenbrier stem tips   boiling water
1 teaspoon salt   commercial French dressing

Boil stem tips in salted water for 2 minutes. Drain and cool. Pour dressing over stem tips and serve.

Remarks: Numerous common names reflect people's experiences with these plants. Catbrier (*S. rotundifolia*) probably refers to the catlike scratches people get when trying to penetrate these vines. Wait-a-bit is a common name in the West Virginia hill country and suitably describes attempts to make progress through the dense tangles of *Smilax*. Blaspheme vine probably refers to the epithets muttered by unaware travelers.

Because *S. herbacea* flowers have a fetid odor, the plant is also called carrion flower. The Asian species of *Smilax* have been found to contain steroidal sapogenins that are used medicinally as cortisone and hormone precursors. A Central American species is the source of Jamaican sarsparilla. The plants are dioecious, which means that male or staminate flowers occur on one plant while female or pistillate flowers occur on a separate plant. The tendrils are modifications of the stipules. Some taxonomists include the greenbriers in the Liliaceae (lily family). *Smilax* is from the Greek *smile*, which means rasping and probably refers to the prickles of some species. *Rotundifolia* describes the round leaves and *herbacea* the soft, nonwoody stem.

HIGH-BUSH CRANBERRY
(Cranberry viburnum)

Viburnum trilobum Marsh.
Caprifoliaceae

10–20'

Characteristics: This deciduous shrub or small tree can grow to a height of 17 feet. The opposite, simple leaves are maplelike, with three long-pointed lobes and coarse teeth. Petioles bear 1 to 6 dome-shaped glands near the leaf base. A pair of slender stipules occurs at the base of the petiole. Clusters of white flowers are present from May to July. Larger flowers are to the outside of the flower cluster. The bright red, translucent, berrylike fruits are actually one-seeded drupes and occur in September and October. The seed is flat.

Habitat: Moist woods, stream banks.

Distribution: Widely scattered in Pennsylvania and Ohio, but more common northward into Canada.

Edible parts: Fruit.

Food uses: Cooked fruit, jelly, cold drink, wine.

Precautions: *V. opulus* or guelder rose may be confused with *V. trilobum*. Its fruit is bitter and not edible. In the vegetative condition, some bushy maples and other viburnums may be confused with high-bush cranberry.

Preparation: Collect the mature fruit from late September through the winter. The fruit is generally too sour to eat raw. Adding sugar to the cooked fruits produces a dish that resembles cranberry sauce. The large, flat seed poses a chewing problem and should be removed by straining.

Recipes:

High-bush Cranberry Jelly

2 quarts high-bush cranberries	1 teaspoon lemon juice
5 cups sugar	1 package pectin

Squeeze cranberries or use blender. Place cranberries in a saucepan and bring to a boil. Strain the berries through a jelly bag and save 4 cups of juice. Add sugar and lemon juice to the cranberry juice and boil hard for 1 minute. Stir constantly. Remove from heat and add pectin. Boil and stir for 1 minute. Skim off foam. Pour into hot, sterilized jars and seal with paraffin.

High-bush Cranberry Sauce

4 cups high-bush cranberries	1 package orange gelatin
¼ cup water	2 tablespoons orange peel (grated)
1 cup sugar	

Heat berries in water and bring to boil. Press through sieve or jelly bag to remove skins and seeds. Place clear juice in saucepan over medium heat. Add sugar, gelatin, and orange peel and stir until all is dissolved. Boil for 5 minutes. Cool and serve with pork or lamb.

Remarks: High-bush cranberry is not a cranberry, nor is it closely related to that species. It does, however, have a red, sour fruit that is similar to cranberry in appearance, taste, and use. High-bush cranberry is in the genus *Viburnum*, which is also often used as its common name. The outside ring of large flowers in the flower cluster are sterile. The fruits are high in vitamin C. The best season to collect the fruits is after the first heavy frost. Continued cold weather seems to improve the taste of this sour fruit. Long after the shrub has lost its leaves, the fruits continue to add a splash of red to the white of winter. High-bush cranberry is more common to Canada, and Pennsylvania marks its southern limit in the eastern United States.

NANNYBERRY
(Sheepsberry, Black haw)

Viburnum lentago L.
Caprifoliaceae

10–20′

Characteristics: Nannyberry is a tall deciduous shrub or tree that averages 10–20 feet but may grow to 30 feet tall. The opposite, ovate leaves are finely toothed. All or some petioles have an irregular wing. White flowers are produced in dense, rounded clusters in May and June. The bluish-black fruit has a whitish bloom. Each oval fruit contains a single flat seed. Fruits occur on slender, reddish stalks that often droop.
Habitat: Moist woods, along roadsides and stream banks, edges of wetlands.
Distribution: Found generally throughout the area south to New Jersey and in the mountains to the west and then south.

178

Edible parts: Fruit.

Food uses: Snack, cooked fruit, jelly, pudding, pie.

Precautions: Nannyberry is often found along wet roadsides, where it may be covered with road dust and exposed to pesticides and auto-exhaust pollutants.

Preparation: Wash the fruit and use as a snack. Seeds can be removed before cooking or by straining the cooked fruit through a colander. Clusters of fruits can be hung to dry in a warm dark place and stored and used like raisins or dates. The best time to collect the fruits is when the leaves begin to fall.

Recipes:

Nannyberry Pudding

4 cups nannyberry fruits	1 cup sugar
3¼ cups water	½ teaspoon cinnamon
3 tablespoons lemon juice	⅓ cup cornstarch
1 teaspoon lime rind (grated)	

Boil the nannyberry fruits in 1½ cups water for 10 minutes. Remove from heat and mash fruits. Strain fruit through a collander to obtain 1 cup of liquid pulp. Add lemon, lime rind, sugar, cinnamon, and ¾ cup water to the pulp. Bring to a boil and then simmer for 15 minutes. Mix cornstarch with 1 cup water and add to the hot nannyberry mixture. Cook slowly for 20 minutes. Pour into pudding dish and cool.

Nannyberry Jelly

8 cups washed nannyberries	3 cups sugar
1 cup water	1 package pectin
3 tablespoons lemon juice	

Add berries to water in saucepan. Bring to a boil and then simmer for 20 minutes. Place in jelly bag and collect juice. Add lemon and sugar to juice and bring to a boil. Stir constantly. Add pectin and bring to a rolling boil. Boil 1 minute. Skim off foam, ladle into hot, sterilized jars, and seal with paraffin.

Remarks: The common name of nannyberry indicates the resemblance of the fruits to the fecal pellets of goats and sheep. West Virginians know this plant as black haw. The plant is a valuable food source for wildlife. Many species of mammals and larger birds use the fruits for food. The dry, large-seeded fruits do not appeal to everyone as an edible wild plant. Large flower clusters, which can be more than 5 inches across, and a shrubby growth form make this plant a popular ornamental. It is reported to be rich in vitamin C. By blending nannyberries with miniature marshmallows, you can create an interesting dessert that has the flavor of chocolate.

HAWTHORN
(White thorn, Haw, Red Haw)

Crataegus spp.
Rosaceae

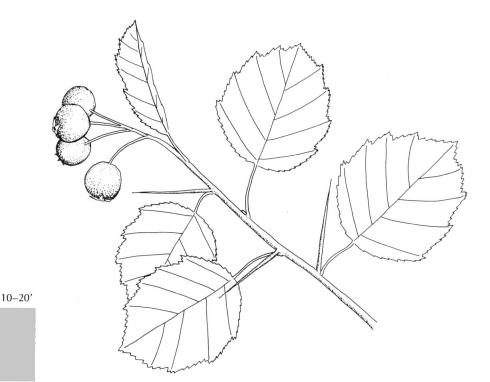

10–20'

Characteristics: Hawthorns are deciduous shrubs and small trees that grow to 20 feet tall. They have crooked stems with long, stiff, sharp thorns. The alternate, simple leaves are toothed, often double-toothed, and often lobed. The white or pale pink flowers have five petals. Flowering occurs from April to June. The ripe fruit is usually red, but varies in color to almost black. Fruits resemble small apples with the familiar dried calyx at the bottom.

Habitat: Wet or dry rocky woods, disturbed areas, pastures, old fields, edges of forests, stream thickets.

Distribution: Found throughout the area.

Edible parts: Fruit.

Food uses: Jelly, tea, nibble.

Precautions: The quality of the fruit varies from tree to tree. The raw fruit can be eaten, but it is dry and mealy and the seeds are bothersome. Too many raw fruits can cause an upset stomach.

Preparation: Collect fruit in fall.

Recipes:

Hawthorn Jelly

10 cups washed hawthorn fruits	6 cups sugar
½ cup water	2 tablespoons lemon juice

Combine hawthorn fruits and water. Bring to boil. Stir. Strain through jelly bag and collect 4 cups of juice. Combine hawthorn juice, sugar, and lemon juice and bring to a boil. Stir. Boil for 1 minute. Remove from heat and skim off foam. Ladle into hot, sterilized jars and seal with paraffin.

Hawthorn Tea

3 tablespoons crushed hawthorn fruits	sprig of spearmint

Boil water. Pour water on hawthorn fruits and spearmint. Steep for 5 minutes.

Remarks: The hawthorns are distinctive as a group, but difficult to identify as individual species. A few are distinguishable by the layman, but identification of the majority of hawthorn species is usually left to plant taxonomists who specialize in this genus. Taxonomists who are considered "lumpers" categorize the hawthorns by fewer than 100 species, while the "splitters" divide the genus into more than 1,000. The dense canopy provides an ideal nesting site for birds, and the fruit provides food for birds and mammals throughout the winter. The fruit contains pectin, which eliminates the need to add the commercial form when making jelly. The thorns have been used as awls for making holes in leather and as fishhooks. Crab apples have buds and leaves on their "thorns" while hawthorns do not.

STAGHORN SUMAC
SMOOTH SUMAC
(Lemonade tree, Vinegar tree)

Rhus typhina L.
Rhus glabra L.
Anacardiaceae

10–20′

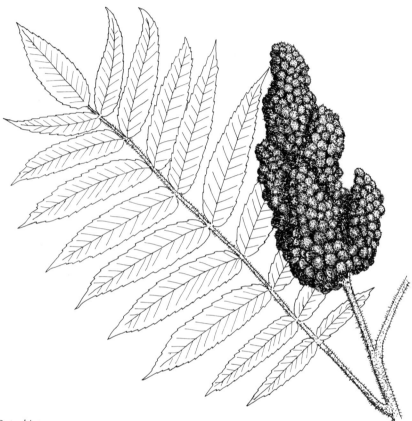

R. typhina

Characteristics: These are shrubs or small trees that vary in height from 10 to 30 feet. When broken, the young twigs exude a thick, milky juice. Fruits are produced in dense, cone-shaped clusters. The fruits are rounded, berrylike, and covered with dark red hairs. The pinnately compound leaves are about 14 to 24 inches long and composed of 11 to 31 pointed leaflets, each 2 to 5 inches long. Staghorn sumac has hairy stems while the stems of smooth sumac are hairless.
Habitat: Common and widespread; fields, margins of woodlands, abandoned farmlands, thickets.
Distribution: Found throughout the area.

Edible parts: Fruit.

Food uses: Drink, jelly.

Precautions: Anyone having a known allergy to any member of the Anacardiaceae (poison ivy, poison sumac, cashews, mangoes, etc.) should probably avoid using these edible sumacs. Poison sumac resembles smooth sumac, but it has white fruits. Some people develop a temporary dermatitis from handling the hairy sumac fruits.

Preparation: Gather the fruit clusters in late summer or early fall, but before heavy rains leach the flavor out of the red hairs on the fruits. Separate fruits from twigs and rinse. Although fruits persist on the tree through the fall and winter, they are not usable at that time.

Recipes:

Sumac Elder Jelly

2 quarts sumac fruits   4½ cups sugar
1 quart elderberry fruits   1 package pectin

Cover the sumac fruits with cold water and crush the fruits. After 10 minutes, strain mixture through a cloth. Keep 2 cups of sumac juice. Squeeze 1 quart of elderberries to obtain 2 cups of juice. Combine the juices and boil for 3 minutes. Add sugar. Bring to a hard boil. Boil 1 minute. Remove from heat. Add pectin. Boil for 1 minute. Skim off foam. Pour into hot, sterilized jars and seal with paraffin.

Sumac Drink

Use several red fruit clusters. Crush the fruits and soak in a quart of cold water. Filter the mixture through a cloth. Sweeten the filtered liquid to taste with sugar or honey. Add cloves or cinnamon for a spicy drink. Use cold for "sumacade" or serve hot for sumac tea. Boiling hastens the process, but bitter tannic acid will be released in addition to the flavorful malic acid.

Remarks: The common name for staghorn sumac probably refers to the hairy stems that resemble a stag's antlers when they are in the velvet stage. A brown dye used by European shoemakers accounts for the pronunciation of sumac as "shoe-mock" as opposed to "sue-mack." In addition to poison ivy, poison oak, and poison sumac, this family (Anacardiaceae) also includes the cashew. In the early 1700s the colonists exported the red fruits to Europe, where they were used as a preferred tobacco ingredient. The milky sap is used in natural glues. Spiles for tapping maple trees are made by hollowing the stems with a round file, round hardwood stem, or hot wire.

PAWPAW
(Indian banana, False banana)

Asimina triloba (L.) Dunal
Annonaceae

10–20′

Characteristics: Pawpaw can be a small deciduous tree up to 40 feet tall or somewhat shrubby. Commonly its height is between 8 and 20 feet. The alternate leaves are dark green above and lighter beneath. The long, thin leaves are simple and entire. The bell-shaped purple flowers have six petals in two whorls. Flowers appear with the emergence of the leaves. The large, fleshy fruits mature in the fall and resemble stubby brown bananas when ripe. There are long, naked, hairy, dark brown terminal buds. The pith is chambered.

Habitat: Stream banks and ravines of rich, moist woods. Sometimes it appears in cleared areas such as pastures.

Distribution: Found throughout southern Pennsylvania and Ohio southward, but localized northward and absent in the northernmost areas.

184

Edible parts: Fruit.

Food uses: Raw fruit, puddings, breads, wine.

Precautions: Some people develop a slight dermatitis from handling the fruit. Others find the sweet smell of the ripening fruit in the house to be overwhelming. The consumption of the fruit has been reported to be disagreeable to some individuals.

Preparation: Collect the fruits when mature or while still green and keep in the house until they ripen. The sweet yellow pulp can be eaten raw.

Recipes:

Pawpaw Pudding

1 tablespoon cornstarch	2 cups uncooked pawpaw pulp
½ cup milk	1 teaspoon cinnamon
4 egg yolks (beaten)	1 teaspoon ground ginger
½ cup sugar	

Meringue:

4 egg whites	¾ teaspoon cream of tartar
¼ cup sugar	

Mix cornstarch in milk and add to egg yolks and sugar. Heat until smooth. Add pawpaw pulp to mixture and stir. Add cinnamon and ginger and mix. Refrigerate. Before serving, prepare a meringue by beating egg whites with sugar and cream of tartar. Pour pawpaw mixture into a casserole dish. Cover with meringue and put under broiler just long enough to brown.

Pawpaw Ice Cream

3 cups uncooked pawpaw pulp	1 cup orange juice
5 tablespoons lemon juice	1½ cup honey
1 lemon peel (grated)	3 cups cream

Whip pawpaw pulp, lemon juice, lemon peel, orange juice, and honey until fluffy. Stir in cream. Pour into cake pan and freeze.

Remarks: The common name for Annonaceae is the Custard Apple family. *Asimina* is the only temperate-zone member of this mainly tropical family. The name *Asimina* may be derived from the word *asiminier,* which was the name used by the French colonists for this plant. Some authorities, however, believe that *Asimina* is derived from the American Indian name for pawpaw. Another spelling of pawpaw is papaw. This spelling, however, is usually used for the West Indian papaya that also grows wild in Florida. *A. triloba* is often referred to as tall pawpaw and the more southern *A. parviflora* as dwarf pawpaw. The bruised foliage is ill-scented and apparently not palatable to cattle. USDA and Purdue University scientists found that pawpaw bark yields a natural pesticide that is effective against bean beetles and blowfly larvae.

CRAB APPLE   *Malus coronaria* (L.) P. Mill.
                              Rosaceae

20–40'

Characteristics: Deciduous trees or tall shrubs that grow to 30 feet tall. Thorn or thornlike projections are found on the branches. The simple alternate leaves are irregularly and sharply toothed, but are also often lobed. The five-petaled flowers are white to pinkish and occur in May. The fruit resembles a miniature apple. The sour fruit is yellowish-green or red.
Habitat: Moist woods and thickets, old pastures, road sides, fencerows.
Distribution: Throughout the area.

186

Edible parts: Fruit.

Food uses: Jelly, preserves, cider, apple butter, relish, crab-apple sauce, drink.

Precautions: The crab apple has a sour taste and is usually not eaten raw. Eat as a cooked fruit. The seeds, bark, and leaves contain hydrocyanic acid and should not be eaten.

Preparation: Collect after several hard frosts. Insects and fungi do little damage to crab apples, but if present, cut away damaged parts. If a neighbor has flowering crab apples and does not spray with pesticides, collect the fruits from those trees. The red crab apples from flowering crabs make an attractive jelly and sauce.

Recipes:

Grapple Punch

2 quarts crab apples	1 quart ginger ale
2 quarts wild grapes	ice ring
1 to 2 cups sugar	

Remove stems from crab apples and grapes. Wash crab apples, then chop them into a saucepan. Cover with water and simmer for 30 minutes. Wash and crush grapes into a separate saucepan, cover with water, and simmer for 30 minutes. Strain each fruit through a strainer or cheesecloth to remove pulp. Save the juices and cool. Just prior to using, pour juice into bowl and add ginger ale and sugar to taste. Then add the ice ring.

Crab-apple Mint Jelly

2 pounds crab apples	sugar
2 cups water	6 sprigs fresh mint
1 teaspoon citric or tartaric acid	

Wash crab apples and place in a large saucepan with water and citric acid. Bring to a boil and simmer slowly until fruit is pulpy and all the juice is released (about 1 hour). Strain through a fine sieve or jelly bag. Measure juice and return to pan with ¾ pound sugar to each 2 cups juice. Add the mint, tied in a bunch. Stir until boiling and boil briskly about 10 minutes, or until jelly sets when tested on a cold plate. Remove mint, pour into hot, sterilized jars, and seal with paraffin.

Remarks: The cultivated apple is probably a native of western Asia, but was introduced into Massachusetts by the Pilgrims. The crab apple, however, is a native of North America. The crab-apple species tend to hybridize with each other and with wild apples and are therefore difficult to identify as individual species. Because they are very high in pectin, crab apples are often used in combination with low-pectin fruits to make jellies. Wild apple is also common throughout the area and can be used the same as crab apples. Horticultural varieties, called flowering crabs, are often planted as ornamentals. *Malus* is the Latin name for apple.

JUNEBERRY
(Serviceberry, Shadbush,
Saskatoon berry, Shadblow)

Amelanchier spp.
Rosaceae

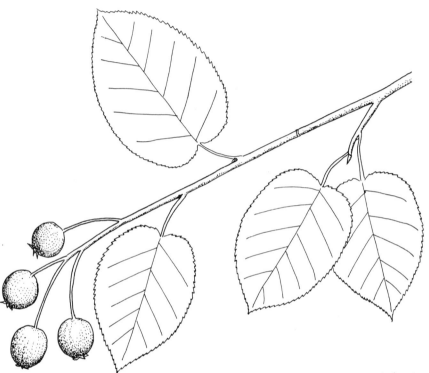

A. laevis

20–40'

Characteristics: Juneberries are deciduous trees or shrubs. Between species they vary in height from trees that are 30 feet tall to small shrubs that grow in dense colonies. Simple toothed leaves occur alternately on thornless branches. White flowers with five petals occur from March to June and usually before the leaves expand. The dark red to black fruit contains ten seeds. The end of each fruit has five toothlike projections that are the remains of the calyx. Some trees have a distinctive smooth gray bark with longitudinal black streaks.

Habitat: Varies with the species from moist woods, clearings, edges of woods, and swamps to dry, rocky slopes and sandy soils.

Distribution: Throughout the area.

188

Edible parts: Fruit.

Food uses: Raw fruit, jams, jellies, pies, wine, dried fruit, pemmican, sauce.

Precautions: Taste and juice content varies with the species and is influenced by the weather. Some fruits are sweet and juicy while others are dry and bland.

Preparation: Birds, small mammals, and bears also enjoy the fruits, so obtaining a sufficient amount may be a problem. The seeds are large and soft and add an almond flavor to the cooked fruit.

Recipes:

Juneberry Sauce

2 tablespoons cornstarch	2 cups Juneberries
¼ cup water	honey

Mix cornstarch and water in saucepan. Stir until cornstarch is dissolved. Add berries and enough water to cover. Simmer until berries are soft and liquid is thick. Add honey to taste.

Juneberry Pie

1 quart Juneberries	½ teaspoon cinnamon
½ cup raisins	¼ cup flour
1 piecrust shell and top crust	2 tablespoons lemon juice
½ cup sugar	¼ cup butter
1 teaspoon salt	

Mix Juneberries and raisins and place in pie shell. Mix sugar, salt, cinnamon, and flour and sprinkle over Juneberry-raisin mixture. Sprinkle with lemon juice and dot with butter. Cover with piecrust. Cut vents into piecrust. Brush melted butter on surface and lightly sprinkle with sugar. Bake for 45 minutes at 375° F or until done.

Remarks: This native of North America has been used for centuries by native North Americans. It was a major component of pemmican. The city of Saskatoon, Saskatchewan, is named after the corrupted Indian name for *A. alnifolia*, which grows abundantly in that region. The showy white trees that are observed in March and April in the leafless Pennsylvania forests are usually Juneberry. Fruits begin to ripen in June, which accounts for the name Juneberry. Other common names reflect the application of phenology. The name shadbush refers to the correlation of the flowering to the migration of shad. Serviceberry or sarvisberry shows the synchronous occurrence of the flowering of Juneberry and the appearance of the preacher to perform services in the spring after a winter absence. Another story attributed to the common name of serviceberry relates its resemblance to a pearlike English fruit called service. Although Juneberries are excellent edible wild plants, beating the birds to the ripe berries is a problem. Foraging robins make a tree appear to be boiling as they squabble for Juneberries. *Amelanchier* is derived from *amelancier,* which is a common provincial name for a French species.

WILD GRAPE

Vitis spp.
Vitaceae

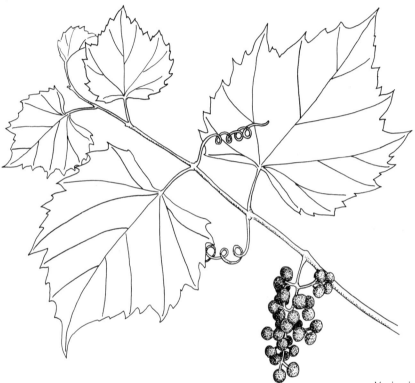

V. riparia

20–40′

Characteristics: Wild grapes are thornless, high-climbing vines with a dark stem and shredding bark. The alternate, deciduous, simple leaves are generally heart-shaped with teeth and lobes. A single tendril may be opposite the petiole. The small green flowers are arranged in a panicle and later develop into juicy berries. Each berry contains up to four ovoid seeds. Flowering occurs in May and June.
Habitat: Riverbanks, thickets, deciduous forests.
Distribution: Throughout the area.

Edible parts: Young leaves, fruit.

Food uses: Cooked vegetable, fruit, jelly, juice, wine, raisins, pie.

Precautions: May be confused with moonseed (*Menispermum canadense*), which is poisonous. The roots of grape are reported to be poisonous. Not all wild grapes are tasty.

Preparation: Collect the leaves in late spring or early summer and use the same as cabbage leaves. The fruit is collected in the early fall.

Recipes:

Stuffed Grape Leaves

2 cups onions (finely chopped)	1/3 cup olive oil
2 tablespoons parsley (minced)	2 tablespoons dill
1/4 cup chestnuts	1/4 cup currants
2 cups lamb (minced)	1 teaspoon pepper
1 teaspoon salt	20 fresh young grape leaves
2 eggs	2 cups chicken broth
2 cups cooked rice	

Combine all ingredients except grape leaves and chicken broth. Spread grape leaves and spoon 2 to 3 tablespoons of mixture on each leaf. Roll grape leaf and secure with toothpick. Be sure to tuck in ends. Arrange leaves in a casserole dish. Pour chicken broth over stuffed leaves. Bake at 250° F for 1 1/2 hours.

Grape Pie

5 cups grapes (washed)	1/4 teaspoon ground cinnamon
1/2 cup water	1/4 teaspoon salt
1 1/2 cups sugar	1 piecrust shell and top crust
2 tablespoons flour	3 tablespoons butter
1 egg (beaten)	2 tablespoons milk
1 tablespoon lemon juice	1 tablespoon sugar

Squeeze skins from grapes. Simmer the pulp in water until it begins to fall apart. Press pulp through sieve to remove seeds. Chop skins into small pieces. Combine chopped skins, strained pulp, sugar, flour, egg, lemon juice, cinnamon, and salt. Pour mixture into pie shell. Dot with butter. Add top crust and pinch edges together. Brush crust with milk; sprinkle with sugar. Bake at 425° F for 15 minutes. Then lower to 350° F and continue to bake for 35 minutes longer or until crust is golden.

Remarks: *Vitis* is the Latin name for vine. European or Old World grapes have been in cultivation for thousands of years. Columbus is said to have brought European grapevines to the New World. Early Spanish missionaries also brought many grapevines to America. About half of the world's grape species are native to the United States. Fox, red, Catawba, and Concord are well-known commercial American varieties. The purple-colored label stamped on meat products is made from grape skins. Grape-seed oil is used to make mayonnaise and potato chips. Many species of mammals and birds feed on the wild grape. Ruffed grouse and wild turkeys are especially fond of the fruits. Although not as large, more tart, and with larger seeds than cultivated grapes, wild grapes are as valuable to the modern forager as they were to the Indians and pioneers.

WHITE MULBERRY
RED MULBERRY

Morus alba L.
Morus rubra L.
Moraceae

20–40′

M. rubra

Characteristics: Mulberries are deciduous trees that grow to a height of 60 feet. The simple, alternate leaves have palmate venation. Leaves are toothed and may also be lobed. Unlobed leaves are somewhat heart-shaped. From 2 to 5 lobes may occur on the leaves. Twigs and petioles have a milky sap. The blackberrylike fruit may be reddish-black or white. Fruits are ripe in June and July.

Habitat: Rich, moist woods.

Distribution: Both are widely distributed throughout the region. Red mulberry is more common in the Ohio River drainage and white mulberry often escapes from cultivation and is more common east of the Appalachians.

192

Edible parts: Fruits.

Food uses: Raw fruit, pies, jelly, jam, breads, dried fruits.

Precautions: The white sap is reported to cause dermatitis in some individuals. Use only the ripe fruit.

Preparation: Mulberries can be dried and used as raisins. Dried white mulberries are especially popular for use in breads. Rather than working with the whole fruit, put them in a blender and use the pulp.

Recipes:

Mulberry Jelly

1 quart ripe mulberries	2 cups sugar
¼ cup water	1 package pectin
4 teaspoons lemon juice	

Remove stems from mulberries and wash in cold water. Mash the mulberries and squeeze through a jelly bag or several layers of cheesecloth. Save 2 cups of mulberrry juice. In a saucepan, combine mulberry juice, water, lemon juice, and sugar. Mix thoroughly. Bring to a full boil. Add pectin and stir constantly. Keep mixture at a hard boil for 1 minute. Skim off foam. Quickly ladle into hot, sterilized jars. Seal with paraffin.

Mulberry Pie

4 cups ripe mulberries	1 teaspoon cinnamon
2 tablespoons lemon juice	1 teaspoon nutmeg
1 cup sugar	1 piecrust shell and top crust
3 tablespoons tapioca	

Remove stems from mulberries. Wash berries in cold water and drain. Combine all ingredients. Pour filling into piecrust shell and cover with top crust. Seal edges and cut vents in top of crust. Bake at 325° F for 40 minutes or until golden brown.

Remarks: The white mulberry is a native of Asia. It provides the food for silkworm caterpillars. The British introduced the white mulberry to the colonies in an attempt to establish the silk industry, but the venture failed. Mulberry fruits are eaten by many species of birds and mammals. Two problems with collecting the fruits are competing with the birds and tedious picking. The fruits are not easily detached from the woody stem. In addition, the green fruit stalk will stay attached to the fruit. The word *rubra* means red and *alba* is white. *Morus* is the Latin name for mulberry.

SASSAFRAS
(Mitten tree)

Sassafras albidum (Nutt.) Nees
Lauraceae

20–40'

Characteristics: This small to medium-sized tree grows to 90 feet tall, but is normally from 10 to 50 feet in height. The young twigs are green. The alternate leaves vary from an entire, ovate leaf to two-lobed, three-lobed, and, rarely, five-lobed. Twigs, bark, and leaves have a spicy aroma. The fruit is dark blue on a red stem.
Habitat: Old fields, forest-field ecotones, roadsides, dry open woods.
Distribution: Throughout the area.

194

Edible parts: Leaves and roots.

Food uses: Tea, soup thickener, seasoning, jelly.

Precautions: Sassafras oil is 80 percent safrole, which at concentrations of 0.5 and 1 percent in the diet has induced liver cancer in rats. The carcinogenic property of sassafras prompted the FDA to remove the plant from the list of nonharmful medicinal plants. Oil of sassafras may be narcotic and addictive, and may cause dermatitis in some individuals.

Preparation: Wash the roots. Cut thin strips of bark off the roots. Dry the strips of bark in the oven, attic, or similar location. Leaves can be used fresh or dried.

Recipes:

Spicy Sassafras Tea

1 cup sassafras root bark	½ teaspoon allspice
3 quarts water	½ teaspoon cinnamon
½ teaspoon ground cloves	¼ teaspoon ginger

Simmer the sassafras root bark in water for 30 minutes. Strain and refrigerate. This is the stock solution. Each time that you want to make some sassafras tea, take 2 cups of stock solution and add 4 cups of water plus all of the spices listed above. Simmer for 10 minutes.

Sassafras Jelly

3 cups strong sassafras tea	½ teaspoon citric acid
1 package pectin	4 cups sugar

Add pectin to warm sassafras tea. Stir and add citric acid. Bring to a boil, stirring constantly. Add sugar. Stir and bring to a boil for 1 minute. Pour into hot, sterilized jars and seal with paraffin.

Remarks: Sassafras oil has been used to flavor a number of commercial products: candy, tobacco, root beer, perfumes, soap, lotion, and toothpaste. It is also used medicinally. Rural people still use sassafras tea as a spring tonic to "thin the blood" and remove impurities that have built up over the winter. To repel moths and ants, try sassafras twigs. In the South a fish gumbo is thickened with crushed, dried sassafras leaves. Look for right- and left-handed mitten leaves on the same tree. Trees are either male or female, so look for the blue fruits on female trees. Many scientific names are used as common names. Sassafras is a good example. Others are trillium, petunia, taxus, chrysanthemum, oxalis, amaranth, rhododendron, zinnia, begonia, cosmos, aster, ilex, dahlia, clematis, wisteria, verbena, and salvia. Sarsaparilla, birch, and sassafras roots were the major ingredients of root beer made in colonial days. An orange dye can be extracted from the bark.

PERSIMMON
(Wild fig, Winter plum)

Diospyros virginiana L.
Ebenaceae

40′+

Characteristics: A medium-sized tree that averages 30 to 50 feet tall, but may grow to 130 feet in height. The alternate, oval leaves have an entire margin. The very dark buds with two scales and the false terminal buds characterize the winter stem. The pith is sometimes chambered. Flowering occurs in May and June. The yellowish-brown oval fruit is a berry that matures in the fall. The dark bark is deeply divided into blocks.

Habitat: Mostly found in dry woodlands or at margins of fields and to a lesser extent in rich bottomlands.

Distribution: Mostly a southern tree that is rare within the area of Wisconsin glaciation.

Edible parts: Fruit.

Food uses: Fresh fruit, jams, jellies, pudding, pie, breads.

Precautions: The fruit is strongly astringent when green. The fruit flavor varies on different trees. Be careful of yellow jackets when collecting windfalls off the ground.

Preparation: Collect fruit only when mature. If in doubt about maturity, wait until after the first frost or until leaves begin to fall. Ripe fruits should be yellowish-brown on the outside, but very soft and orange on the inside. Use the strained fruit to make jams, jellies, pudding, and pies. The persimmon can also be used as a dried fruit.

Recipes:

Persimmon Pudding

½ stick butter	1 teaspoon salt
2½ cups persimmon pulp	2 cups sifted flour
1 cup milk	2 teaspoons baking soda
2 cups sugar	1 teaspoon nutmeg
1 cup dates	3 teaspoons rum (optional)
2 eggs	4 teaspoons cinnamon

Melt the butter. Except for the cinnamon, combine all ingredients. Mix at low speed. Butter a small cake pan and pour mixture into pan. Sprinkle cinnamon on top. Bake at 300°F for about one hour.

Persimmon-Walnut Bread

2 cups flour	¾ cup butter
1 teaspoon baking soda	2 eggs (beaten)
1 teaspoon cinnamon	1 cup persimmon pulp
1 teaspoon nutmeg	½ cup walnuts (chopped)
1 cup sugar	

Sift together flour, baking soda, cinnamon, and nutmeg in a bowl. In another large bowl combine sugar, butter, eggs, and persimmon and mix at slow speed. Add flour mixture and continue mixing at slow speed. Add nuts and continue mixing. Grease two bread pans. Place half of batter in each pan. Bake at 325° F for 60 minutes.

Remarks: Ebenaceae or ebony family refers to the dark wood characteristic of members of this family. Most of the commercial ebony wood comes fron *Diospyros*. Golf-club heads and textile-industry shuttles are made from the wood of the common persimmon and attest to its hardness. The word *Diospyros* comes from the Greek *dios* meaning divine and *pyros* for wheat. It has been literally interpreted to mean "celestial food," "fruit of Zeus," or "bread of the gods." *Virginiana* means that the "bread of the gods" came from Virginia. Technically the persimmon fruit is a berry—the largest berry produced by an American forest tree. The word persimmon is of Indian origin and means "dried fruit." Female trees have flowers that have non-functional stamens.

BUTTERNUT
(White walnut)

Juglans cinerea L.
Juglandaceae

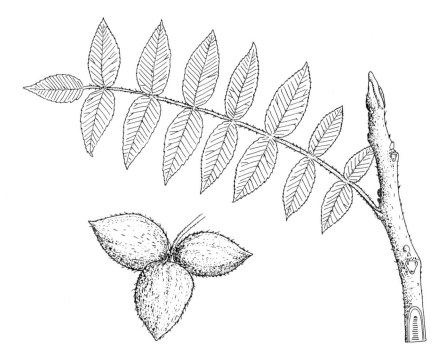

40'+

Characteristics: A medium-sized deciduous tree that can grow to 90 feet, but is usually from 50 to 70 feet tall. The pinnately compound leaves are arranged alternately and are composed of eleven to seventeen sticky, toothed leaflets. The terminal leaflet is usually present. The chambered pith is dark brown. Fruits are hairy, sticky, and about twice as long as thick. A thick fleshy husk surrounds the indehiscent fruit. Each fruit contains a two-parted nut that has a grooved, jagged shell.

Habitat: Rich, moist soils; often found along fencerows, edges of deciduous woods, small open woodlots.

Distribution: Generally throughout the area, but not along the Atlantic coast.

Edible parts: Nuts, sap, fruit.

Food uses: Nuts, flour, candy, oil, sugar, syrup, pickles, vinegar.

Precautions: The hands can be stained while handling the fruits. Some individuals are squeamish about the sticky, hairy fruit. Nuts are difficult to open and require a hammer.

Preparation: Collect fruits in September as they fall to the ground. Let fruit dry before removing the husk. Nuts should be dried for several weeks before cracking. Collect green, immature butternuts in early summer, when a needle will penetrate the husk, for use in pickling. Sap is obtained in the same manner as for maples and made into syrup or sugar or fermented into vinegar. To obtain oil or nut butter, smash the nuts and boil in water. Oil will float on the surface and can be skimmed off. Nut meats will also float to the surface, where they can be collected, dried, and ground into flour.

Recipes:

Butternut Pancakes

1 cup pancake flour	1 egg (beaten)
1 cup buttermilk	2 tablespoons soft butter
1 teaspoon sugar	1 cup butternuts (chopped)
¼ teaspoon salt	

Combine flour and buttermilk. Add other ingredients to mixture and blend thoroughly. Let mixture sit for 10 minutes. Blend mixture again and add more milk to get desired consistency. Cook in heavy skillet until golden brown.

Butternut-Maple Syrup

4 tablespoons butter	1 cup maple syrup
½ cup butternuts (chopped)	

Heat butter in small saucepan over low heat. Add butternuts and cook for 1 minute. Stir constantly. Add maple syrup and heat for 2 minutes. Serve with butternut pancakes.

Remarks: The black walnut will live to 250 years, but the white walnut only lives for about 75 years since it is often the victim of fungal attacks. The wood is used to make furniture and cabinets, but does not have the commercial value of black walnut. A tan dye is made from the husks and bark. During the American Civil War many confederate uniforms were dyed at home with butternut hulls. The color of the uniform and the soldiers were called "butternuts." The *cinerea* part of the scientific name means ashy gray and probably refers to the bark of the mature tree. *Juglans* is thought to be derived from the Latin *Jovis glans* or the nut of Jupiter.

BLACK BIRCH
(Cherry birch, Sweet birch)
YELLOW BIRCH

Betula lenta L.
Betula alleghaniensis Britt.
Betulaceae

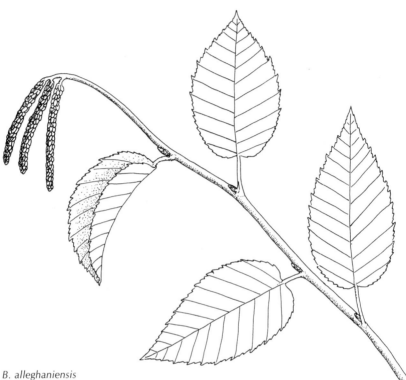

B. alleghaniensis

Characteristics: These are deciduous trees with the yellow birch reaching 90 feet tall and the black birch slightly less. The bark and leaves have the smell of wintergreen. The oval leaves have fine teeth and straight veins. Prominent lenticels occur on the young bark. Bark on older trees separates into thin layers and gives a shaggy appearance to the trunk. Flowers are catkins and the fruit is winged. Yellow birch has yellow bark and black birch has black bark.

40'+

Habitat: Black birch occurs on rich upland forested areas. Yellow birch is found in moist woodlands and along streams and swamps. Yellow birch is often associated with hemlock.

Distribution: Yellow birch is a dominant tree of the hemlock-hardwood forests of New York and Pennsylvania. Outside of the area it is infrequent, but does occur in central Ohio. Black birch is found in the same general geographic area, but extends southward to Alabama.

200

Edible parts: Sap, inner bark, twigs, leaves.

Food uses: Sugar, syrup, flour, tea, beer.

Precautions: These two species are the only edible birches.

Preparation: Collect the inner bark and sap in early spring. The sap can be boiled until a molasses-flavored syrup remains. The inner bark can be eaten raw or dried at room temperature and then boiled like noodles, ground into flour, or used for tea. Steep fresh or dried inner bark, twigs, or leaves to make tea.

Recipes:

Birch Beer

4 gallons birch sap	4 quarts fine birch twigs (cleaned)
1 gallon honey	1 cake yeast

Boil sap and honey for 15 minutes. Pour over fine twigs in a crock. Cool, strain to remove twigs. Add yeast. Pour back into crock. Cover and ferment for 1 week or until cloudiness settles. Bottle and cap tightly.

Birch Syrup

In late winter or early spring, bore a half-inch-diameter hole two to three inches into the tree trunk. Insert a spile into the hole and hang a container on the spile to collect the sap. It takes forty-five to fifty gallons of sap to get one gallon of syrup. Slowly boil the sap until a molasseslike syrup remains.

Remarks: The oil of wintergreen that is used in medicines, soft drinks, and household products was originally obtained from the twigs and bark of black birch. Today the commercial oil of wintergreen is usually made synthetically. The bark of yellow birch makes a good tinder for starting a campfire and will even burn when wet. Indians and frontiersmen are reported to have made bread from the flour made from the inner bark. The syrup is used as a sugar substitute. Black birch is not a good common name for *B. lenta* because it may be confused with river birch (*B. nigra*), whose specific name, *nigra*, means black. In construction, birch wood is used for doors, paneling, and interior finishes. The next time you make tea, substitute a handful of young birch twigs for the tea bags.

SUGAR MAPLE
(Hard maple, Rock maple)

Acer saccharum Marsh.
Aceraceae

40'+

Characteristics: Sugar maples are deciduous trees that usually grow from 50 to 90 feet tall. The simple, opposite leaves are about as wide as long, with five-toothed lobes and palmate venation. The sinuses between the upper lobes are U-shaped. The dry fruit is winged. No milky sap is present.
Habitat: Rich, moist, but well-drained forests.
Distribution: Throughout the area.

Edible parts: Sap.

Food uses: Syrup, sugar, vinegar.

Precautions: Strain the sap to remove debris. To avoid contamination, clean tubing and spiles.

Preparation: Bore a ½-inch hole, 3 inches deep, into the tree trunk. Slant hole slightly upwards. Insert commercial or homemade spile into hole. Hang pail from spile. Average-sized trees can take two or three spiles. A mild vinegar can be made from the fermented sap.

Recipes:

Maple Syrup

About 45 gallons of sap are needed to produce one gallon of syrup. It is best to boil the sap outdoors because a lot of steam is produced and things get quite sticky. Have a large supply of hardwood available for firewood. Place sap in the largest available pot. Boil slowly. As sap thickens, continually stir until desired consistency is reached for syrup. Filter syrup and store in sterilized jars. Commercial production of maple syrup involves a careful observation of temperatures, but this general description will enable you to obtain a worthwhile product.

Maple Sugar

Boil maple syrup in a saucepan. Keep stirring until the syrup is about the consistency of thick molasses. Cool. While still warm, pour the thick liquid on waxed paper and allow to harden.

Remarks: Tapping maple trees is a technique that the Indians taught the early colonists. Except for Norway maple, all maples can be tapped for their sap. Other trees, such as hickory, black walnut, and the birches, can also be tapped. Sugar maple, however, yields the greatest amount of sap and produces the best-flavored syrup.

Trees can be tapped from late January until the buds swell in April. The best time to collect sap is during the "Sap Moon" in March. Warm days and freezing nights cause the greatest amount of sap flow. Except for the labor involved in chopping firewood, the major problem with maple-syrup production is time. To reduce the time involved in the project, some individuals freeze the sap. The sugar is concentrated in the center bottom of the ice block. Thawing the outside of the block of ice and discarding the water leaves a more concentrated sugar solution. Continued thawing and freezing can concentrate the sugar further.

Sugar maple is a valuable lumber tree. It is also planted in cities as a shade tree. The name *saccharum* refers to the sugar present in the sap. The winged fruits are technically called samaras, but common names include fly-aways, airplanes, and keys. The samaras are also reported to be edible. The sugar-maple leaf is the emblem of Canada. In Nova Scotia, maple coffee is made by combining ¾ cup strong coffee, ¼ cup maple syrup, and a dash of whiskey, then topping with whipped cream.

OAKS

Quercus spp.
Fagaceae

Q. alba

Characteristics: In general the oaks in this region are tall deciduous trees with a star-shaped pith, multiple terminal buds, and a fruit that is commonly called an acorn. The leaves are alternate, but the margins vary from lobed, toothed, and lobed with bristle tips to entire. The white oak group has lobes while most of the red oak group has bristle tips. White oaks are usually from 60 to 80 feet tall but may reach heights of 150 feet.

Habitat: The white oaks occur in well-drained upland soils of mature deciduous forests.

Distribution: Found throughout the area.

40'+

Edible parts: Acorns.

Food uses: Flour, candy, coffee, nuts.

Precautions: Many cases of livestock poisoning have been reported as a result of the consumption of acorns from the red-oak group or immature acorns.

Preparation: Although white-oak acorns are considered to be sweet acorns and can be eaten raw in small quantities, all acorns contain various amounts of tannin, which makes them bitter. The red-oak group contains a great deal of tannin. Leach the tannin from the acorns before using by removing the shells and boiling the nutmeats in several changes of water until no further brown coloration occurs. Dry the nutmeats and grind into a flour or chop into pieces. The flour will be a brown color.

Recipes:

Acorn Cookies

½ cup butter	¼ teaspoon almond extract
½ cup maple syrup	½ cup acorn flour
½ teaspoon vanilla extract	1½ cups all-purpose flour
2 eggs (beaten)	1 teaspoon baking powder

Melt butter and combine with maple syrup. Add vanilla, eggs, and almond extract. Beat all. Add flours and baking powder. Mix gently to make a stiff dough. Add more flour if necessary. Drop by spoonfuls onto greased cookie sheets. Bake 15 minutes at 350° F or until light brown.

Acorn Coffee

Leach and dry acorn nutmeats. Place on a cookie sheet and roast at 300° F until very dark brown and hard. This will take from thirty to forty-five minutes. Cool roasted nutmeats and grind. Use 1 tablespoon of ground acorns for each cup of brewed coffee. Use percolator or boil grounds in water for 15 minutes and strain. Add milk, cream, or sugar if desired. A sprinkle of cinnamon also adds an interesting flavor.

Remarks: Of all the oaks found throughout the region, white oak is the best choice for an edible. It is very common and has a relatively sweet acorn. Burr oak has a sweeter acorn, but is not as common in this region. Acorn flour was a staple for many Indian tribes. Indians leached the bitter tannin by putting the acorns in a cloth or basket and soaking them in a stream for several days or by mixing the acorns with wood ash and burying them for several months.

Oaks are valuable lumber trees and provide about half the hardwood lumber in the United States. White oak is used to make barrels. Three-hundred-year-old white oaks are not uncommon. These are valuable trees for food and shelter for many species of wildlife. Several delicious fungi are typically associated with oaks. Look for sheepshead, boletes, and the yellow honey mushroom under these trees. Medicinal values include a bark decoction for diarrhea and the inner bark for pyorrhea. Tannin has been associated with malignancies of the sinuses of woodworkers and people who work with leather cured with tannin. The oak has long been considered a symbol of strength and is celebrated in legend and mythology. In southern France, pigs are fattened on acorns.

BLACK CHERRY
(Wild cherry)

Prunus serotina Ehrh.
Rosaceae

40'+

Characteristics: A deciduous tree that grows from 60 to 80 feet tall. The young bark has prominent raised, circular lenticels that later become transverse lines. The simple, lance-shaped leaves are finely toothed and arranged alternately. The white flowers are arranged in a raceme. The fruit is a one-seeded drupe that is dark purple or black when mature. One or two pairs of glandular dots occur on the upper part of the petiole near the base of the leaf blade. The inner bark has an almond smell.
Habitat: Mixed hardwood woodlands. Abundant as a weed tree in wasteland.
Distribution: Common throughout the area.

Edible parts: Fruit.

Food uses: Fresh fruit, jelly, jam, pies, wine, cold drink.

Precautions: May be confused with chokeberry. Wilted leaves and fruit pits contain the poisonous hydrocyanic acid.

Preparation: Pick cherries in August and September when the fruits are fully ripe. Rinse in cold water and pit the cherries.

Recipes:

Cherryade

4 cups black cherries (pitted)
8 cups water
½ cup lemon juice
2 cups sugar

1 teaspoon cinnamon
2 teaspoons ground ginger
10 spearmint leaves

Put cherries in a large saucepan, cover with water, and bring to a boil. Stir constantly. Simmer for 20 minutes. Set aside. In another saucepan combine water, lemon juice, sugar, cinnamon, and ginger. Bring to a boil. Strain cherry solution to remove cherry pulp. Combine strained cherry solution and spiced solution. Add more sugar if necessary. Chill and add spearmint leaves.

Cherries Jubilee

4 cups cherries (pitted)
1 cup boiling water
sugar

cornstarch
vanilla ice cream
½ cup warmed brandy

Slowly cook cherries in boiling water until tender. Add sugar a little at a time until sweetened. Strain and keep juices. Set cherries aside. For each cup of juice, add another tablespoon of sugar and a tablespoon of cornstarch. Stir constantly until mixture is clear and thickened. Add 2 cups of cooked cherries. Place cherry mixture on vanilla ice cream and top with brandy. Serve flaming.

Remarks: Early lumbermen denuded the hemlock-hardwood forests of its stands of hemlock and white pine. As the forests regenerated, hardwoods replaced the conifers. Black cherry was one of the dominant hardwood species to occupy these sites. Today black cherry is a valuable lumber species in areas formerly dominated by the hemlock-hardwood forests. The best logs sell for $800–$900 and are usually used for veneer. This strong, close-grained, beautiful wood is also valuable for furniture. *Serotina* refers to late summer and probably describes the time of fruit ripening. Domestic stock have been poisoned by eating wilted leaves. Convulsions and paralysis can cause death within one hour. Pin cherry (*P. pensylvanica*) and chokecherry (*P. virginiana*) also have edible fruits. Indians often used dried chokecherries in pemmican. Dried cherries and the inner bark are used to make a tea to treat coughs.

BLACK WALNUT
(American walnut)

Juglans nigra L.
Juglandaceae

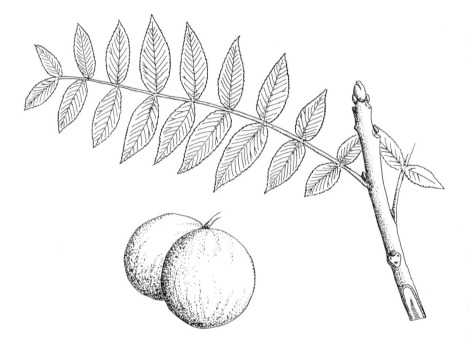

40'+

Characteristics: Black walnut is a deciduous tree that grows to 120 feet tall, but usually ranges from 70 to 100 feet in height. The pinnately compound leaves have an alternate arrangement. The leaves are composed of 15 to 23 leaflets that are hairy on the undersurface. The terminal leaflet is usually missing or very small. A longitudinal section of the stem shows a light-brown chambered pith. The spherical, indehiscent fruit has a thick fleshy husk covering a two-parted seed that is deeply grooved.
Habitat: Rich, moist soil such as lowlands and river bottoms. Once common in deciduous forests.
Distribution: Generally found throughout the area.

Edible parts: Fruit, nuts, sap.

Food uses: Nuts, flour, candy, oil, sugar, syrup, vinegar.

Precautions: A strong dye is found in the husks, so gloves are in order when handling the fruits. The nuts are difficult to crack and require the use of a hammer and a nut pick. Chemicals in the plant have been reported to have mitogen properties.

Preparation: Collect in September as the fruits fall from the tree. Allow the fruits to dry first, then remove the husks. Let the nuts dry for several weeks before cracking and removing nutmeats. Nuts can be eaten raw or added to breads and cookies. Sap can be obtained as with maples and made into syrup, candy, or sugar. The nuts are dried and ground into flour. Oil is obtained from the nuts.

Recipes:

Walnut Bread

2 cups flour (sifted)	1 cup sugar
1 teaspoon baking soda	½ cup soft butter
½ teaspoon salt	1 teaspoon lemon juice
2 eggs (beaten)	1 cup walnuts (chopped)
⅓ cup milk	

Sift flour, baking soda, and salt together. Combine eggs, milk, sugar, butter, and lemon juice. Blend thoroughly. Add dry ingredients to liquid mixture. Blend and stir in walnuts. Grease a bread pan. Pour in batter. Bake at 350° F for 1 hour or until light brown.

Walnut-Honey Balls

2 cups dates	1 tablespoon lemon juice
2 cups black walnuts	1 tablespoon rum or brandy
¼ cup honey	

Chop dates and nuts separately in food chopper. Mix together dates and half of the nuts. Moisten the mixture with honey, lemon juice, and rum or brandy. Form into small balls and roll them in the remainder of the chopped nuts.

Remarks: Black walnut is a commercially valuable wood that is used in making veneers, furniture, and gunstocks. A quality tree is worth at least $5,000. An Ohio tree was reportedly sold for $35,000. For that reason, making veneer is the best way to get maximum use from a walnut log. The chemical juglone is a natural herbicide produced by the tree and accounts for the death of tomatoes and other crops planted nearby. A rich brown dye can be extracted from the bark and fruit husks. A common winter activity of pioneers was to sit around the fireplace at night cracking walnuts and removing the nutmeats. At one time the crushed nut husks were used to poison fish to be used for food. Trappers dye their traps by boiling them in a walnut husk solution.

SHAGBARK HICKORY
(Shellbark)

Carya ovata (Mill.) K. Koch.
Juglandaceae

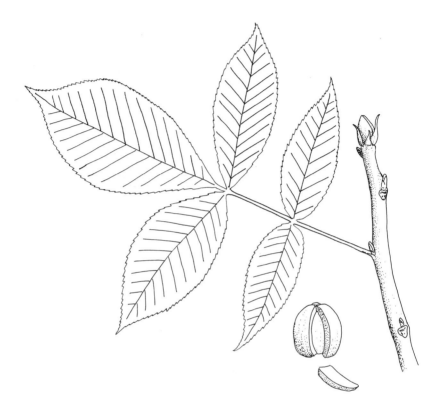

40′+

Characteristics: Hickories are deciduous trees with straight trunks and spreading crowns. Their average height is between 60 and 90 feet. Young bark is smooth and gray, but later splits into long strips that give the trunk a shaggy appearance. The pinnately compound leaves are alternate and composed of five to seven leaflets. The lower two leaflets are smaller and the terminal leaflet is the largest. Tufts of hair occur on the leaflet teeth. The fruit is nearly round and contains a single nut that is four-ridged and sharply pointed at one end. The fruit husk splits into four parts when ripe.
Habitat: River bottoms to upland forested slopes; moist rich woodlands.
Distribution: Throughout the area.

Edible parts: Nuts, sap.

Food uses: Raw nuts, desserts, confections, oil, flour, syrup.

Precautions: Cracking the hard-shelled nut requires the use of a hammer, stone, or vise.

Preparation: Collect nuts after they have fallen, which is usually at leaf fall or later. Air-dry nuts for 3 weeks for easier removal. Sap can be collected and made into syrup as with maples. Nuts can be eaten raw or used in any desserts or confections calling for nuts. Oil and flour are made from the nuts.

Recipes:

Hickory Christmas Balls

2 cups hickory nuts	¼ cup honey
2 cups dates	2 tablespoons rum

Put nuts and dates separately through food chopper or blender. Mix together chopped dates and half of the nuts. Add the honey and rum to this mixture. Stir well and form into small balls. Roll balls in remainder of chopped nuts. Chill in refrigerator and serve cold.

Hickory Cookie Balls

1½ cups butter	¼ cup honey
½ cup brown sugar	½ teaspoon baking powder
½ teaspoon salt	1 tablespoon vanilla
2 cups hickory nuts (finely chopped)	2 cups flour
2 cups dates (chopped)	½ cup confectioner's sugar

Cream butter. Add brown sugar and salt and cream until fluffy. Blend in hickory nuts, dates, honey, baking powder, and vanilla. Gradually mix in flour. Form balls of mixture the size of golf balls. Place on ungreased cookie sheet. Bake at 325° F for 15 minutes. Roll in confectioner's sugar.

Remarks: All hickory nuts are edible, but some, such as bitternuts and to a certain extent pignuts, are bitter. Shagbark, mockernut, and pecan are the most important species for edibility. Shagbark and pecans are available commercially. Shagbark wood is strong and heavy. It is used for tool handles, baseball bats, bows, skis, and golf clubs. Pioneers used hickory wood to make yokes, wheel spokes, gunstocks, baskets, handles, and barrel hoops.

Hickory is excellent for firewood because it produces a great amount of heat. A high grade of charcoal can be made from the wood. Hickory-smoked ham, bacon, fish, and fowl are very popular. The pollen from the wind-pollinated hickories is included with the elms, oaks, and box elders as producing the most troublesome spring hay fever allergens. Crushed green nut husks have been used as a fish poison. *Carya* is the Greek name for walnut. The large leaf scars and terminal buds of the winter twigs make this species a valuable teaching tool when instructing students on twig characteristics.

AMERICAN BEECH
(White Beech)

Fagus grandifolia Ehrh.
Fagaceae

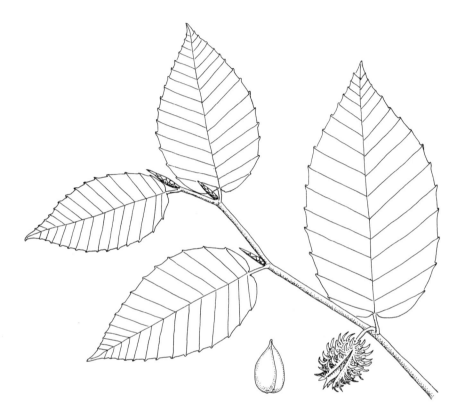

40'+

Characteristics: Sharply pointed, inch-long, slender buds characterize this 50- to 90-foot tree. The simple, ovate leaves are arranged alternately. Straight veins run to each tooth. The bark is smooth and light gray to bluish-gray. Two three-angled nuts are found in burred pods in September and October. Catkins appear in April and May.
Habitat: Mixed deciduous forests with rich, moist soils.
Distribution: Although uncommon along the coast, it is abundant in the Appalachians, especially in the western portion, and extends through Ohio.

212

Edible parts: Nuts.
Food uses: Flour, oil, coffee, nibble.
Precautions: Collect in September or October after the first hard frost.
Preparation: Separate burrs from nuts. Spread nuts in an open, warm area to dry. Remove nutmeats. Dry nutmeats and grind flour. Oil can be obtained by boiling crushed nutmeats and skimming off the oil. For a coffee substitute, grind the roasted nutmeats. Nutmeats can be eaten raw as a nibble.
Recipes:

Oatmeal-Beechnut Pie

½ cup beechnuts	½ cup shredded coconut
3 eggs	1 cup dark corn syrup
¾ cup quick oatmeal	¾ cup sugar
½ cup melted margarine	9-inch unbaked pie shell

Finely chop the beechnuts. Beat the eggs. Combine all ingredients. Pour ingredients into unbaked pie shell. Bake at 350° F for 45 minutes.

Beechnut Muffins

1 cup beechnut flour	2 eggs (slightly beaten)
1 cup cornmeal	1½ cups milk
1 cup flour	2 tablespoons melted margarine
3 teaspoons baking powder	½ cup beechnuts (chopped)
1 teaspoon garlic salt	

Sift together beechnut flour, cornmeal, flour, baking powder, and garlic salt. Beat eggs and milk together and stir in margarine. Add liquid to dry ingredients. Mix in chopped nuts. Pour into greased muffin pans and bake 20 minutes at 375° F.

Remarks: The flour made from the nutmeats was once a staple food of many American Indian tribes. Passenger pigeons relied to a large extent on beechnuts for food. Turkeys, wood ducks, squirrels, bears, grouse, and many other animals eat beechnuts. Old beech trees provide valuable dens for a number of mammal and bird species. American beech is often planted as an ornamental for its shade and strikingly beautiful trunk. Its smooth gray bark is quite distinctive but often vandalized by love-smitten teenagers or individuals who want to be sure that everyone knows that they were there. Beech is not highly valued as lumber because the wood shrinks considerably during drying and also has low resistance to decay. The wood, however, is used for railway ties, handles, flooring, and barrel staves. *Grandifolia* means large leaves.

EASTERN HEMLOCK

Tsuga canadensis (L.) Carr.
Pinaceae

40' +

Characteristics: Hemlocks are coniferous evergreen trees with a pyramid shape and a straight trunk. The tree averages between 70 and 90 feet tall. An Ohio tree has been reported to be 149 feet tall. The blunt, flattened single leaves have two white lines beneath. The leaves appear to be two-ranked, which gives the branches the appearance of flat sprays. The leaves are less than one inch long and grow on a stalk. The cones are slightly longer than one inch.

Habitat: Upland and rocky ridges, scattered through deciduous forests, and common in deep gorges.

Distribution: Found from Canada to Georgia and westward to the Allegheny Plateau sections of Ohio.

214

Edible parts: Leaves, inner bark of the young twigs.

Food uses: Tea, nibble.

Precautions: Although some reportedly enjoy hemlock tea and the inner bark, consider this a survival food. Hemlock seedlings are often confused with the poisonous yew (*Taxus*).

Preparation: Use young, bright green leaves that occur in the spring. The inner bark can be eaten raw as a nibble or boiled.

Recipes:

Hemlock Tea

Place 1 tablespoon of fresh needles in a cup. Pour boiling water over the needles and let steep for 5 to 7 minutes. Strain. Add honey or sugar to taste.

Inner Bark Nibble

Peel the bark from this year's growth. Separate the dark, outer bark from the light, green inner bark. Eat the inner bark raw as a nibble.

Remarks: Although many scientific names are Latin or Latinized, some are from other languages. *Tsuga* is the Japanese common name for the native hemlock of Japan. Entire hemlock forests were destroyed and the wood discarded to obtain the inner bark for tanning leather. The wood is not highly valued for lumber. Because the needles drop quickly as the cut tree dries, hemlock makes a poor Christmas tree. Hemlock is the state tree of Pennsylvania. This is not the same species, nor is it closely related to the poison hemlock that killed Socrates. Poison hemlock is classified in the parsley family and therefore related to wild carrot (Queen Anne's lace), which it closely resembles.

Some American Indian tribes made a tea from the inner bark to treat colds and pain. The plant is high in vitamin C. The inner bark of the tree trunk can also be eaten, but collecting it may result in the death of the tree. Removing the inner bark from around a tree trunk is called girdling. This destroys the cambium layer which produces the vascular tissue that transports food and water. Rabbits, porcupines, and elk girdle trees when they eat the bark. To avoid root or stump sprouts from a tree that is to be removed, girdle the tree several years before cutting it down. Lumberjack tea is made by using the young needles of either hemlock or white pine.

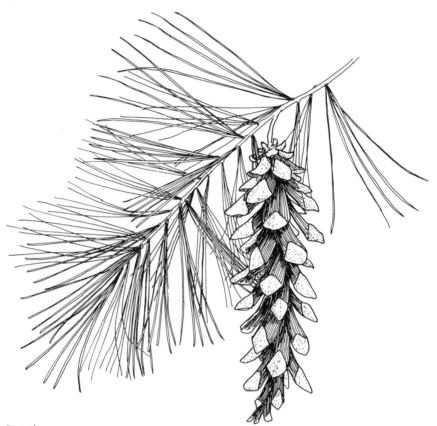

P. strobus

40'+

Characteristics: Evergreen trees or shrubs that produce male and female cones. The male cones occur in clumps in the spring and fall off after shedding their pollen. The female cones become woody and persist on the tree for two to three years until mature. The leaves are reduced to needles that appear in bundles of two to five on very short, dwarf branches.

Habitat: Variety of habitats from dry, sandy soils to swamps.

Distribution: Throughout the area.

Edible parts: Inner bark, young needles.

Food uses: Tea, candy, flour, nibble.

Precautions: Meals prepared with pine have a definite piney flavor and odor which for some make pine dishes more of a survival food item than a delicacy. Do not confuse pines with yews (*Taxus*), which are poisonous.

Preparation: The young needles make a better tea than the older needles. The inner bark from the young shoots can be eaten raw as a nibble. The inner bark from the trunk can be used for candy or flour. Only use small portions of the tree bark and never girdle the tree.

Recipes:

White Pine Tea

1 cup water for each cup of tea   honey to taste
1 tablespoon pine needles for each cup of tea

Boil water in kettle. Place pine needles in hot teapot. Cover needles with boiling water. Let steep for 10 minutes. Strain. For a more intense flavor, chop the needles and place in a tea ball before convering with boiling water.

White Pine Bark Candy

2 cups inner white pine bark   1 cup honey
2 cups water

Boil the inner bark in a mixture of water and honey until the bark is pliable. Cool and use as a gum-type candy.

Remarks: White-pine needles are rich in vitamins A and C and were used by Indians and pioneers to prevent scurvy. Other species of the Pinaceae (fir, spruce, pine, hemlock, and larch) are apparently edible in the same manner as that described for pines.

In the 1600s Great Britain had trouble finding suitable mast wood for its sailing vessels. The white pines (*P. strobus*) of the New World provided a source of light, strong masts. At that time the white pine was called the Weymouth pine after the British Navy captain who first brought it to England from the New World. Crown lands were established and choice trees marked with the King's Broad Arrow. The rebellious colonists burned and destroyed these trees as the Revolutionary War approached. The single figure on the first American flag was the white pine.

In Scotland each clan had a screeching tree, where family members could privately express their feelings. The screeching trees were Scot's pines (*P. sylvestris*). White-pine bark is used in cough remedies. The chemical pinene is found in pines and can cause a contact dermatitis. Pine nuts from the pinon pine are sold commercially. *Pinus* is the Latin name for pine and *strobus* refers to the cones.

Nutrient Composition of Selected Edible Plants
(per 100 grams)

Plant	Energy (C)	Protein (g)	Fat (g)	Total Carbohydrate (g)	Calcium (mg)	Phosphorus (mg)	Iron (mg)	Vit.A (IU)	Thiamine (mg)	Riboflavin (mg)	Niacin (mg)	Vit.C (mg)
Amaranth (raw)	36	3.5	.5	6.5	267	67	3.9	6,100	.08	.16	1.4	80
Asparagus (raw spears)	26	2.5	.2	5.0	22	62	1.0	900	.18	.20	1.5	33
Beans (snap raw)	32	1.9	.2	7.1	56	44	.8	600	.08	.11	.5	19
Beets (raw)	43	1.6	.1	9.9	16	33	.7	20	.03	.05	.4	10
Blackberries (raw)	58	1.2	.9	12.9	32	19	.9	200	.03	.04	.4	21
Blueberries (raw)	62	.7	.5	15.3	15	13	1.0	100	(.03)	(.06)	(.5)	14
Cabbage (raw)	24	1.3	.2	5.4	49	29	.4	130	.05	.05	.3	47
Carrots (raw)	42	1.1	.2	9.7	37	36	.7	11,000	.06	.05	.6	8
Chicory (raw, green)	20	1.8	.3	3.8	86	40	.9	4,000	.06	.10	.5	22
Corn, sweet (raw)	96	3.5	1.0	22.1	3	111	.7	400	.15	.12	1.7	12
Cranberries (raw)	46	.4	.7	10.8	14	10	.5	40	.03	.02	.1	11
Dock (raw) curly or nar-rowleaf dock, broadleaf dock, and sheep sorrel	28	2.1	.3	5.6	66	41	1.6	12,900	.09	.22	.5	119
Elderberries (raw)	72	2.6	(.5)	16.4	38	28	1.6	600	.07	.06	.5	36
Gooseberries (raw)	39	.8	.2	9.7	18	15	0.5	290	—	—	—	33

Grapes (raw)	69	1.3	1.0	15.7	16	12	.4	100	(.05)	(.03)	(.3)	4
Hickory nuts	673	13.2	68.7	12.8	trace	360	2.4	—	—	—	—	—
Jerusalem artichoke (raw)	7	2.3	.1	16.7	14	78	3.4	20	.20	.06	1.3	4
Lamb's-quarters (raw)	43	4.2	.8	7.3	309	72	1.2	11,600	.16	.44	1.2	80
Leeks, bulb & lower leaf (raw)	52	2.2	.3	11.2	52	50	1.1	40	.11	.06	.5	17
Lettuce, Iceberg (raw)	13	.9	.1	2.9	20	22	.5	330	.06	.06	.3	6
Peas (raw, mature seeds)	340	24.1	1.3	60.3	64	340	5.1	120	.74	.29	3	—
Persimmons (raw)	127	.8	.4	33.5	27	26	2.5	—	—	—	—	66
Poke, shoots (raw)	23	2.6	.4	3.7	53	44	1.7	8,700	.08	.33	1.2	136
Potatoes (raw)	76	2.1	.1	17.1	7	53	.6	trace	.10	.04	1.5	20
Purslane, leaves & stems (raw)	21	1.7	.4	3.8	103	39	3.5	2,500	.03	.10	.5	25
Raspberries, red	57	1.2	.5	13.6	22	22	.9	130	.03	.09	.9	25
Spinach (raw)	26	3.2	.3	4.3	93	51	3.1	8,100	.10	.20	.6	51
Strawberries (raw)	37	.7	.5	8.4	21	21	1.0	60	.03	.07	.6	59
Sunflower seed kernels (dry)	560	24.0	47.3	19.9	120	837	7.1	50	1.96	.23	5.4	—
Walnuts, black	628	20.5	59.3	14.8	trace	570	6	300	.22	.11	.7	—
Watercress (raw leaves and stems)	19	2.2	.3	3.0	151	54	1.7	4,900	.08	.16	.9	79

Note: Numbers in parentheses denote imputed values. Dashes denote lack of reliable data for a constituent believed to be present in a measurable amount.
Source: B. K. Watt and A. L. Merrill, 1963. Composition of Foods. Agricultural Handbook No. 8, USDA.

TOXIC LOOK-ALIKES

Butterfly Weed (*Asclepias tuberosa* L.) is a milkweed that does not produce a milky sap. This hairy, herbaceous perennial grows to 30 inches tall. It has opposite and/or alternate, lanceolate, simple leaves. The flowers are usually orange-red in color. The fruit is an egg-shaped, pointed follicle that is held erect. The flattened seeds are tipped with silky hairs.

Daffodil (*Narcissus pseudonarcissus* L.) is an herbaceous perennial that has linear, basal, nearly erect leaves with parallel venation. The 10–20-inch plant grows from a bulb. The single flower occurs at the end of a long peduncle. A yellow tubular crown grows above the three yellow petals and three yellow sepals.

Death Camas (*Zigadenus venenosus* S. Wats.) is a 1–2 foot perennial herb that grows from a bulb. The narrowly linear, grasslike leaves occur at the base and lower part of the stem. The numerous whitish flowers occur on the end of an upright, unbranched flower stalk. The fruit is a capsule with three chambers.

Dogbane (*Apocynum androsaemifolium* L.) and Indian Hemp (*A. cannabinum* L.) are perennial herbs that grow from a rhizome. Indian hemp grows to 5 feet and is shrublike while dogbane is shorter at 1–2 feet. The opposite, simple leaves are entire. The regular flowers are white (Indian hemp) or pink (dogbane). The follicle bears many seeds that are tipped with silky hairs. The long, thin fruits occur in pairs. All parts of the plants are milky. The plants grow in fields, roadsides, and forest margins.

False Hellebore (*Veratrum viride* Ait.) is a perennial herb that grows from a short rhizome. The coarse, unbranched plant varies from 3 to 6 feet tall. The large alternate, three-ranked leaves appear to be pleated. A panicle of nonshowy, greenish flowers terminates the flower stalk of those few plants that do flower. False hellebore usually occurs in wet areas as a rather large colony.

Iris (*Iris* spp.), which is also known as flag, includes a variety of cultivated and native species. The habitat of these perennial herbs may vary from the flower garden to open woods to wetlands. The sepals and petals are not easily distinguishable, but the outer three are nearly horizontal while the middle three are erect. The showy flowers, which vary in color from yellow to blue to purple, later form a capsule with seeds in one or two rows in each chamber. The 2–4 foot tall, swordlike leaves grow in an alternate pattern from a rhizome and form a dense clump.

Jack-in-the-pulpit (*Arisaema triphyllum* [L.] Schott) has a corm that usually produces two leaves that are each divided into three leaflets. The three leaflets are not identical or equally spaced. The two basal leaflets occur across from each other and tend to fold downward. Between the leaves grows a fleshy spadix, which is surrounded by a green to purple-brown spathe. The veins of the leaflets are parallel from the midrib to the marginal vein. Their habitat includes rich, moist woods and boggy areas.

Moonseed (*Menispermum canadense* L.) is a 6–15-foot perennial vine that has simple, alternate, palmately veined leaves. The petiole is attached to the lower surface of the blade rather than to its base. The leaf margin is somewhat lobed to shallowly toothed. The black fruits occur in clusters similar to grapes. Each fruit contains a single crescent-shaped seed. The plant usually grows in moist woods and thickets.

Poison Ivy (*Toxicodendron radicans* [L.] Kuntze) has alternate, compound leaves composed of three leaflets that are broadest near their base. The terminal leaflet has a longer stalk than the other two leaflets. The leaflet margins vary from entire to coarsely toothed. The growth form ranges from a low shrub to a vine. The white fruits are organized into grapelike clusters. Fence rows, forest edges, open woods, waste areas, disturbed sites, and areas around buildings are likely places to find poison ivy.

Poison Sumac (*Toxicodendron vernix* [L.] Kuntze) grows in wetlands such as swamps and bogs. The white-berried shrub grows to about 15 feet tall. The pinnately compound, alternate leaves have seven to fifteen entire leaflets. The twigs and buds are hairless.

Red-berried Elder (*Sambucus racemosa* L.) is a deciduous shrub that grows from 9 to 12 feet tall. The opposite, pinnately compound leaves are composed of five to seven toothed leaflets. Large purplish buds and a brown pith characterize the twigs. The small white flowers are arranged in a paniclelike inflorescence. The berrylike fruits are bright red and contain three to five small seeds. It often occurs in mountainous forests.

Rhubarb (*Rheum rhaponticum* L.) leaves are usually from 2 to 4 feet long and occur in a basal clump. The smooth leaves vary in shape from round to heart-shaped and have a wavy margin. The petioles are long, usually reddish, and often flattened on one side. A tall, hollow stalk supports the cream-colored inflorescence, which later forms the three-winged fruits.

Swamp Milkweed (*Asclepias incarnata* L.) is an erect perennial herb that grows from 3 to 4 feet tall. The pink to red flowers are arranged in an umbel. The opposite leaves are lance-shaped, usually pointed, and entire. Flowering occurs from June to August. The fruit is a follicle. Found in wet areas, but not in standing water. Common along the edges of lakes, streams, and ditches.

Yellow Sweet Clover (*Melilotus officinalis* (L.) Pallas) and White Sweet Clover (*M. alba* Medic.) are found in disturbed sites, waste areas, roadsides, and old fields. These biennials grow to a height of 7 feet. The stems show little branching and are weak. The alternate, compound leaves are composed of three finely toothed leaflets with the terminal leaflet on a stalk. The small white or yellow flowers occur in dense racemes. Improperly dried sweet clovers get moldy, which in turn produces the anticoagulant coumarin.

Sweet Pea (*Lathyrus latifolius* L.) and its relatives are also known as vetch, vetchlings, wild pea, and flat pea. The alternate leaves are pinnately compound and terminate in a tendril. Below each leaf is a pair of lanceolate stipules. This climbing or trailing perennial herb grows from a rhizome. Four to ten pink to white irregular flowers form a raceme. Each flower develops into a flat pod with several seeds.

Wild Indigo (*Baptisia tinctoria* (L.) R. Br.) is a 3-foot perennial herb that grows from thick rhizomes. The much-branched plant bears compound leaves that are composed of three leaflets that blacken upon drying. The yellow flowers are organized into racemes, which are found at the end of almost every branch. Pods later form from the flowers. It is primarily found in dry soils.

Yew (*Taxus canadensis* Marsh.) is an evergreen shrub whose growth form is low and straggly, but may reach a height of 3 feet. The single, flat needles are stalked, sharp-pointed, and green on both sides. The lower leaf surface has two pale green lines. The red "fruits" are berrylike and contain a single, hard, dark seed. The cultivated yews (*T. baccata* and *T. cuspidata*) are also poisonous.

223

GLOSSARY

• Entries preceded by a bullet are illustrated.

ACHENE. A small, dry, one-seeded indehiscent fruit.

AEROALLERGENS. Allergens that are carried by air.

ALKALINE. Having a pH of more than 7 and often referred to as basic.

ALKALOID. Class of nitrogen-containing organic compounds found largely in seed plants.

ALLERGEN. A substance that induces allergies.

ALLICIN. Natural antibiotic found in *Allium*.

• ALTERNATE. Used to describe the arrangement of leaves
on a stem where one leaf occurs on one side of the
stem and the next further along the stem, but not in the
same line.

ANNUAL. Plant that flowers, produces seeds, and dies in
the same year.

• ANTHER. The expanded tip of a stamen in which pollen
is formed.

ANTIRHEUMATIC. Substance that eases the discomfort of
rheumatism.

ANTISCORBUTIC. Substance that is used in the treatment
and prevention of scurvy, which is caused by a deficiency of vitamin C.

ANTISEPTIC. A substance that prevents or destroys micro-
organisms that could cause infection.

APHRODISIAC. Something that promotes sexual desire.

AROMATIC. Having a pleasant or strong spicy odor.

ASARONE. Hallucinogenic principal found in *Acorus*.

ASTRINGENT. Substance that causes the soft external tissues to contract.

• AXIL. The angle between a branch or leaf and the axis
from which it projects.

AXILLARY. Situated in or growing from an axil.

BIENNIAL. A plant that completes its life cycle in two
years.

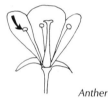

Alternate

Anther

Axil

Bundle Scar

BISEXUAL. Both sexes occur in the same flower.

BRACT. Modified leaves found directly below and adjacent to the inflorescence.

• BUNDLE SCAR. Scar left on stem by vascular bundles broken during leaf fall.

CALYX. A collective term for all of the sepals of a flower.

CAMBIUM (vascular). A layer of dividing cells that produces xylem and phloem and results in growth in circumference.

CAPSULE. A dry dehiscent fruit developed from a compound ovary.

CARCINOGEN. A substance or agent capable of causing cancer.

CARMINATIVE. A substance used to expel gas from the alimentary canal.

CHEMOTHERAPEUTIC. The use of chemical agents in the control of diseases.

CITRONELLA. A fragrant oil.

CLEAVE. To adhere firmly.

CLEISTOGAMOUS. An unopened flower that is self-pollinated.

• COMPOSITE. An inflorescence composed of a compact mass of flowers; also called a head.

• COMPOUND (LEAF). A leaf blade divided into several separate parts that form leaflets.

CONIFEROUS. Cone-bearing plants.

CORM. An enlarged, fleshy, solid underground stem that looks like a bulb but is covered with dry scales.

COROLLA. A collective term for all of the petals of a flower.

CORTEX. The main outer tissue of a root or stem between the epidermis and the central core.

COSMOPOLITAN. Broad distribution in most parts of the world under various ecological conditions.

DECIDUOUS. Sheds all of its leaves at one time, usually at the end of the growing season.

DEHISCENT. Opening or splitting at maturity.

DERMATITIS. Inflammation of the skin.

• DISK (FLOWERS). The central flowers in a composite inflorescence, such as sunflower.

DIURETIC. Substance that tends to increase the flow of urine.

DOCTRINE OF SIGNATURES. A belief that parts of certain plants can be used to cure ailments of the part of the human body that they resemble.

Composite

Compound (leaf)

Disk (flowers)

Fiddlehead

Frond

Inflorescence

DOWSER. A person who uses a divining rod to search for water, oil, or natural gas.

DRUPE. A fleshy fruit with a single hard seed.

DRUPLET. A small drupe; one of the individual parts of a clustered fruit such as a raspberry.

EMETIC. A substance that causes vomiting.

ENTIRE. Smooth leaf blade edge that is devoid of teeth or lobes.

EPITHET. The second term in a scientific name.

EVERGREEN. Having green foliage throughout the year.

FASCIOLIASIS. A disease caused by liver flukes.

FERTILE. A flower capable of producing fruit or a fern frond that produces spores.

FETID. Having a definite offensive smell.

• FIDDLEHEAD. The early growth stage of a fern frond that resembles the head of a violin.

FLORAL CLOCK. Using the time of opening and closing of the flowers as a clock.

FLUKE (liver). A parasitic worm.

FOLLICLE. A dry dehiscent, one-celled, many-seeded fruit that splits open along one side.

• FROND. The leaf of a fern.

GALLINACEOUS. Relating to the bird order Galliformes, which includes pheasants, grouse, and turkeys.

GIRDLE. A ring made by the removal of bark around a plant stem.

GLUTEN. Elastic protein that gives cohesiveness to dough.

GLYCOSIDE. A large group of plant compounds that are sugar derivatives.

HERBACEOUS. Nonwoody plants.

HERBIVORE. A plant-eating animal.

HYBRID. Offspring of two plants of different varieties or species.

INDEHISCENT. Remaining closed at maturity.

• INFLORESCENCE. A complete cluster of flowers.

INTERNODE. The part of the stem between two nodes.

• IRREGULAR (FLOWER). Having bilateral symmetry with the upper half unlike the lower half.

LATERAL ROOT. The root that grows from another, older root.

LEACH. Subjected to percolating water.

LEAFLET. A subdivision of a compound leaf.

LEAVEN. A substance used to produce fermentation in dough and subsequently its rising.

Irregular (flower)

Lenticel

Margin

Node

Opposite

Pinnate-pinnatifid

LEGUME. A member of the Fabaceae family (pea or bean).

• LENTICEL. A pore in the stem of a woody plant through which gases can be exchanged.

LOBE. A rounded projection on the margin of a leaf.

LYMPHOCYTE. A type of blood cell.

Pith

• MARGIN. The outer edge of a leaf.

MESCALINE. A hallucinatory compound.

MIDRIB. The central vein of a leaf.

MITOGEN. A substance that disrupts normal mitosis.

MITOSIS. The process in which two-cell nuclei form that have the identical number of chromosomes as the parent nucleus.

MUCILAGE. A gelatinous substance.

MUTAGENIC. A substance that has the ability to cause mutations.

Prickle

MYCORRHIZAE. The symbiotic association of the hyphae of certain fungi with the roots of a plant.

• NODE. The point on a stem to which branches or leaves are attached.

NOXIOUS. Physically harmful or destructive.

OBOVATE. Widest above the middle.

Raceme

• OPPOSITE. Describing leaves that are arranged in pairs on opposite sides of the stem.

OVARY. The enlarged, rounded basal portion of the pistil that develops into the fruit.

OVATE. Widest at the middle.

OXALATE. A salt or ester of oxalic acid.

PALMATELY (COMPOUND). Having leaflets that resemble the shape of a hand with the fingers spread.

Ray (flowers)

PANICLE. A compound inflorescence that is longer than it is thick with a branched main axis that bears loose flower clusters.

PEDICEL. A stalk that supports an individual flower within an inflorescence.

PEDUNCLE. The stalk that supports an entire inflorescence.

PEMMICAN. A concentrated food consisting of dried meat and fat.

Regular (flower)

PERENNIAL. A plant having a life cycle of more than two years.

PETIOLE. The stalk of a leaf.

PHENOLOGY. A branch of science dealing with the relationship between calendar time and biological events.

PHOTODERMATITIS. A light-induced inflammation of the skin.

Rosette

PINNA. The leaflet of a frond.

PINNATELY (COMPOUND). Having leaflets in a featherlike arrangement.

• PINNATE-PINNATIFID. A frond with lobed pinnae.

PISTIL. The female reproductive organ of a plant.

PISTILLATE. Having only pistils.

• PITH. The central core of tissue in stems.

PODOPHYLLIN. A resin produced from mayapple rhizomes.

POLLINATION. The transfer of pollen from the anther of one plant to the stigma of another plant.

POLYSACCHARIDE. A complex carbohydrate that is composed of many units of simple sugars.

POULTICE. A medication that is placed on cuts, bruises, and sores and is used to draw out the infection.

POTHERB. Cooked greens prepared by boiling or steaming.

• PRICKLE. A sharp-pointed growth arising from the outer tissues of a stem.

PROBOSCIS. The elongated tubular mouthpart of an invertebrate.

PROSTRATE. Trailing on the ground.

• RACEME. An inflorescence having the elongated unbranched axis bearing flowers in continuation toward the apex.

• RAY (FLOWERS). The outer petallike flowers in a composite inflorescence, such as a sunflower.

• REGULAR (FLOWER). Having radial symmetry.

RHIZOME. An elongated horizontal stem that lies at or just below ground level.

• ROSETTE. A cluster of leaves in crowded spirals usually close to the ground.

RUBIFACIENT. A counter-irritant that tends to make the skin redder.

RUMINANT. A cud-chewing mammal.

SALINE. Containing or consisting of salt.

• SAMARA. An indehiscent, dry, usually one-seeded, winged fruit.

SAPOGENIN. A plant chemical that produces foam when combined with water.

SCALLION. An onion that forms a wide basal portion and a very small bulb.

• SEPAL. A flower part that resembles a leaf and occurs directly below the petals.

• SHEATH. The lower part of the leaf which encompasses the stem.

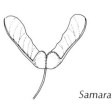

Samara

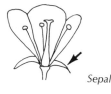

Sepal

Sheath

Simple

Spadix

Spathe

- SIMPLE. Refers to a leaf blade that is in one solid piece.
  SOLUBLE. Capable of being dissolved.
  SOMATIC CELLS. Cells that compose body tissues of multi-cellular plants as contrasted to sex cells.
- SPADIX. A short inflorescence that contains a dense arrangement of staminate and/or pistillate flowers and is enclosed in a leaflike structure.
- SPATHE. A large leaflike bract that often encloses an inflorescence.
  SPILE. Spout inserted into a tree to extract the sap.
- SPUR. A hollow tube protruding from the corolla or calyx.
  STAMEN. The male reproductive organ of a flower.
  STAMINATE. Having only stamens.
  STERILE. Incapable of producing fruit or spores.
- STIPULE. Either of the pair of leaflike appendages at the base of the leaf.
  STOLON. A stem that creeps horizontally over the soil surface.
  STRIGOSE. Having bristles or scales which lie flat against the stem.
- STYLE. The "neck" part of the pistil.
  SYMBIOTIC. The intimate living together of two different species in a mutually beneficial relationship.
  TANNIN. Complex phenolic compounds produced by plants.
  TAPROOT. A main root that grows vertically downward.
  TAXONOMY. The science of classification of plants and animals.
- TENDRIL. A coiling modified leaf, stipule, or stem.
  TERMINAL. Growing at the end of a stem or branch.
  TETRAPLOID. Having four sets of chromosomes.
  TOXIC. Poisonous.
  TRANSVERSE. Lying crosswise or horizontal.
  TUBER. A short, fleshy, enlarged underground stem growing at the end of a rhizome.
- UMBEL. A type of inflorescence whose pedicels all radiate from the same point.
  UNISEXUAL. Restricted or relating to one sex.
  VASCULAR PLANT. A plant with conducting tissue.
  VENATION. The system or arrangement of veins.
- WHORL. An arrangement of flower parts or leaves in a circle around a point.
  WOODY. Containing an abundance of xylem, which makes a hard stem.

Spur

Stipule

Style

Tendril

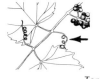

Umbel

Whorl

LIST OF
RECOMMENDED BOOKS

Baily, L. H. *How Plants Get Their Names*. New York: Dover Publications, 1963.

Beatty, B., and B. Beatty. *Wild Plant Cookbook*. Happy Camp, CA: Naturegraph Publishers, 1987.

Berglund, B., and C. E. Bolsby. *The Edible Wild*. Toronto: Pagurian Press, 1971.

Boxer, A., and P. Back. *The Herb Book*. New York: W. H. Smith Publishers, 1986.

Brackett, B., and M. Lash. *The Wild Gourmet: A Forager's Cookbook*. Boston: Godine, 1975.

Brill, S. *Shoots and Greens of Early Spring in Eastern North America*. Jamaica, NY: Steve Brill. n.d.

Brown, T., Jr. *Tom Brown's Guide to Wild Edible and Medicinal Plants*. New York: Berkley Books, 1985.

Busch, P. S. *Wildflowers and the Stories Behind Their Names*. New York: Charles Scribner's Sons, 1977.

Coats, A. M. *Flowers and Their Histories*. New York: McGraw-Hill, 1956.

Crowhurst, A. *The Flower Cookbook*. New York: Lancer Books, 1973.

Crowhurst, A. *The Weed Cookbook*. New York: Lancer Books, 1972.

Darnall, J., and M. Darnall. *Wild Plants to Eat*. North Fork, CA: Outdoor Eduquip, 1975.

Ditmer, W. P. *Pennsylvania Weeds*. Harrisburg, PA: Pennsylvania Department of Agriculture, 1961.

Dobelis, I. N. (ed.). *Magic and Medicine of Plants*. Pleasantville, NY: The Reader's Digest Association, 1986.

Durant, M. *Who Named the Daisy? Who Named the Rose?* New York: Dodd, Mead, 1976.

Elias, T. S., and P. A. Dykeman. *Field Guide to North American Edible Wild Plants*. New York: Van Nostrand Reinhold, 1982.

Elliott, D. B. *Roots: An Underground Botany and Forager's Guide*. Old Greenwich, CT: The Chatham Press, 1976.

Fernald, M. L. *Gray's Manual of Botany*, 8th ed. New York: Van Nostrand Reinhold, 1950.

Freitus, J. *The Natural World Cookbook*. Washington, DC: Stone Wall Press, 1980.

Furlong, M., and V. Pill. *Edible? Incredible! Pondlife.* Happy Camp, CA: Naturegraph Publishers, 1980.

Gibbons, E. *Stalking the Healthful Herbs.* New York: David McKay, 1966.

Gibbons, E. *Stalking the Wild Asparagus.* New York: David McKay, 1962.

Gleason, H. A. *The New Britton and Brown Illustrated Flora.* Lancaster, PA: Lancaster Press, 1952.

Hall, A. *The Wild Food Trailguide.* Canada: Holt, Rinehart and Winston, 1973.

Hall, W., and N. Hall. *The Wild Palate.* Emmaus, PA: Rodale Press, 1980.

Hardin, J. W., and J. M. Arena. *Human Poisoning from Native and Cultivated Plants.* Durham, NC: Duke University Press, 1974.

Harrington, H. D. *Edible Native Plants of the Rocky Mountains.* Albuquerque, NM: The University of New Mexico Press, 1967.

Harrington, H. D. *Western Edible Wild Plants.* Albuquerque, NM: The University of New Mexico Press, 1972.

Hill, R. J. *Poisonous Plants of Pennsylvania.* Harrisburg, PA: PA Department of Agriculture, 1986.

Hill, S. R., and P. K. Duke. *100 Poisonous Plants of Maryland.* College Park, MD: The University of Maryland Cooperative Extension Service, 1985–86.

Lehner, E., and J. Lehner. *Folklore and Symbolism of Flowers, Plants, and Trees.* New York: Tudor Publishing, 1960.

Lewis, W. H., and M. P. F. Elvin-Lewis. *Medical Botany: Plants Affecting Man's Health.* New York: John Wiley and Sons, 1977.

Martin, L. C. *Wildflower Folklore.* Charlotte, NC: Fast and McMillan Publishers, 1984.

McPherson, A., and S. McPherson. *Wild Food Plants of Indiana and Adjacent States.* Bloomington, IN: Indiana University Press, 1977.

Millspaugh, C. F. *American Medicinal Plants.* New York: Dover Publications, 1974.

Muensher, W. C. *Poisonous Plants of the United States.* New York: Macmillan, 1951.

Newcomb, L. *Newcomb's Wildflower Guide.* Boston: Little, Brown, 1977.

Niering, W., and N. Olmstead. *The Audubon Society Field Guide to North American Wildflowers, Eastern Region.* New York: Knopf, 1979.

Niethammor, C. *American Indian Food and Lore.* New York: Collier-Macmillan, 1974.

Palmer, E. L., and H. S. Fowler. *Fieldbook of Natural History.* New York: McGraw-Hill, 1975.

Peterson, L. A. *A Field Guide to Edible Wild Plants of Eastern and Central North America.* Boston: Houghton Mifflin, 1977.

Peterson, R. T., and M. McKenny. *A Field Guide to Wildflowers of Northeastern and Northcentral North America.* Boston: Houghton Mifflin, 1968.

Petrides, G. A. *A Field Guide to Trees and Shrubs.* Boston: Houghton Mifflin, 1972.

Phillips, R. *Wild Food.* Boston: Little, Brown, 1986.

Roberts, J. C. *Born in the Spring.* Athens: Ohio University Press, 1976.

Robinson, D. *Appalachian Hill Country Cookbook.* Charleston, WV: Jalamap Publications, 1980.

Runyon, L. *Lawn Food Cook Book (Groceries in the Backyard)*. Warrensburg, NY: The Runyon Institute, 1985.

Stokes, D. W., and L. Q. Stokes. *A Guide to Enjoying Wildflowers*. Boston: Little, Brown, 1985.

Strausbaugh, P. D., and E. L. Core. *Flora of West Virginia*. Grantsville, WV: Seneca Books, 1977.

Szczawinski, A. F., and N. J. Turner. *Wild Green Vegetables of Canada*. Ottawa: National Museums of Canada, 1980.

Tatum, B. J. *Billy Joe Tatum's Wild Food Cookbook and Field Guide*. New York: Workman Publishing, 1976.

Tull, D. A. *A Practical Guide to Edible and Useful Plants*. Austin: Texas Monthly Press, 1987.

Turner, N. J., and A. F. Szczawinski. *Edible Wild Fruits and Nuts of Canada*. Ottawa: National Museums of Canada, 1979.

Turner, N. J., and A. F. Szczawinski. *Wild Coffee and Tea Substitutes of Canada*. Ottawa: National Museums of Canada, 1978.

Weatherbee, E. E., and J. G. Bruce. *Edible Wild Plants of the Great Lakes Region*, 1959.

Wigginton, E. *Foxfire II*. New York: Anchor Press-Doubleday, 1973.

INDEX OF FOOD USES

Page number in **bold** indicates that a recipe is included

235

INDEX OF SCIENTIFIC NAMES OF FAMILIES AND COMMON AND SCIENTIFIC NAMES OF SPECIES

239

241